music theory:
problems and practices
in the middle ages
and renaissance

Alleluia. Facsimile of Montpellier, Fac. des Medecins, H. 196, fol. 40v. Reprinted with permission from Yvonne Rokseth, *Polyphonies de XIIIe siècle*, L'Oiseau-Lyre, Paris, 1935-1939.

music theory:
problems and practices
in
the middle ages
and
renaissance

By lloyd ultan

Professor and Chairman
Departments of Music and Music Education
University of Minnesota

UNIVERSITY OF MINNESOTA PRESS □ MINNEAPOLIS

Library of Congress Catalog Card Number 77-75597

ISBN 0-8166-0802-4

Example 8.3, p. 105, is reprinted from *The Notation of Medieval Music* by
Carl Parrish (Fig. 43, m. 1-3, p. 96). By permission of W. W. Norton &
Company, Inc. Copyright © 1957 by W. W. Norton & Company, Inc.

dedication

To

Roslye, my wife

Wendy
Alicia
Jacqueline
Deborah

pReface

The study of music theory is the study of musical style by carefully attending to the minutiae of compositional technique in the perspective of the broad organizational concept of an entire composition. This study is directed toward the cultivation of a deep concern for and consciousness of the smallest details in the analysis and creation of music as well as toward cultivating an awareness of the manner by which these small components have served composers in the development of expansive musical forms.

Traditionally the formal study of music theory has been confined to the styles and techniques of the eighteenth and nineteenth centuries. Occasional token homage has been paid to the works of Palestrina, and the music of the twentieth century has been approached with trepidation and diffidence. It is the purpose of the present volume to study the theory of music through the perspective of history and, by introducing subject matter not normally included in the undergraduate curriculum, to achieve a degree of equity between the several historical periods of Western music and the respective degrees of difficulty posed by their various limitations, characteristics, and aesthetic concerns.

The academic program this volume is designed to serve is intended to supplant in part the traditional music-major theory curriculum. The volume was developed to serve two semesters of a three-year theory program. Ideally, in such a program the traditional courses in harmony, counterpoint, form, and ear training would be incorporated into a two- to three-year historical theory sequence.

This volume is revolutionary in concept because it suggests that theoretical problems of the Middle Ages and Renaissance be presented to freshmen and sophomores. This has traditionally been done on the graduate level, and even then it was rarely approached from a creative theoretical point of view. We recognize that the curriculum of each institution has special limitations and requirements. Therefore the volume has been designed to provide materials for beginning a logical continuum of study, while enabling each faculty to adapt the materials to its own needs.

The author assumes that students will bring to this study a basic musical background such as may be acquired in a strong fundamentals of music class that provides an introduction to the concepts of line, rhythm, vertical relationships, notations, and forms. Students are expected to have developed a good, basic reading ability. In addition, an understanding of fundamental concepts like the following is highly desirable: the balance between unity and variety in the design of music; the constantly changing attitudes toward consonances and dissonances; the rudiments of acoustics (at least to the extent of understanding the relationships of the overtone series); and the concept of the graphic representation of sound—students must be flexible in their understanding of the concept if they are to successfully approach the early notational efforts of the Middle Ages as well as the diverse experiments of the twentieth century.

It should be fully understood by students and teachers that this book is not intended to be a musicological treatise providing results of new research or treating a narrow subject in depth. Nor can it be equated with the traditional harmony or counterpoint textbook designed to serve present theory curricula. It has been conceived, rather, to assist students in developing analytical and compositional techniques by studying selected works in historical sequence. Only a tiny sampling of the vast literature available has been made to serve the particular needs of given theoretical problems. Unquestionably many other works could have been selected to accomplish the same ends. Likewise it would have been possible to devote attention to some subjects that are mentioned in passing or that have been completely ignored. It was the author's judgment that only topics that would contribute directly to the evolution of students' techniques in both analysis and composition and that were sufficiently important in the evolution of compositional style in general or of individual techniques in particular would be included in this study. Undoubtedly the omission of some specific subjects allows room for debate about the value they might have offered in this context. It is possible that

there are readers who will consider some of the subjects covered to be un-
necessary or unimportant relative to things they are more interested in. It is
the author's experience in having developed and taught theory classes that the
materials presented are the most effective for the purposes defined and are
both interesting and challenging to students. This is especially so when work
with this volume is coordinated with the accompanying workbook/anthology.
However, each class reflects the unique cumulative talents of its participating
students and the interests, talents, and personality of its teacher. The author
encourages expanding or contracting the content of this volume to suit the
particular needs and interests of the individuals concerned.

In light of the many parallels between historical periods, even at opposite
ends of the time spectrum (comparisons between the Middle Ages and the
twentieth century are more and more frequently employed and can be remarkable in their clarity), flexibility should be cultivated in the minds of all
students. The study of music theory can be a marvelous vehicle for the
achievement of that goal if it is understood that the seemingly severe limitations imposed by many styles provide an almost infinite source of choices
which challenge the imagination, knowledge, and technical facility of students. The emphasis throughout this study should be on the development of a
sensitivity to the music and a recognition of the artistic premises that pervade
the thinking of all composers. Students should be discouraged from cold,
matter-of-fact adherence to rules and should be encouraged to understand the
malleability of all styles and techniques. The development of musicality must
be the primary goal, and the achievement of computerlike representation of
sharply defined practices should be considered the greatest failing.

No volume of this complexity and dimension can be realized without the
sympathetic assistance and advice of many people. One, beyond all others,
has made the existence of this book possible. Through her intense efforts in
obtaining materials, her devotion and care in proofreading, her understanding
of my various problems and frustrations, and her incisive evaluation and
provocation always directed toward achieving greater refinement and clarity,
my wife Roslye made it possible for this project to be completed with whatever merits it may have achieved.

It is impossible to express appreciation to all who have contributed to this
volume. However, I do wish to acknowledge those whose contributions have
been most significant: Dr. George C. Schuetze Jr.; the late Dr. Esther William-
son Ballou; James L. McLain; Alan Mandel; John Marlow; Douglas Dawson;
Tommie Carl; Dr. Meredith Little, all associated with The American Univer-

sity; Phillip Buttall, student reader from the Royal College of Music, London; Dr. John Morehen, assistant organist, Windsor Castle; The American University for the opportunity it provided for academic exploration; and the many students at The American University with whom I have worked and whose efforts in the development and refinement of this volume I have valued so very much.

L. U.

Edina, Minnesota
September 8, 1976

contents

part one

the middle ages

notation

When considering the problems and practices of musical composition in the Middle Ages, it is essential to begin with notation. The extent to which composers' expressive possibilities were limited by the inadequacies of their graphic tools is approximated in but one other historical period — the present. It is possible to trace in the Middle Ages an evolution from ambiguity to increasing clarity in the development and use of symbols. The reverse can be shown to be true in the notational problems and experiments throughout the twentieth century.

The difficulties encountered in studying the music of the medieval period are enormous. In the earliest stages, notation was clumsy and at times indecipherable or, at best, debatable. This was compounded by its dependence upon poetic forms and rhythms or upon the requirements and limitations of a liturgy it was designed to serve. The problems are largely unlike those of later periods. But with an awareness of them, students may find consolation in knowing that this period provides many of the artistic and technical foundations upon which the evolution of Western music is predicated to the present.

Although a wide variety of notations can be distinguished during the period under consideration (c. 800-1400 A.D.), discussion in this chapter will be confined to three of the principal early forms of notation which contributed to the evolution that led to our current notation. These may be identified as plainsong, rhythmic modal, and Franconian. The periods during which these notations were used may be loosely defined as:

Plainsong . . . . c. 1000 to the present
(This notation is still used
for the music of the Catholic
liturgy.)
Rhythmic modal . . . . . . c. 1150-1250
Franconian . . . . c. 1250-1325

The latter two were clearly short-lived. However, these dates should and accurately do indicate that vigorous activity was taking place in music during this period and that increasingly shorter periods of time were needed to solve notational problems after graphic forms had been developed for the basic delineation of pitch and time.

The three forms of notation are discussed here to indicate to students the limitations they impose and to provide students with a set of boundaries within which to confine their musical thinking. The constricting nature of these notations is not an arbitrary pedagogical device chosen to provide a more sharply focused study of narrow parameters (although it accomplishes this well); this is an accurate representation of the respective styles.

Plainsong Notation

The four-line notation of plainsong that is still used today in collections of Catholic liturgical music (e.g., the *Liber Usualis*), was devised by a monk, Guido d'Arezzo, at the beginning of the eleventh century. His treatise, *Micrologus* (c. 1025), clarified and challenged earlier practices and provided new techniques in the evolution of Western music.

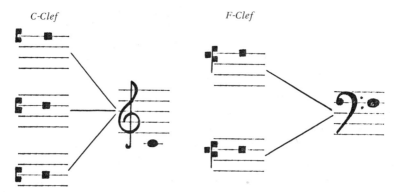

Example 1.1. Interpretation of the *C* and *F* Clefs.

A variety of devices for the notation of pitch definition had been explored for centuries before the four-line staff and the two clefs which necessarily accompany it were adopted. The clefs, *C* and *F*, identify respectively the location of middle C and the F below middle C on our present keyboard. These clefs are movable to accommodate the range of a given melody within the four lines and to avoid the use of more than one leger line above or below the staff. It is not uncommon to find a clef change in the middle of a line that changes the pitch orientation according to the relocation of the clef. The common positions of the two clefs are shown with their modern equivalents in Example 1.1.

A system of identifying pitches was devised from symbols dating back to directional chant indications over the text in ancient Hebrew music. These symbols, or *neumes*, indicated one or more pitches set apart as single melodic entities. Over a period of time and through usage, they were classified into four different categories based on complexity and function. A few of the more common neumes are shown with their Solesmes interpretations in Table 1.1. The shapes of the neumes date from approximately the thirteenth cen-

Table 1.1. Selected Neumes

Name	Shape	Interpretation
Virga		
Punctus		
Podatus (or Pes)		
Clivis		
Torculus		
Porrectus		
Climacus		
Scandicus		
Salicus		
Pes Subpunctus		
Pressus		

tury. With the vertically paired pitches (e.g., the *podatus*), the lower pitch is sung first. The starting and ending positions of the oblique lines (e.g., the *porrectus*) indicate which notes are to be sung.[1] Students will find it relatively easy to gain a basic working facility with square-note notation. In addition to using the example in the workbook/anthology, it is suggested they turn to the *Liber Usualis* for sight-singing practice in the chant of the period — an excellent means of developing sensitivity to the sacred music of the Middle Ages.

Reference was made to rhythmic symbols. It should be understood that no means were available to specifically delineate time values in plainsong notation. Only the most general suggestions were offered for phrasings, for lengthening the prevailing general referential values, and for phrase ritards. Even these suggestions developed at a somewhat later date and remain a subject for heated debate. Rhythmic interpretation was essentially left to the good taste and judgment of the individual performer within only the most general guidelines. (See Appendix.)

This approach sufficed for the music of the Church but was inadequate for secular music. In the former, a free-flowing chant contributed to the spiritual character of the environment within which the music was to be presented. This extramusical function relegated music to a service role in which it was the vehicle for the expression of a spiritual idea. Secular music, however, which drew upon poetry for its texts and was not infrequently associated with the dance, was severely handicapped by the lack of a precise means for indicating time values.

Rhythmic Modal Notation

In the early evolution of notation, the most complex problem that faced composers was the development of some system for representing the division of time — a rhythmic notation. This process began with simple components which some scholars have suggested were initially derived from the Greek poetic meters.[2] These meters were the rhythmic modes which in their earliest stages of usage (secular monophony) were not notated but were understood to be derived from the rhythmic patterns inherent in the text. Because there was no clearly defined notation for the rhythmic values, there were many interpretations for some pieces.

As the use of rhythmic modes became more widely recognized as a means for defining time divisions, a notation developed in the thirteenth century based essentially on the virga-shaped neume as a long value (now referred to as *longa*) and the punctus-shaped neume as the short value (*breve*) — an early, simple adaptation of square notation for rhythmic purposes.[3] However, this solution to the rhythmic problem was not as satisfactory as a cursory glance might suggest since the rhythmic modes inherently implied two different gradations for the longa. Consequently the notation had to allow for essentially three different rhythmic values which bore the ratios 1:2 and 1:3 (i.e., a short value; an imperfect long value or altered breve equal to two short values; and a *perfect* long value that equaled three short values).

Whether a given longa was to be interpreted as a perfect or an imperfect was solely dependent upon its position relative to the other longae and the breves adjacent to it. As this notational system developed, certain conventions were established which provided a guide to the interpretation of the rhythmic notation. This entire system of rhythmic notation was conceived in such a way to ensure that the music would flow in a series of perfections (i.e., three-to-one relationships), each perfection producing the equivalent of three

Table 1.2. The Rhythmic Modes[a]

Group	Mode Number	Mode Name	Square Notation Pattern	Modern Equivalent	Poetic Value
A	I	Trochaic			— ◡
	II	Iambic			◡ —
B	III	Dactylic			— ◡ ◡
	IV	Anapaestic			◡ ◡ —
C	V	Spondaic			— — —
	VI	Tribrachic			◡ ◡ ◡

[a]The horizontal bar set in the half circle is provided to make it easier for students to visualize the difference between the breve and the altered breve.

breves. It must be emphasized that the decision of whether a longa-breve relationship was perfection or imperfection (i.e., a two-to-one relationship) was
dependent on the position of the notes in relationship to each other and not
on the shape of the notes. The six rhythmic modes are presented in Table 1.2
with their modern equivalents and their poetic rhythmic values.

In the literature of the period during which the rhythmic modes were
used, Modes I and III were favored, Mode II was used less often, and Mode IV
was almost never used. Mode V was ordinarily used only in the tenor. Mode
VI was widely used in *organum* (to be discussed in a later chapter) but not in
the tenor.

It is widely held that these modes are to be interpreted in triple or compound meters; but there is some disagreement, with a number of scholars contending that some music of the period is more accurately interpreted in duple
meters. I shall not enter into this debate but for the purposes of this discussion shall accept the former interpretation.

To clarify the use of the rhythmic modes Example 1.2 is provided for
study. It should be noted that the Dactylic pattern is consistent throughout
and since the concept of perfections must be retained, the vertical half bar is
interpreted as a rest equivalent to the second half of the Dactylic pattern.

Au   tans   d'a - oust   que   fuil - le   de   bo - schet

Au   tans d'a--oust   que fuil--le   de bo---schet

Example 1.2. Excerpt and Transcription of *Au tans d'oust.* Jean Beck, *Les Chansonniers des Troubadours et des Trouveres*, University of Pennsylvania Press, Philadelphia, 1927, Vol. I, fol. 13d.

This example is typical because it consists of a rhythmic pattern (Dactylic)
which continually recurs, forming larger groups of patterns (to the half bar).
These larger groups are termed *ordines* (*ordo* — singular). The total number of
single notes used determines the size of the ordo, i.e., a seven- or a nine-note
ordo.

Frequently groupings of two or three notes were used to supplant a single
breve or longa. These forms derived from the square plainsong notation and
were termed *binaria* and *ternaria* respectively. *Quarternaria* (four-note group-

Table 1.3. Characteristic Patterns of the Rhythmic Modes[a]

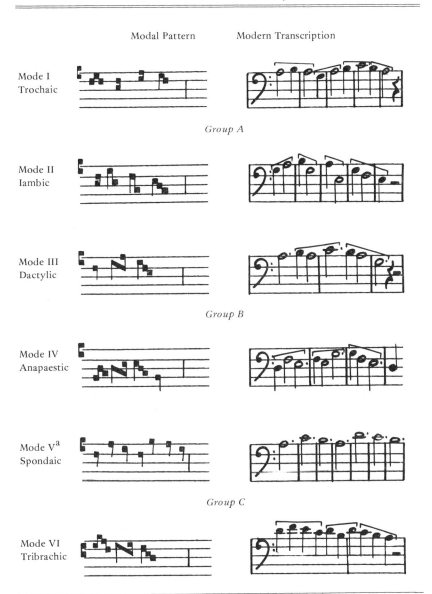

Modal Pattern   Modern Transcription

Mode I
Trochaic

Group A

Mode II
Iambic

Mode III
Dactylic

Group B

Mode IV
Anapaestic

Mode V[a]
Spondaic

Group C

Mode VI
Tribrachic

[a]Ligature groups of three notes followed by a quarter bar are occasionally used for this mode when the flow of the music is appropriate (producing three dotted half notes followed by a dotted half rest).

ings) were also used but much less frequently, except as they appeared naturally in the basic pattern of Mode VI (see Table 1.3).

When the ordo patterns were used without modification (especially in sacred music), conventional groupings were employed, which immediately identified each of the modes. One might expect that a single mode would persist
from beginning to end, but a good number of examples could be cited in
which changes of mode or deviations from the basic pattern within a mode
complicate interpretation. The basic ordo patterns for the rhythmic modes
are shown in Table 1.3.

In the basic *ligature* patterns (e.g., binaria and ternaria) that constitute the
ordines, the final note should always be interpreted as having the same value
as the first note in the modal pattern. Thus an unaltered ordo beginning with
a breve ended with a breve followed by the necessary length of rest to complete the mode (e.g., the Dactylic ending was followed by a perfect longa
rest — all rests, regardless of value, appeared as half or quarter bars).

Table 1.4. Interpretation of Substituting Ligatures in Modes I and II[a]

basic modal pattern (Trochaic)		=	
binaria substitute for imperfect longa		=	
basic modal pattern (Trochaic)		=	
ternaria substitute for imperfect longa		=	
basic modal pattern (Trochaic)		=	
binaria substitute for breve		=	
basic modal pattern (Trochaic)		=	
ternaria substitute for breve		=	

[a]Although all patterns are shown in the Trochaic mode, a simple reversal of
the order of the longa and breve will produce the equivalent patterns for the Iambic mode.

To provide for the possible division of individual members of a given pattern, the same ligatures were employed. Each ligature that fell on a single syllable replaced a single note, whether it was a longa or a breve. When the binaria was used to replace a single note, it divided equally into two parts to the next smaller note value. When the ternaria replaced a single note, the first two members each assumed one-quarter of the value of the original and the last member equaled one-half of that note. This can be more clearly understood by careful study of Table 1.4.

As with many aspects of the music of this period, there is a disagreement among scholars about these interpretations. Students should recognize that several different versions of a single example can result from different interpretations of the symbols. For the ternaria, for example, some scholars divide the three notes into equal values in the form of a triplet.

The third and fourth modes introduce another element to the discussion. That is, there was a perfect longa, a breve, and a third value which, because of

Table 1.5. Interpretation of Substituting Ligatures in Modes III and IV[a]

basic modal pattern (Dactylic)	*(musical notation)*
binaria substitute for perfect longa	*(musical notation)*
basic modal pattern (Dactylic)	*(musical notation)*
ternaria substitute for perfect longa	*(musical notation)*
basic modal pattern (Dactylic)	*(musical notation)*
binaria substitute for altered breve	*(musical notation)*
basic modal pattern (Dactylic)	*(musical notation)*
ternaria substitute for altered breve	*(musical notation)*

[a]Although all patterns shown are in the Dactylic mode, simple reversal of the perfection patterns in each example will produce the equivalent pattern for the Anapaestic mode.

its shape (of another breve), will be termed an altered breve. Substitutions for the breve were the same as those shown in Table 1.4. The alterations that occurred when substituting for the longa and the altered breve are shown in Table 1.5. Modes V and VI usually were not altered, and for the purposes of this study no alterations will be considered.

Another alteration of the flow of a basic pattern within any mode when ligatures are used necessarily results from the repetition of a note. Under such circumstances it becomes necessary to break a ligature into its respective parts (breves and longae) and to interpret the groupings from the context and placement of the text against these several individual notes.

Because of the difficulties inherent in this notation, it is often helpful, after determining the mode, to transcribe at the same time the rhythm from both the beginning and the end of the ordo. This can help to clarify the position and function of substituted single notes or substituted groups of notes or ligatures. A great many factors influence the interpretation of passages involving departures from the basic patterns. These factors are best pursued in greater detail in volumes primarily devoted to the study of early notations.[4]

One additional device, however, should be understood before we leave this notation. The *plica*, widely used throughout the early developmental stages of

Table 1.6. Rhythmic Interpretation of the Plica[a]

Perfect longa with plica	
Imperfect longa with plica	
Breve with plica	
Plica on the final note of ligature: (some possibilities)	
Perfect longa (Dactylic)	
Imperfect longa (Trochaic)	
Breve (Iambic)	

[a]In modal notation there is no consistency of practice regarding length or location of the vertical line; only direction is indicated. The value of the notes (and the resulting plica) is determined by their location in the modal pattern and not by the shape of the note or the location of the plica.

rhythmic notation, is a note that had an auxiliary or embellishing function and is frequently difficult to interpret in terms of both pitch and rhythm. Its symbol is an ascending or descending vertical line attached to a single note or to the end of a ligature. Often the note head itself is slightly turned in the direction of the plica motion. The rhythmic interpretation is dependent upon the value of the note to which it is attached but, as with so many aspects of this notation, differences of opinion exist about proper interpretations. In Table 1.6 a basic reference for one possible interpretation of the different values of plicae in this notation is provided.

Pitch determinations cannot be as easily dispensed with. That is, it is necessary to judge each plica in terms of its position in the line. For example, if the two notes that surround the plica (i.e., the one to which it is attached and the one to which it is going) are a third apart, it is logical that the plica is a passing tone between them. However, if the two notes are on adjacent pitches (i.e., a second apart), the plica may move to a position of anticipation of the following note or it may skip a third and return by step to the note that follows.

Other uses of the plica (e.g., in elongated note patterns) are beyond the purview of this brief study, but interested students could pursue the subject further in such works as those cited earlier (see n. 4). It should be stated that authors have employed different means of indicating plicae in transcriptions. Possibly the most common method is the use of a smaller note with a slur connecting it to the preceding note to which it was attached in the original.

In closing the discussion of modal notation, it should be observed that essentially two different variants were used. The first variant was characterized by the extensive use of single notes to a syllable and, consequently, by relatively few ligatures. This is especially characteristic of the secular literature of the period in which complete ligature-pattern ordines were almost never used. On the other hand, the sacred music, characterized by a frequently melismatic (many notes to a single syllable) treatment of the texts, required a more concise system of notation (parchment was often at a premium) which gave rise to the ligature patterns discussed earlier. Of course the single-note notation was also employed by the Church when it was appropriate to the treatment of the text.

Although it has been suggested that multiplicity of modes is not likely to be found in single works, the statement is most accurately applied to the monophonic literature. In compositions of two or more parts, it is quite characteristic for the upper part or parts to be in one mode and the lower part or parts to be in another, typically the Spondaic. The two-voiced excerpt in Example 1.3 demonstrates a combination of the Dactylic and Spondaic modes and includes a few passing-note plicae. Note the use of the three-note ligature and the individual longa in the tenor. As the piece is transcribed, it becomes apparent that the first member of each pair of single longae must be interpreted as a double longa to accommodate the flow of the music. The need to make such rhythmic interpretations is frequent and must be exercised with care and discretion.

Tenor

Transcription

Example 1.3. Motet: *O Maria—Nostrum*, (Excerpt). London, British Museum, Add. 30091, fol. 1, thirteenth century.

Franconian Notation

In his treatise *Ars Cantus Mensurablis* (c. 1260), Franco of Cologne codified a rhythmic notation that gave precise values for the member pitches of the ligatures used in modal notation. This system provided composers with increased flexibility in their efforts to achieve greater variety and expression in composition and was clearly the result of an extension and modification of the ligature practices developed earlier.

Table 1.7. Some Basic Franconian Ligatures

Values[a]	Franconian Ligatures				Modern Equivalents				Propriety and Perfection
	Ascending		*Descending*		*Ascending*		*Descending*		
	Binaria	Ternaria	Binaria	Ternaria	Binaria	Ternaria	Binaria	Ternaria	
B(B)L									with propriety and perfection
L(B)L									without propriety with perfection
B(B)B									with propriety without perfection
L(B)B									without propriety without perfection
SS(B)[b]									with opposite propriety
SS(L)									with opposite propriety

[a] It should be noted that all longa are subject to perfect or imperfect interpretation depending upon context. Bracketed values show the location of the third member of a ternaria.

[b] All ligatures that begin with two semibreves are considered to be with opposite propriety.

The principle in modal notation of having the music flow in a series of perfections remained essentially unchanged (although the duple versus triple controversy became more acute in this later notation). Within these perfections, various patterns or rhythmic values were possible, as has already been suggested. When describing the rhythmic structure of these patterns, theorists have used the terms *propriety* and *perfection*. A ligature is said to have propriety when the first note is a breve and to have perfection when the final note is a longa. The four basic possibilities are shown in Table 1.7: (1) with propriety and perfection; (2) without propriety but with perfection; (3) with propriety but without perfection; (4) without propriety or perfection.

It is quite apparent that this new system evolved from the earlier modal notation — employs the same ligatures as a point of departure. However, an essential characteristic of Franconian notation which was not true of modal notation is that the *appearance* of the ligature was a vital element in determining the rhythmic components that constitute it.

The values of single notes in Franconian notation were the same as in modal notation. To these (perfect longa, imperfect longa, breve, and altered breve) was added one smaller value which usually appeared in pairs — the *semibreve*. This new value was notated by adding a vertical stroke to the beginning of a ligature which transformed the first two notes of the ligature into semibreves as shown in Example 1.4.

Example 1.4. Notation of Semibreves.

The semibreve pairs took the place of a single breve and were frequently attached to compound ligatures, as shown above. This type of ligature, with or without semibreves, was quite common in Franconian notation when several notes were to be sung to a single syllable. Owing to the clarity of the symbols used in this notation, even large groupings of notes were not obscured when treated in this manner. See Example 1.5.

Transcription

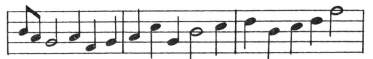

Example 1.5. Attached Groups of Ligatures.

One of the most significant contributions of Franconian notation was the establishment of precise values for the symbols used for rests, which provided composers with considerably greater freedom. Parts could assume more individuality, new textures could be introduced with greater control over the change, and various expressive devices could evolve (e.g., *hocket*, which will be discussed in a later chapter).

The symbols for rests in this notational system were vertical bars of varying lengths. In addition to the double bar that concluded a piece, five values of rests were recognized: the perfect longa; the imperfect longa; the breve; and the major and minor semibreves. The last distinction refers to the possible division of the breve into thirds. The major semibreve rest functioned as two-thirds of a triplet breve whereas the minor semibreve rest functioned as one-third of a triplet breve.

The plica was used infrequently in the Franconian system. When it did ap-

Table 1.8. Rhythmic Interpretation of the Plica

Perfect longa with plica (longer line on the right ascending or descending)	
Imperfect longa with plica (longer line on the right ascending or descending)	
Breve with plica (longer line on the left either ascending or descending)	
Plica on the final note of a ligature (vertical line ascending or descending from the head of the last member of the ligature)	

pear, and this was true of all other elements of the notation system as well, it had a more definite shape that was associated with its rhythmic role. Whereas in modal notation the plica simply consisted of a pair of vertical stems pointing in the appropriate direction from the note to which it was attached, in the Franconian system the stems of the plica had a specific location and direction for each rhythmic function it (the plica) assumed. Some uses of the plica are demonstrated in Table 1.8.

One interesting peculiarity of the notation of this period should be noted before this discussion closes. Score form as we know it (several parts aligned vertically) was used in a variety of sacred forms (e.g., *organum*). In the thirteenth century, especially in the motet, a unique layout of the voice parts was used. There were several varieties, but the most widely used seems to have

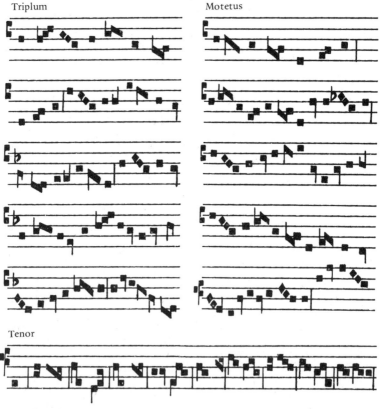

Example 1.6. Motet: *Se valours—Bien me—Hic factus est*. Bamberg, Staatsbibliothek, Ed. IV 6, fol. 9ro.

d

been one in which the *triplum* (uppermost sounding part) appeared on the upper left side of the page; the *motetus* (middle voice part) was on the upper right side of the page; and the *tenor* (lowest sounding voice part) was written across the bottom of the page. Since in many instances the tenor part was apparently intended for instruments and since most frequently the longest rhythmic values were associated with it, the use of compound ligatures was quite common and the part itself quite compressed compared with the other two parts. See Example 1.6.

This example is interesting because it reflects the historical phenomenon that change generally takes place gradually not suddenly, although the contributions of some individuals may, at times, give the impression that the reverse is true. The upper two voices in this example are clearly in Franconian notation whereas the lowest voice is in modal notation. Because notation evolved rapidly in this period, it is not uncommon to find examples of various notational developments and practices in a single manuscript.

One further notation of the Middle Ages remains to be discussed, the *Ars Nova*. However, since the balance of our work in this period will be undertaken in this notation, it will be considered in a separate chapter.

If students are to grasp fully the inherent limitations and characteristic styles of the notations considered up to this point, a few basic premises must be recognized. First, composers of the period wrote solely for the male voice and usually stayed within the comfortable compass of the respective voices (rarely more than a tenth). This naturally resulted in the use of few movable clefs and never more than a single leger line above or below the staff.

The second and clearly more involved premise relates to the evolving concept of rhythm. In plainsong notation only the most general suggestions of rhythmic variance were provided, and these appeared late in the development of this notation. Rhythmic interpretation of musical/textual phrases was left to the discretion of the singer, which may have resulted in regular chanting with little or no alteration or in a free rhythmic presentation based on any one of a number of practices. Modal and Franconian notations, however, were based on the concept of perfection and imperfection. All groupings of notes were expected to move in perfections, although individual notes could be perfect or imperfect. It is on this ternary or compound metrical concept (e.g., Trochaic and Dactylic, respectively) that the interpretation of all symbols was based. If one adds to this the absence of rest symbols having specific values in modal notation and the limited rest possibilities in Franconian notation, it is obvious that the system was quite restrictive. Rhythms that were possible and impossible or unstylistic during this period are given in Table 1.9. The possibilities must be interpreted, of course, within the limitations of the

Table 1.9. Basic Rhythmic Possibilities and Limitations of Modal and Franconian Notation[a]

Possible values

Values added by use of the plica

Impossible or unstylistic values

[a] 𝅗𝅥. = longa;   𝅗𝅥 = imperfect longa or altered breve;   ♩ = breve.

rhythmic modes and the symbols employed in each of the notational systems. Students should also take cognizance of earlier remarks regarding the different interpretations prevalent among scholars in the field.

Summary

Following the development of the square notation system for pitch definition, the evolution of notation was almost exclusively concerned with devising a functional rhythmic notation. The earliest steps toward the development of a means of notating rhythm reflect an adaptation of plainsong's square symbols and of the poetic modes into a viable modal notation. This system appeared in two forms: one used patterns of ligatures (formerly compound neumes) which followed certain conventions for interpretation in an essentially melismatic organum style (to be discussed in the next chapter); the other was based on the interpretation of the former virga as having two degrees of long value and the former breve as having the referential short value in a basically syllabic style. The first was associated with sacred literature and the second with both sacred and secular literature.

The Franconian system of notation was, in part, a codification of practices before Franco's treatise and was particularly innovative in the further refinement of rhythmic notation. This system draws fully upon existing notational devices but is distinguished by the assignment of specific values to specific note shapes. Of particular importance in the development of the Franconian system was the definition of rests. Before this period, rests simply assumed the value remaining after a given passage (e.g., an ordo) was concluded and did not have the freedom and clarity that the Franconian system provided.

Both the sacred and secular forms throughout the period were predicated on the concept of perfection. This required that the music flow in a series of perfect longae or the equivalent, i.e., in groupings of three pulses. Some of the music of the Franconian period is believed by some scholars to be more accurately transcribed in duple meter (imperfections).

Substitution ligatures in modal notation, the use of plicae in both systems, and the smaller values recognized in Franconian notation provided greater rhythmic-value possibilities than is suggested by the three basic values upon which the rhythmic concept is based (i.e., perfect longa, imperfect longa, and breve). The appearance and wide use of the semibreve in the Franconian system served to project the breve value into the more important role of unit-of-measure reference and opened up the notational and musical systems for a rather rapid accumulation of smaller note values in the period immediately following.

One final characteristic peculiar to Franconian notation in the entire history of notation (until some very recent experiments) is that ligatures could be grouped together in rather large numbers without losing clarity of pitch or rhythmic definition.

Throughout the period of approximately 300 years (c. 1000-1300) during which the notations discussed in this chapter evolved, a large number of the most basic characteristics of Western music were defined and initially explored (e.g., multipart writing, canonic and imitation techniques). The recognition of some of these as informal practices impelled theorists to seek and devise workable notations, and the development of the notations impelled composers to explore new compositional techniques. The two are totally interdependent and inseparable.

plainsong

Plainsong is a monophonic form of music embodying a vast literature, much of which reflects a refined and sophisticated concept of melody. Large collections of secular and sacred monophonic music exist that date from the Middle Ages and have a number of unifying characteristics.

The linear concept of this literature is strongly conjunct, i.e., many seconds and thirds, fewer fourths and fifths, very few sixths and octaves, practically no sevenths, and no intervals larger than an octave. Its range normally remains within the comfortable span of the human (male) voice — approximately a tenth. Only one chromatic alteration (Bb) is used and that to avoid a linear tritone and to provide subtle nuances of line. The natural and flat forms of the B are never used immediately adjacent to each other (a practice referred to as *degree inflection*).

As suggested in Chapter 1, there is no formal rhythmic scheme, but performance practices have resulted in some consistency of interpretation. Relatively short phrases characterize this music. These may vary in length from a few notes to as many as twenty pitches. The tempo is usually not indicated in the manuscripts but has been described as being derived from the speed of such human functions as heartbeat or a walking pace — what today may be interpreted as approximately a moderato tempo.

The form or broad architectural design of the music of this period is usually determined by the text. However, some purely musical structuring elements can be identified (e.g., return to musical phrases with or without the same text). The modest levels of linear pitch-determined tension and resolve which may assume a structural function derive their relative value from the respective positions of the pitches in the prevailing ecclesiastical modes. There is a sense of internal unity and logic in this modal music.

Dynamic variation is not shown in the music but is left to the performer who, traditionally, departs only slightly from the *mp-mf* performance levels. Some dynamic variation results naturally from the frequent use of alternating soloist and choir.

Plainsong is further characterized by three melodic styles and three performance classes. The former refers to the number of individual pitches sung to a single syllable of text in any given section of a chant or in the piece as a whole. The latter provides a basic architectural or form delineation. The melodic styles of plainsong — *syllabic*, *neumatic*, and *melismatic* — are demonstrated in Example 2.1

Syllabic: usually confined to one note for each syllable

Do - mi - ne De - us

Neumatic: a few notes are sung for most syllables (usually
             neumes of two or more notes)

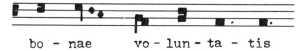

bo - nae   vo - lun - ta - tis

Melismatic: a florid passage with many neumes (of all
              types) sung to single syllables)

Chri - - ste

Example 2.1. Melodic Styles of Plainsong. The Syllabic and Neumatic are from the *Liber Usualis*, Gloria, p. 86, and the Melismatic is from the same volume, Kyrie IX (*O Pater Excelse*), p. 85. Reprinted with permission from the 1963 edition of Desclee & Co., Tournai-Doornik, Belgium.

The three basic performance classes of chant, which will be discussed more extensively in Chapter 3, are: *strophic*, in which all stanzas of a text are sung to the same music (e.g., hymns); *psalmadic*, including both responsorial and antiphonal psalmody, in which sections are repeated, with choir answering soloist or two choirs answering each other; and *through-composed*, in which new musical ideas unfold from the beginning to the end of the piece (e.g., the typical Gloria and Credo sections of a Mass).

The Ecclesiastical Modes

All the factors considered to this point are finally dependent upon the fundamental distinguishing characteristics of the modal system, which largely make it possible to distinguish one chant from another. At the same time, certain of these characteristics also serve to establish groupings of melodic figures resulting from the relationship between tones and the varied functions of the tones that comprise the ecclesiastical modes. Although the names of these modes are derived from the Greek melodic modes, there is only a limited relationship between the two. See Example 2.2.

Each ecclesiastical mode has certain defining components beyond the simple scale patterns shown in Example 2.2. Some of the elements that contribute to the definition of these modes are:

> *finalis*: the tone that functions as the focal point for the mode. It is often used as the final tone, although this is not essential.
>
> *reciting tone*: (also referred to as *tenor* or *confinalis*). This tone serves as a primary focal point in the melody (particularly internally) and as a substitute for the finalis; it is also the reciting tone in the psalms.
>
> *range*: the prescribed range of each mode is rarely exceeded by more than a tone above or below.
>
> *musica ficta*: the use of an altered tone (only Bb in plainsong) often in Modes I and V, frequently in Modes II and VI, and virtually never in Modes III, IV, VII, and VIII.
>
> *melodic patterns*: the melodic figures associated with the mode that contribute to its unique quality.
>
> *absolute initial*: a confusing term used by at least one author to refer to one of the many possible starting tones characteristic of each mode – for some modes as many as six of the possible seven tones are defined as "absolute initials."

The first four components listed above are presented for convenient reference in Table 2.1 (the fourth is shown indirectly in the Half-Step Locations column). The fifth component will be discussed more fully below, and the sixth

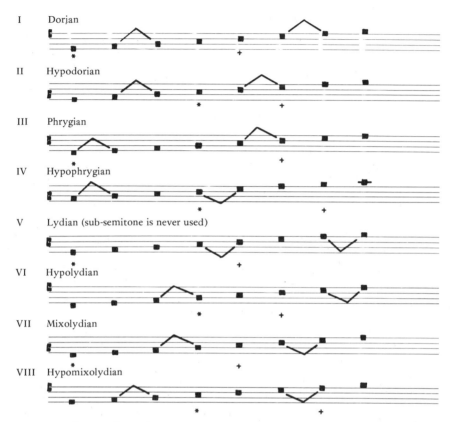

Example 2.2. The Ecclesiastical Modes. An asterisk indicates the finalis; a plus, the reciting tone; and the large and inverted carets, the location of the half steps. Plagal modes (II, IV, VI, and VIII) seldom use the notes below the finalis.

Table 2.1. Characteristics of the Ecclesiastical Modes

Mode	Authentic	Plagal	Range	Finalis	Reciting Tone[a]	Half-Step Locations
I	Dorian		d-d′	d	a′	2-3 and 6-7
II		Hypodorian	a-a′	d	f	2-3 and 5-6
III	Phrygian		e-e′	e	c′	1-2 and 5-6
IV		Hypophrygian	b-b′	e	a′	1-2 and 4-5
V	Lydian		f-f′	f	c′	4-5 and 7-8
VI		Hypolydian	c-c′	f	a′	3-4 and 7-8
VII	Mixolydian		g-g′	g	d′	3-4 and 6-7
VIII		Hypomixolydian . .	d-d′	g	c′	2-3 and 6-7

[a]The reciting tone is referred to by some authors as either the *confinalis* or the *tenor*.

will be dropped from further consideration since it seems to contribute confusion rather than clarity.

It should be noted that the modes, as they appear in Example 2.2, are more closely akin to our tonal representations than to modal representations. Little more than a convenient reference to the most basic modal attributes can be provided in such an example. Scale associations are so integral to the tonal system to which most of us have been conditioned that this approach may be helpful in terms of our orientation, but it can be quite misleading when considering the spirit of the modes. The principal attributes of the modes are not simply those associated with their scale-pattern intervallic relationships. The modes are more accurately represented by the elements that contribute to the sense of mood with which each mode can be identified — that is, the elements delineated in Table 2.1 — and the melodic figurations, such as those provided in Table 2.2. The latter may historically have greater significance and may be more subtle than the former. Also such a practice can be shown to be closely related to the musical practices of Hindu and Arabic cultures in which small

Table 2.2. The Ecclesiastical Modes: Characteristic Melodic Figures[a]

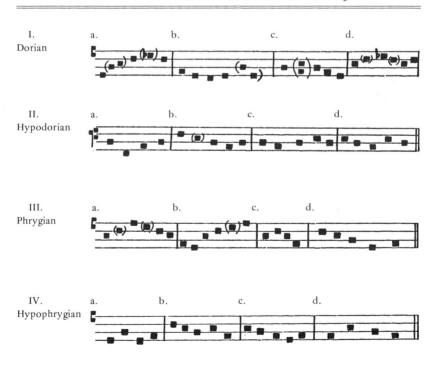

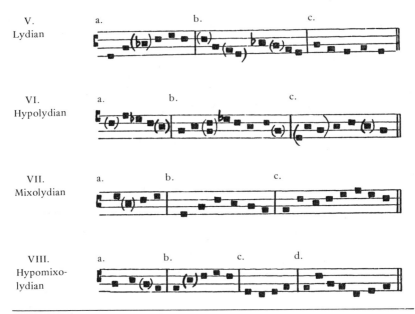

[a]These melodic patterns occur often enough in the respective modes that they may be considered characteristic and may contribute to the definition of the mode. The note (or notes) enclosed in parentheses may or may not appear and thus may be considered relatively incidental in the figure. The basic melodic contour and the notes of arrival at the principal positions in that contour are the most important elements.

melodic components provide the bases for lengthy compositions through various embellishments and extensions.

The melodic figures shown in Table 2.2 are examples from the numerous possibilities that exist for each mode. The use of figures such as these is necessarily subject to considerable discussion and to flexibility in interpretation. Some figures appear in different modes in the same or similar forms, and some seem, by their very nature, to be universal as simple melodic figures. However, those in Table 2.2 appear more consistently in prominent melodic positions in the respective modes and seem to have a more definitive function in these modes. Particularly important are the patterns that appear either at the beginning of a given mode or at a cadence (internal or final). The largest number of the figures provided are employed in this manner.

Although these melodic components are found in some form in many examples of plainsong, it is unusual to find them in close proximity or relatively unadorned. The first section of the *Kyrie Orbis Factor* provides a clear, melodic Dorian scheme. In Example 2.3 three of the four patterns listed in Table 2.2 for this mode are given: patterns d, a, and b (in order of their appearance). The d pattern is quite straightforward; the a pattern is a free interpretation of the skip of a fifth in close proximity with the notes g and b^b in something of a free retrograde form; and the b pattern is complete and unadorned.

Example 2.3. *Kyrie Orbis Factor* (first section). *Liber Usualis*, p. 85. Reprinted with permission from the 1963 edition of Desclee & Co., Tournai-Doornik, Belgium.

Another example which is reasonably clear and employs the three figures provided for Mode V in the order they appear in Table 2.2 is *Kyrie Altissime* (see Example 2.4). None of these are unembellished and some flexibility is necessary when interpreting the passage in this fashion.

Example 2.4. *Kyrie Altissime* (first section). *Liber Usualis*, p. 81. Reprinted with permission from the 1963 edition of Desclee & Co., Tournai-Doornik, Belgium.

The first of these, to the asterisk, uses all the required tones from the pattern provided but is elongated by the c'-a'-c' motion (notes four, five, and six) before stating its two final notes. The b pattern is most obscured by the embellished descent to the a' which is suggested in Table 2.2 by the optional notes. The c' of the climacus is again an embellishing tone before the balance of the pattern is stated. The c pattern interlocks with the end of the preceding pattern and is elongated by embellishing oscillations between the member notes.

These two examples should make it apparent that the patterns (and these are but a sampling) can vary in value from providing great clarity to requiring considerable freedom of interpretation.

Plainsong Line

The principles of good plainsong line provide the foundation for evolving concepts of linear writing throughout the ensuing history of Western music.

Each era has molded and shaped these principles to suit its own concepts of beauty and to express its own historical temperament, but all owe their basic premises to this literature.

The first principle in the search for beauty in any time and with any style is freedom of expression and avoidance of rigidity. Rules that theorists have established in retrospect must be understood to be no more than honest efforts to explain the creative processes which led to the resulting styles. The creative mind never works in a vacuum but always enjoys rich resources of knowledge. However, it also enjoys and vigorously protects the privilege of free choice and the exercise of personal aesthetic judgment. It is in light of this first principle that all suggested guides to the study of style must be interpreted.

Plainsong line has been described as essentially conjunct — lines unfold mostly in steps with a moderate number of thirds. The thirds do not detract from but rather contribute to this conjunct sense by providing a modest shading of variety of effect within a narrow intervallic context. A fluid line with a distinguishable sense of forward motion must always be sought.[1] That exquisite linear flow can be achieved within such limitations is clearly reflected in the excerpt in Example 2.5, a piece which has intrigued composers for a thousand years and has been used in the works of many, even in electronic music.

Di - es ir - ae, di - es   il - la,   Sol-vet sae - clum in fa-vil- la

Example 2.5. *Dies Irae* (first two incises). *Liber Usualis*, p. 1810. Reprinted with permission from the 1963 edition of Desclee & Co., Tournai-Doornik, Belgium.

Larger intervals should be used freely but with discretion. It is relatively rare to find several large intervals in close proximity. More commonly they are used to emphasize the effects of a contour, to create a stronger sense of motion, and to provide variety in the flow of a line. The *Kyrie* in Example 2.6 demonstrates the beautiful and typical use of a single large skip (a fifth) in a conjunct setting.

Ky - ri - e   * e - -- le - i - son. iij

Example 2.6. *Kyrie Orbis Factor* (first two incises). *Liber Usualis*, p. 85. Reprinted with permission from the 1963 edition of Desclee & Co., Tournai-Doornik, Belgium.

The principal tones in a line are the primary tones in the mode in which that line has been conceived — that is the finalis and the reciting tone. However, it is not uncommon for the tones located a third or fourth above the finalis to assume roles of prominence. Definitive rules for such selections are impractical and would require so many qualifications that they would be useless. It is better for students to work initially with the finalis and reciting tones as focal points until they become more confident and have developed a sensitivity to the spirit of the literature. Then as each line unfolds it should be permitted to provide its own reference points to perceptive and sensitive composers. This kind of flexibility, predicated upon as extensive an exposure to the plainsong literature as possible, should produce the desired results for the music students.

The tritone should be avoided at all times, both directly and indirectly. Consequently it is necessary to insert the Bb in the modes in which both the *b* and *f* have melodic prominence. Certainly this is not going to be true with the appearance of every *b*. Such generalizations are dangerous if interpreted literally for every occurrence. However, three characteristic uses can be delineated: (1) between two *a*'s as an upper neighboring tone; (2) to avoid a tritone skip (i.e., from *f* to *b*^{b} instead of *f* to *b'*); (3) in a descending scale line from above the *b'*. The second of these three possible uses of the flat is observed strictly, the first and third more freely. It should also be understood that the use of this flat is restricted to Modes I, II, V, and VI. It rarely occurs in the other modes, except when a passage becomes modally unstable and a sense of Modes I, II, V, or VI is sought. Characteristic uses of the B flat are shown in Example 2.7.

Example 2.7. Use of the B Flat in Plainsong.

Placement of Text

A few simple guides should be sufficient for the intelligent placement of a text to a plainsong line. Of primary importance is that no change of syllable or word can take place in the middle of a neume. This should immediately suggest the graphic appearance of the several performance styles. That is, melismatic plainsong will have many multipitched neumes to each syllable or word whereas the syllabic type will exculisvely have punctus with an occasional two-note neume (rarely more). Neumatic plainsong will, of course, have a syllable or word for longer neumes or small groupings of simpler neumes.

In the Kyrie section of a Mass, the last syllable of both the Kyrie and the Christe (i.e., the *e* sound) is usually treated melismatically. In that same section the first syllable of *eleison* is treated melismatically which often produces the effect of a single word (e.g., *Kyrieleison*). The extension of a word over many pitches in melismatic and neumatic singing is always done with an open vowel sound. In the *alleluia*, the second syllable (the *le*) is usually treated very melismatically.

No strict practice appears to have been defined regarding whether the beginning, middle, or end of a word should receive the most melismatic treatment. Although there is consistency of practice in such instances as those described above, in general the division of a word is left to the good taste of the composer. An effort should certainly be made to have these changes occur at points in the melody that are compatible with its contour, with the relative degree of openness of the sound of the syllable to the pitch possibilities, and with the smooth sense of the line. Abruptness should be avoided in all aspects of plainsong writing because it is diametrically opposed to the spirit of the style.

Solmization

In an effort to facilitate learning and memorizing the melodies of the plainsong literature, especially needed for the long melisma sections, Guido d'Arezzo developed a system of neutral syllables which could be used in any mode, could move freely between modes, and provided each interval with a specific set of possible syllable relationships. A particular emphasis was placed on the half step and on the maintenance of the same syllable pattern for that interval

Example 2.8. *Ut queant laxis. Liber Usualis*, p. 1504. Reprinted with permission from the 1963 edition of Desclee & Co., Tournai-Doornik, Belgium.

throughout the system. The syllables he used were taken from the first sylla-ble of each incise of the hymn *Ut queant laxis*. In Example 2.8 this hymn is shown with the syllables underlined that were extracted to produce this sys-tem.

This is known as the *Hexachord System* because it employs a set of six syl-lables which is moved from one order of six notes to another, as necessary, to retain the position of the mi-fa (half step) relationship. Three such hexa-chords are identified by the presence or absence of *b* and the form of that note. If no *b* is present (i.e., the hexachord that begins on *c*), the hexachord is called *naturale* (natural). With a *b* natural present (i.e., the hexachord that be-gins on *g*), the hexachord is called *durum* (hard). The final hexachord, begin-ning on *f*, is referred to as *molle* (soft) owing to the presence of the *b flat*. No other hexachords are possible for they each contain the pattern two whole steps, one half step, and two whole steps, and are limited to the use of a single altered tone—*b* flat.

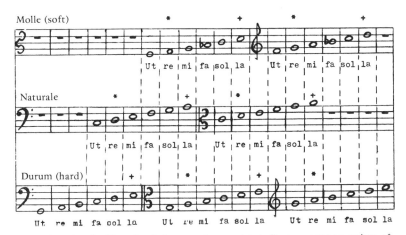

Example 2.9. The Hexachord System. An asterisk indicates common points of mutation ascending; a plus, common points of mutation descending.

Movement from one hexachord to another, frequently necessitated by range and variance between *b'* and *b'* flat in relatively close proximity, is re-ferred to as *mutation*. Certain syllables in each of the hexachords serve as convenient points of change from one hexachord to another. The three hexa-chords together with the points of most convenient change are shown in Ex-ample 2.9. Often a repeated pitch may provide the most convenient position

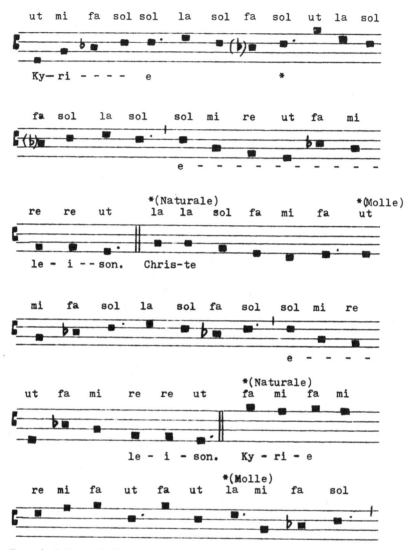

Example 2.10. *Kyrie de angelis* (excerpt). *Liber Usualis*, p. 37. Reprinted with permission from the 1963 edition of Desclee & Co., Tournai-Doornik, Belgium.

for change from one hexachord to another. Example 2.10 demonstrates hexachord usage with mutation between molle and naturale.

Summary

The monophonic literature of the Middle Ages exists in large quantity, was reasonably consistent in compositional practice, and was notated in a system that proved to be the foundation of the notational evolution that continued into the twentieth century.

Three notable performance styles developed which were largely dictated by the length or function of the text. The entire literature is conceived within the bounds of the ecclesiastical modes which essentially define patterns of intervallic relationships and tone functions within each mode.

Plainsong line is predominantly conjunct, but there is a discreet use of some wide skips. It should be relaxed and free-flowing within the comfortable range of the male voice and should never create a sense of strain which could detract from the central purpose of the music — i.e., serving as a vehicle to reinforce the textual idea.

To facilitate the process of learning the plainsong literature, Guido d'Arezzo devised a solmization system of six syllables which, by retaining the identity of the half step and adjusting pitch names, permitted free motion with intervallic security throughout the possibilities of the modal system.

monophonic forms

Monophonic music of the Middle Ages derives its broad organizaitional logic from phrases, sections, and larger structures or forms which fall into several general categories. In many of the forms, the music is through-composed (i.e., there is no reference in the latter part of a piece to the musical materials presented in the earlier portion — a continuous unfolding of new ideas).

Sacred plainsong was composed to serve two principal services of the Catholic Church — the Mass and the Offices. Each of these consists of several different sections which have a clear service function. Some sections of the text vary with the Church seasons or with special occasions, but others remain the same for all services. The portion of the Mass for which the texts are unchanging is referred to as the Ordinary of the Mass.[1] The variable sections are known as the Proper of the Mass. The texts of the Ordinary have remained the same for over a thousand years and have been set as major compositions by leading composers of every historical period.

The five musical sections of the Ordinary of the Mass invite, by the varied lengths of their texts, differing musical treatments. The section with the shortest text (the Kyrie eleison) tends to be the most melismatic and the section with the longest text (the Credo) is usually highly syllabic. Also, the relative clarity of the textual forms of the Kyrie and Agnus sections produces a definable musical form for each. To a lesser degree this is true for the Sanctus section. However, the textual structure of both the Gloria and the Credo usually produces through-composed music. The formal and stylistic treatment of the Ordinary may be summarized as follows:

> *Kyrie eleison*: melismatic; generally in some variety of a broad three-part form such as *A-B-A*, *A-B-C*, or *A-A-A*.[2] Since each section of the text is repeated three times before the next is stated (producing, in reality, a nine-part form), variations on the simple three-part patterns mentioned above may be employed by altering one or more of the repeated sections musically (e.g., *aab*, *ccc*, *ddd* or *abc*, *ddd*, *abc*, with the sections between the commas retaining the same text).
>
> *Gloria*: syllabic or partially neumatic and through-composed.
>
> *Credo*: syllabic and through-composed.
>
> *Sanctus*: neumatic or melismatic with a variety of three-part structures (the Hosanna and/or Benedictus portions may serve as separate musical ideas).
>
> *Agnus Dei*: syllabic or neumatic (sometimes melismatic) and set in a simple three-part form (e.g., *A-A-A*).

The Proper of the Mass consists of several musical sections with variable texts determined by the occasion in the Church calendar that they are designed to serve. The musical sections of the Proper are: Introit, Gradual, Alleluia or Tract, Sequence (only five remain in use), Offertory, and Communion. These are, for the most part, syllabic and through-composed. Some neumatic writing is used, and melismatic sections do appear, especially in the Alleluia. The Sequence has a distinct form, which will be discussed shortly.

There are eight Divine Offices (Canonical Hours), which occur every three hours beginning at midnight in the following order: Matins, Lauds, Prime, Terce, Sext, None, Vespers, and Compline. The principal musical sections of the Office services include: Antiphons, Psalms, Hymns, and the Magnificat (Mary's song upon learning that she will be the mother of Christ).

Various settings of the musical sections of the Mass and Offices have been explored by composers throughout history from the simplicity of plainsong to the complexities of full orchestral-choral compositions. The formal structure of the Ordinary of the Mass has been significantly expanded in some later treatments (e.g., the *B-Minor Mass* of J. S. Bach). However, the fundamental principles and structures have guided compositional decisions and have remained essentially unchanged (i.e., sections with natural patterns, such as the three-part Kyrie, retain these patterns regardless of dimension).

Other Sacred Forms and Techniques

The Hymn developed as a form acceptable to the Church in the fourth century under St. Ambrose. It may be liturgical or nonliturgical and is thought to have adopted the popular style of its day (often using favorite secular tunes), characterized by simple melodies and syllabic text treatment. The pieces, intended to be sung by the congregation, were in strophic form (i.e., all strophes — stanzas — to the same music). In Example 3.1 compare the first line of music with the third (beginning at the double bar). The same treatment is carried throughout the hymn, i.e., the same music is repeated with each stanza of text.

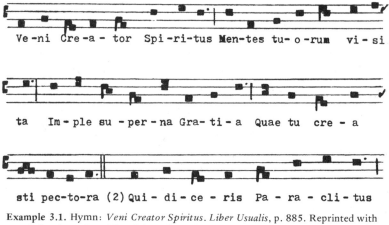

Example 3.1. Hymn: *Veni Creator Spiritus. Liber Usualis*, p. 885. Reprinted with permission from the 1963 edition of Desclee & Co., Tournai-Doornik, Belgium.

The Hymn, as indicated earlier, is one musical part of the Divine Offices. A second, the *Sequence*, has had a somewhat turbulent history. Only five presently remain in use, one of which — the *Stabat Mater* — was abandoned by the Council of Trent but reinstated in the eighteenth century. The remaining four are: *Veni sancte spiritus*, *Victimae paschali laudes*, *Laude Sion*, and *Dies irae*.

The Sequence follows a double versicle structure that consists of melodic couplets (e.g., y . . aa . . bb . . cc . . dd . . . . z). The first and last may form a couplet in the same manner as the internal adjacent pairs, or they may be two separate melodies not paired musically. In Example 3.2 the first phrase is an independent melody which is not paired musically with the final one. The passages beginning with *Agnus* and *Mors* represent the first melodic couplet. *Dic nobis* introduces the tune for the second couplet, the second half of which begins with *Angelicos testes* on the repeat of the tune. The final musical idea in this Sequence is essentially an independent tune, although some relationship can be found between it and the melody of the first couplet (i.e., beginning with *Agnus*).

Example 3.2. Sequence: *Victimae paschali laudes*. *Liber Usualis*, p. 780. Reprinted with permission from the 1963 edition of Desclee & Co., Tournai-Doornik, Belgium.

A technique of interpolating an explanatory nonliturgical text between words of the original text (but not restricted to the language of the original, e.g., the original may be in Latin, the interpolated words in French), developed between the ninth and thirteenth centuries. This technique, *troping*, may have been used with one or two words or with lengthy, descriptive, poetic texts. All tropes were removed by the Council of Trent, but many Kyries are still identified by the opening words of the trope that was once used for them.[3] In Example 3.3 untroped and troped versions of a portion of a Kyrie may be compared. In the original form the Kyrie is repeated three times before the Christe begins. In the troped form, the music for the Kyrie is repeated three times, but a different portion of the trope text is placed against each of the three statements. In the following example, the troped form is shown for the first Kyrie statement and the beginning of the second.

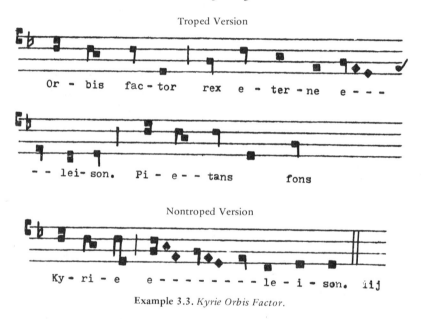

Example 3.3. *Kyrie Orbis Factor.*

An early type of monophonic sacred music that was intended to serve as "an elaboration of a liturgical act" rather than to satisfy the formal musical demands of the liturgy was the *conductus*. The first use of the term is believed to have been in the *Play of Daniel*, a twelfth-century liturgical drama. The music was conceived as accompaniment for processions. Its form is very free, including strophic (hymnlike), double versicle, and through-composed types. The stanzas are uniform as in a hymn.

Example 3.4 is a conductus by the composer Perotin (fl. late twelfth century) of Notre Dame, Paris. The entire first phrase and the melisma (cauda) are repeated.

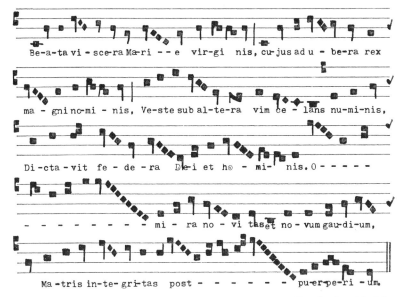

Example 3.4. Conductus: *Beata viscera Marie virginis.* Wolfenbüttel 1099, fol. 156v.

Secular Monophonic Forms and Performance Styles

During the eleventh to fourteenth centuries, a great many secular monophonic forms were developed by the troubadours (southern France), the trouvères (northern France), the Minnesinger and Meistersinger (Germany), and a variety of minstrels (e.g., jongleurs). The musical designs of their works were derived from the form of the poetic texts to which the music was written. The names of these forms varied from one locale to another, but the principal designs remained essentially the same. Although written in simple plainsong notation, these works, it is believed by some authors, derived their rhythmic structure from the poetic meter of the text (as discussed in Chapter 1).

The simplest of the secular monophonic forms is the *vers* which, like the hymn, is a strophic form, i.e., the same melody is repeated for each stanza of the text. The anonymous vers shown in Example 3.5 is accompanied by four additional stanzas of text in the collection from which it has been excerpted, each of which would be sung to the same music as the first stanza (shown).

A three-part form consisting of a repeated musical section followed by a new musical section, each of which had a different text, is represented by the

Example 3.5. Vers: *Au tans d'oust.* Jean Beck, *Les Chansonniers des Troubadours et des Trouveres,* University of Pennsylvania Press, Philadelphia, 1927, Vol. I, fol. 13d.

letter scheme *aab*.[4] This form had several different names depending upon the locale of origin, e.g., *Bar* form in Germany, and the *ballade* form in France. The latter usually appears with a refrain at the end. Example 3.6 is representative of the ballade; the refrain is the single word *pris.*

The *rondeau* is a musical form used by the trouvères consisting of two sections (usually short) that are sung according to a pattern dictated by the poetic form for which the rondeau was devised. The pattern *ABaAabAB* often reflected a performance practice in which a soloist sang the stanzas and a group sang the refrain[5] (the repeated music and text are indicated by the capital letters *AB*). See Example 3.7.

In addition to the two clearly distinguishable forms of the ballade and rondeau, the trouvères also used the *virelai,* a form which gained considerable popularity and appears, in slightly varied interpretations, in the Italian and Spanish music of the period. The virelai, like the ballade and rondeau, consisted of two basic musical phrases *AbbaA,* which occurred according to the pattern of the text. See Example 3.8. A common grouping consisted of three statements of the basic pattern (i.e., AbbaAbbaAbbaA). Similar to the ron-

Example 3.6. Ballade: *Je nuns hons pris*. Jean Beck, *Les Chansonniers des Troubadours et des Trouveres*, University of Pennsylvania Press, Philadelphia, 1927, Vol. I, fol., 62c.

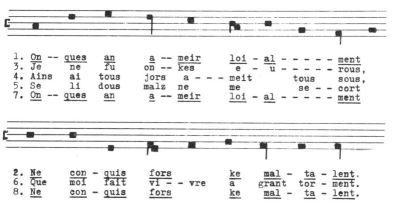

Example 3.7. Rondeau: *Onques an ameir*. Reprinted with permission from the 2nd edition, 1970, of Friederich Gennrich, *Formenlehre des Mittelalterlichen Liedes*, Max Niemeyer Verlag, Tübingen, 1932. This piece is a slight variant of the rondeau in that the fourth line returns with the music of A but employs a different text, producing ABaaabAB rather than the expected ABaAabAB.

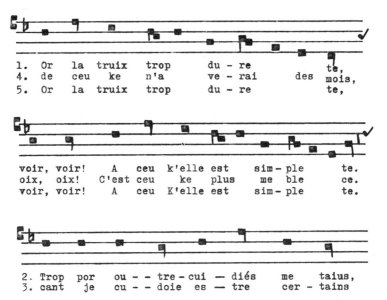

1.	Or	la	truix	trop	du – re		te,
4.	de	ceu	ke	n'a	ve – rai	des	mois,
5.	Or	la	truix	trop	du – re		te,

voir, voir!	A	ceu	k'elle est	sim – ple	te.
oix, oix!	C'est ceu	ke	plus	me ble	ce.
voir, voir!	A	ceu	K'elle est	sim – ple	te.

| 2. | Trop | por | ou – – tre – cui — diés | me | taius, |
| 3. | cant | je | cu – – doie es — tre | cer – tains |

Example 3.8. Virelai: *Or la truix*. Montpellier, Faculté de Medecins, H 196, fol. 338.

deau, the refrain (capital letters) was frequently sung by an informal audience. This form was later (fourteenth century) called *chanson balladée* by the French composer Guillaume de Machaut. Also, the *ballata* in Italy closely resembles it.

The forms described in the preceding pages are the principal ones for which consistent defined patterns can be identified. It should be understood that many other forms existed that were characterized by irregularity of design (e.g., the *lai* and the *rotrouenge*), or were variations on those already discussed (e.g., *ballata* and *villancico* — both variants of the virelai).

Broad generalizations are dangerous and should only be accepted with an awareness of the omnipresent possibility for inaccuracy or inapplicability when applied to a given case. However, it can be observed that there is greater freedom in the melodic construction of the secular monophonic literature than there is in the sacred. The secular tends to be more disjunct with a moderate occurrence of melodic triads — more than is usually associated with the sacred literature. Of course, as has been suggested earlier, secular monophony seems to have employed rhythmic distinctions that are, in part, the natural result of the musical setting of poetic texts — the use of the rhythmic modes. Finally, secular forms employ a considerable amount of melodic repetition resulting, also in part, from text-determined patterns. In sacred monophony, melodic repetitions are far fewer — even when suggested by text construction.

Plainsong Analytical Procedures: Sacred

The analysis of plainsong is essentially limited to the process of attempting to define the salient characteristics of modally conceived line with its several concomitant elements. Although some attention must necessarily be paid to the manner of underlaying the text and to its role in determining form, such considerations as the use of principal tones and their relationship to each other, contour of line, phrase structure and the elements contributing to its definition, and form will command the greatest part of our attention.

The first matter with which we must concern ourselves is mode determination. Reference to Table 2.1 (p. 26) will be helpful in identifying certain elements that contribute to establishing the sense of a given mode (i.e., range, reciting tone, finalis, and half-step location). Table 2.2 (p. 27) also provides a basic set of characteristic patterns associated with each of the modes which, when used with discretion, can be helpful in determining mode.

To ensure that the techniques of analysis are thoroughly understood, Example 3.9 will be used to demonstrate each step of the procedure. At the outset, however, it should be understood that regardless of how sophisticated our techniques may be or how many parameters of the music we find convenient means of delineating, each composition has idiosyncrasies and characteristics that may defy convenient or routine procedures or terminology. The development of a sensitivity to these factors must be considered a vital part of one's analytical technique.

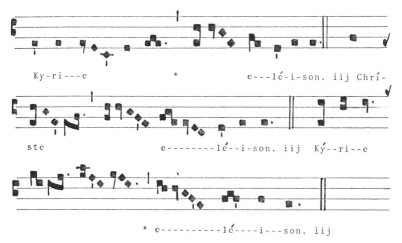

Example 3.9. *Kyrie eleison (O Pater Excelse). Liber Usualis,* p. 85. Reprinted with permission from the 1963 edition of Desclee & Co., Tournai-Doornik, Belgium.

There is no question about which is the principal tone in this example. Both by number of times sounded (22) and melodic position, *g* is the focal point of the piece. It appears in dotted form as the cadential tone at the end of each principal section and in one of the remaining three subordinate cadences. It is used twice as many times as the next most frequently appearing pitch (*a'*, which occurs 11 times). The note *g* is the finalis of Modes VII and VIII, a point to be kept in mind as we attempt to determine mode.

The second most important pitch is *c'*. This decision is based not on the number of appearances (9) — which is duplicated by two other tones (*f* and *d*) and exceeded by another (*a'*) — but on the prominent melodic position of *c*. In three of the four incises that begin with an ascending skip (which, by its nature, in a conjunct context commands the attention of the ear), the tone of arrival is *c'*. Add to this the fact that for two-thirds of the piece, in the prominent position identified, *c'* remains the highest pitch (in the final third *g'* is the top tone).

Although this information might be sufficient to justify a decision that the mode is Hypomixolydian, there can be little doubt about the validity of this decision when a few additional facts are considered. The range is from *d* to *g'*, which allows for a Mixolydian or Hypomixolydian interpretation. If we use the characteristic figures discussed earlier, as they may relate to these two modes, two Hypomixolydian figures become immediately apparent in unadorned form — figure *a*, the final cadence of the piece, and figure *c*, the cadence of the middle (Christe) section. The characteristic skip of a fourth from *g* to *c'* is reflected in figures *b* and *d* of Table 2.2 and apparent in the first two sections of the piece. A modified form of the *d* figure is used as the entire eleison incise of the first Kyrie section. Although some relationships can be drawn with figures from other modes, no set of factors can be defined to support any other mode that even remotely approximates the convincing arguments for the Hypomixolydian mode.

In summary, we have determined the mode through gradually narrowing our focus by

(a) identifying the range, which helped narrow our consideration to two probable modes (VII and VIII);

(b) determining the finalis (*g'*) by frequency of appearance and melodic function;

(c) identifying *c'* as the reciting tone by its linear functional importance;

(d) clearly identifying several characteristic melodic figures associated with a single mode.

A second consideration in the analysis of plainsong is phrase structure. This is essentially a rhythmic concept because it represents melodic expanses of time of greater or lesser length. However, it is especially interesting to note that this essentially rhythmic phenomenon is dependent for its existence in this inherently nonrhythmically varied music on the musical behavior of other musical and even extramusical components (e.g., linear contour, melodic formulae, and text).

In Example 3.9, six phrases can be clearly ascertained by the quarter and double bar divisions notated into the music. This convenient eye reference, a later innovation used throughout sacred literature, cannot be accepted matter-of-factly as part of all plainsong notation, nor does its presence rule out the possibility of the effect of lesser internal phrases. If the presence of a bar line (of whatever length) is accepted as one indication of a phrase ending, another device should be identified immediately as contributing to this effect, i.e., the elongation of the final note before a bar line which is indicated by the dot following the note.

The presence of the half, single, and double bar lines did exert a real rhythmic impact on the literature through the performance conventions that evolved in the church. The half bar was a signal for a slight ritard, and the full and double bars signaled a diminuendo and ritard, which contributed to a decisive sense of cadence (according to the Solesmes interpretation).

In addition to the six phrases in Example 3.9 that are identified by incise or sectional symbols, two shorter but reasonably distinct internal phrases can be identified. Both are five notes in length and appear adjacently in the first incise of the final Kyrie statement, each ending with a dotted note. The halting effect created by these two phrases serves to subdivide the Kyrie melisma into three parts and to reinforce subtly the slight underlying arch shape of the passage.

Other elements that contribute to the division of the piece into smaller parts of varying sizes are: (a) the double bar that defines the three sections of this Mass movement; (b) the repetition sign (iij) that parallels the sections (this compatibility may vary from one example to another); and (c) the asterisk that indicates a change from soloist to choir or from one half choir to another. All these factors must be considered when determining the broad architectural components of a plainsong line.

The final consideration in this analytical process is the definition of the form and its defining features which, when treated with care, will to some extent provide a summary of the piece. The formal structure is presented in outline form.

Nine-Part Kyrie (aaa, bbb, ccc)

Kyrie: Large *A* section (sung three times)
   First incise: three repeated tones (g) descending third and return.
                    embellished tone (g) by using an upper neighboring tone.
   Second incise: ascending skip of a fourth from *g* with embellished return to the *g*.

Christe: Large *B* section (sung three times)
   First incise: after single pitch (a′), the first figure from the second incise of the
                    figure from the second incise of the Kyrie appears with slight mod-
                    ification at the end.
   Second incise: an embellishment reminiscent of the first figure of the second incise
                    of the Kyrie leads to a return to a prominent finalis (*g*).

Kyrie: Large *C* section (sung three times)
   First incise: opening skip of a fifth is reminiscent of the first figure of the second
                    incise of Kyrie *A*. Resemblance ends immediately with a florid
                    free-composed section employing a wider range than any earlier
                    section (an octave).
                    this incise could be considered as suggesting a modal departure (to the
                    Mixolydian) with its principal tone *d′* in the middle as the confi-
                    nalis and with a range from *g-g′* (finalis).
   Second incise: returns through an innocuous scale line to the original mode and the
                    final cadence.

Example 3.10. *Kyrie eleison* (*O Pater Excelse*). Outline analysis of **Example 2.9**.

Plainsong Analytical Procedures: Secular

Analysis of secular monophonic music encompasses the same areas of ex-
amination presented for the sacred literature. Two interrelated additional elements must be considered in the analysis of the secular literature, i.e., the
form as a clearly text-derived entity and the rhythmic flow, which is also
largely derived from the text.

Examples 3.5 to 3.8 demonstrate the principle of musical form resulting
from poetic form. These examples and the many other forms (either variants
on these examples or distinctly different patterns) consist basically of two
musical ideas and a variety of verse-refrain patterns. Occasionally, a single
word will be used as a refrain (e.g., *pris*, the final word of the ballade example). Although the text often plays a role in defining the form of sacred monophony (e.g., the nine-part Kyrie or the three-part Agnus patterns), this literature is much freer and, in very large measure, through-composed.

Another marked distinction between the secular and sacred monophonic
literature is the highly syllabic and partially neumatic conception in the secular as opposed to the abundance of melismatic music in the sacred. This obvious distinction has broader implications than might be revealed in a cursory

glance. That is, whereas sacred monophonic music embodies no graphically expressed note-to-note rhythmic relationships, secular music (by virtue of its text) does. As suggested earlier, the rhythmic flow of the text in secular forms had considerable influence on the rhythmic conception of the music. Long and short values that have a clear relationship to each other and are derived from the poetic meter of the text are an integral part of the secular literature. This extramusical force, inherent in the poetry used in secular music, provided a significant impetus to the development of notational devices for musical rhythmic definition. The evolution of rhythmic notation was one of the most perplexing problems faced by the composers of the Middle Ages (and remains so in the last third of the twentieth century). The performance-style distinction noted above was indicative of the syllable-to-note association that pervaded the secular literature and reflected the rhythmic value associated with each note as being derived from the poetic rhythmic position of that particular syllable or word in the text. Although syllabic treatment of the text is clearly associated with the Gloria and the Credo sections of the Mass, no rhythmic implications should be inferred from this text-music relationship, although stress groupings may be shown.

Compositional Considerations

Efforts at stylistic composition provide, in essence, a means for developing a greater understanding of the information uncovered in the analytical process. A set of rules based on computerlike analyses of works in a given style could easily be (and too often is) postulated. It is this author's contention that rigid adherence to such a procedure devoid of any musical sensitivity to the literature may produce correct examples but is not likely to result in imaginative and musically expressive compositions. Therefore, in presenting the remarks and suggestions that follow it is assumed that students have at least a moderate analytical and performance exposure to the music of this period, and a substantial listening exposure. Conversely, it is understood that just as composition is dependent upon these experiences for its success, it, in turn, contributes immeasurably to the achievement of a greater facility in analysis, performance, and intelligent listening.

The text is of paramount importance in both secular and sacred monophony although the specifics of its role may differ. The character, mood, flow of ideas, relative importance of single words or short phrases, overall length, and inherent form of the text must be studied. It must be accepted as *sine qua non* that the music was created to reinforce the message of the text and not, by any means, to obscure its intent.

With this concept as a working premise, one should proceed to select musical materials appropriate to the nature of the text in a particular example. That is, the mode should be selected on the basis of the individual's subjective judgment of the inherent qualities of the text reflected-in the interval pattern; in the melodic patterns associated with the mode; in the strength of principal tones; and in general impressions of its historical usage in this literature. The text should be set in the selected mode in a style suitable to its length and function (i.e., syllabic, neumatic, or melismatic). In a syllabic setting, one must be sure to musically divide syllables of words in such a way that principal syllables fall on primary rhythmic and melodic positions and secondary syllables or words (e.g., *of, in*) fall on weak positions. Primary rhythmic positions here refer to those implied by the rhythmic implications of the text itself in a secular composition. Principal melodic positions can be seen in both secular and sacred compositions, e.g., large skips, peak of the contour of a rising line. Neumatic writing is approached in essentially the same way except that note groupings rather than single notes serve as the musical reference. However, in melismatic writing, any text change (syllable or word) must take place at a meaningful melodic position, i.e., one which has been conceived in the broader terms of the beginnings and endings of phrases. Relatively incidental (and fewer) changes occur in a melismatic line.

A relatively obvious basic decision is imposed immediately by the text, either by virtue of its inherent form or by traditional practice. That is, the identification of the broad architectural scheme that must be used derives from the secular poetic forms or from the accepted practices of the Church. If one is to write in the forms of this period, sacred or secular texts must be chosen or original texts written in the secular forms discussed. Freedom does exist and should be exploited in the areas of length, degree, and performance-style treatment, as well as in melodic contour. The sensitivity and imagination of the composer will be a prime factor in determining the success of a piece if these guidelines are followed.

Smooth flowing lines should be the goal of anyone attempting to write in this style. Having achieved this, every effort should be made to ascertain the success of the cadences of the piece. Are they the natural result of the line which leads into them or do they present an abrupt effect? Second only to the success of the line itself is the success of the varying degrees of finality sought and achieved at the various cadences in the piece (internal or momentary cadences as compared with final or concluding cadences). It is especially desirable, although not essential, to use the characteristic modal cadential patterns (as in some of the examples presented earlier) at these critical points in a monophonic melody. Students should recognize as early as possible that the problem of bringing a composition to a satisfying close has commanded the attention of composers in all periods and will become an increasingly important problem in the student's ongoing study of music theory.

Summary

Monophonic forms are classified into two basic groups — secular and sacred. In the former, poetic forms dictate the musical design. In the latter, the length, text form, place in the liturgy, and traditional practice determine the musical architecture. Sacred music is predominantly through-composed (with notable exceptions such as the Kyrie eleison section of the Mass), whereas secular music, in the majority of forms, consists of two musical ideas arranged according to varying patterns of recurrence dictated by the text.

Rhythm was not indicated in the earlier notations of this period in the sacred or the secular literature. However, rhythmic interpretation was incorporated into sacred music by conventional practice and a few symbols were developed at a later date — e.g., incise markings, dots, and phrase vertical lines. In secular music, the inherent poetic meter of the text provided the basis for rhythmic decisions until the rhythmic modes gained wide recognition and use as a notational phenomenon.

Three distinguishable performance styles were practiced in sacred monophony: syllabic, neumatic, and melismatic. In secular music, performance style was limited almost exclusively to syllabic with occasional neumatic writing. Examples of highly syllabic sacred singing must include: the Gloria and Credo of the Mass; and the Antiphon and Psalms of the Divine Offices (the latter, although a vitally important part of the liturgical literature, is not included as an integral part of this study owing to a variety of considerations which require digression from the prime concerns of this book.

early polyphony: organum

The development of the precise notational system described in Chapter 1 provided the essential component for the creation and evolution of a multivoiced form of music. This achievement, probably more than any other, provided the basic tool that was necessary to establish subsequently the uniqueness of Occidental music. The gradual development of varying sophisticated styles of counterpoint and harmony, the refinement of chamber ensembles, and the evolution of the orchestra (a precision instrument for artistic musical performance often consisting of as many as one hundred or more members) reflect the magnitude and impact of this innovation on the musical art form of Western civilization.

Primitive types of multipart music existed in many parts of the world before the development of this notational system in the form of *heterophony* (two or more simultaneous albeit slightly varied versions of the same melody by several performers) and drone accompanied melody.[1] The earliest extant manuscript of multipart music in which the parts are specifically defined is in a preneume (Daseian) notation in the *Musica enchiriadis* (c. 900). The music consisted of parallel forms of a plainsong line at the interval of a fourth or fifth below the principal line, which was the chant taken from a liturgical source. This type of early polyphony was termed *organum* (accent on the first syllable) and it appeared in several forms.

Three different classes of organum may be distinguished. The earliest of these, strict organum, may be divided into two types — *diapente* (organum at the interval of a fifth) and *diatesseron* (organum at the interval of a fourth).

The anonymous author of *Musica enchiriadis* recommended that this parallel singing of plainsong have a slow tempo.

The original plainsong of an organum is termed the *vox principalis* (principal voice) and the added voice at the fourth or fifth below, the *vox organalis* (organum voice or duplum). Although other organumlike styles existed (e.g., parallel singing at the third, termed *gymel*), our discussion will be confined to the principal organum at the fourth and fifth.

Strict organum at the fifth seems to have been preferred only by the author of *Musica enchiriadis*; organum at the fourth was favored by Guido d'Arezzo and others of the period.[2] In Example 4.1 diapente organum is demonstrated. The parts begin a fifth away from each other and remain at that interval to the very end.[3]

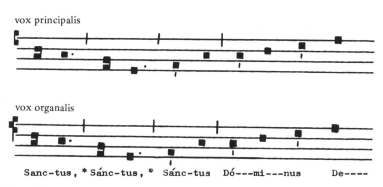

Example 4.1. Diapente Organum. *Liber Usualis*, p. 52. Vox principalis from Sanctus XIII. Reprinted with permission from the 1963 edition of Desclee & Co., Tournai-Doornik, Belgium.

The vertical relationship of the tritone (three whole steps) was rejected immediately in polyphonic music (as it was in monophonic music) and was later termed *Diabolus in musica* (Devil in music). When attempts were made to write strict organum at the fifth, the composer had to be selective in choosing the vox principalis because in these early stages of polyphony the only accidental available was the B♭ and the tritone had to be avoided. Consequently, if the original plainsong arrived at the pitch F, the duplum at a fifth below had to be altered to read B♭ instead of B♮. However, a plainsong line which included B♭ could not be used since it would have been necessary to alter the tone a fifth below it (E) by lowering it a half step (E♭), an unacceptable alteration during this period.

In diatesseron organum (see Example 4.2) the reverse is true. Retaining the interval of a perfect fourth between the two voices worked out easily with the plainsong that included the note B^b since the perfect fourth below is F. However, the line that included B$^\natural$ was not acceptable because the resultant

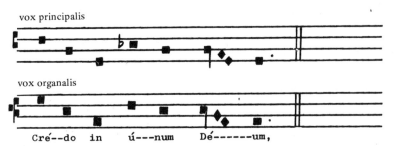

vox principalis

vox organalis

Cré--do in   ú---num Dé------um,

Example 4.2. Diatesseron Organum. *Liber Usualis*, p. 68. Vox principalis from Credo III. Reprinted with permission from the 1963 edition of Desclee & Co., Tournai-Doornik, Belgium.

F#, which had to be used, was, like the E^b, not available.

These two types of strict organum were also conceived as composites with four separate voice parts. In addition to the vox principalis and the vox organalis, two other voices appeared which were simply octave transpositions of the two original voices. The vox principalis was presented an octave lower and the vox organalis an octave higher. Example 4.3 shows composite strict organ-

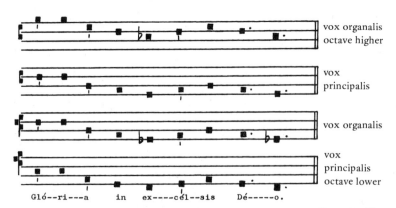

vox organalis
octave higher

vox
principalis

vox organalis

vox
principalis
octave lower

Gló--ri---a   in   ex----cél--sis Dé-----o.

Example 4.3. Composite Strict Organum at the Fifth. *Liber Usualis*, p. 37. Vox principalis from Gloria VIII. Reprinted with permission from the 1963 edition of Desclee & Co., Tournai-Doornik, Belgium.

um at the fifth and Example 4.4 shows composite strict organum at the
fourth.

In closing the discussion of strict organum, it should be noted that it is
questionable whether this kind of polyphony was ever practiced as a performance style. Also, there is some disagreement about the treatment of the tritone. It is only for the purposes of learning this style and avoiding unneces-
sary misunderstanding that the procedures outlined above will be followed.

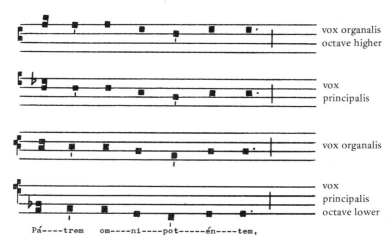

Example 4.4. Composite Strict Organum at the Fourth. *Liber Usualis*, p. 64. Vox
principalis from Credo I. Reprinted with permission from the 1963 edition of
Desclee & Co., Tournai-Doornik, Belgium.

Free Organum

The note-against-note style characterizing strict organum is also used in
free organum. The distinguishing feature is that in free organum the parts
may move in parallel, oblique, or contrary fashion. Several treatises of the period discuss this style of composition, and many differences of opinion are
manifest. An attempt has been made in the following discussion to codify basic guidelines to the style and *not* to provide a set of rules that, if rigidly followed, would produce authoritative replicas of eleventh-century organum.

Three kinds of free organum may be distinguished. The first (c. ninth century) and simplest of the three is a modest step forward from strict writing in
parallel motion. The two parts begin at the unison. One voice remains on the
starting tone while the other proceeds with the plainsong line, or both voices

may move apart from the opening unison until the desired interval is reached. The two voices continue in parallel motion at this interval until the *occursus* (cadence) is reached. The occursus is then treated in the same manner as the beginning of the piece but in reverse motion, altered only to accommodate the motion of the concluding several notes of the vox principalis. The piece ends on a unison. Example 4.5 demonstrates an abbreviated treatment of a plainsong melody in this style.

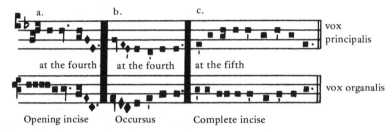

Example 4.5. Free Organum—Form One. Vox principalis from *Liber Usualis* as follows: a. and b. from Kyrie, p. 79; c. from Gloria, p. 57. Reprinted with permission from the 1963 edition of Desclee & Co., Tournai-Doornik, Belgium.

In a. of this example, the vox principalis begins in unison with the vox organalis, and while the latter remains on the same pitch, the former moves up by step until the interval of a fourth is reached. From that point the two parts continue in parallel motion. In b. of the example, the occursus has been reached and the line moves back toward unison. However, since the vox principalis does not simply move down by step to the final tone from the interval of a fourth, the treatment is slightly different. At a point as close to the final tone as is musically convenient, the vox organalis begins through stepwise motion to close the intervallic space between it and the vox principalis. In this instance, the unison is reached at the third note before the final and the two parts proceed to the end of the unison. Either of these solutions may be employed at the beginning or end of an organum section.

The c. portion of this example demonstrates the treatment of a complete incise. The vox principalis does not move by step at either end, and the vox organalis must move in the opposite direction before the interval of organum (the fifth) is reached because of the narrow range of the principal voice. Likewise, the voices are required to converge at the end of the section.

These examples demonstrate that there are several alternatives for moving the two voices to the organum interval and returning to unison. Every effort should be made to move the vox organalis by step to and from the interval of organum.

The second type of free organum (c. eleventh century) is characterized by an extensive use of contrary motion. The occasional appearance of parallel motion (e.g., consecutive fifths) may be observed. The vertical intervals used are normally limited to the unison, fourth, fifth, and octave, but it should be noted that the parts may cross freely.

Although an effort should be made to create as conjunct a line as possible, to comply with the basic premises of this music, the nature of the limitations in this form of free organum tend to produce more angular lines than are generally found in the early polyphonic literature. See Example 4.6.

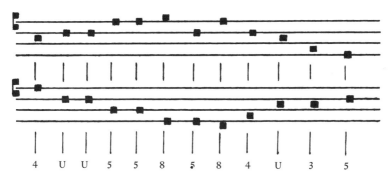

Example 4.6. Free Organum — Form Two. London, British Museum, Add. 36881, fol. 1, twelfth century.

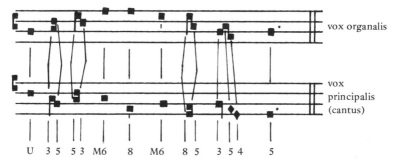

Example 4.7. Free Organum — Form Three. *Liber Usualis*, p. 51. Cantus from Gloria XIII. Note that two-note neumes are answered by two-note neumes and three-note neumes by three-note neumes. Reprinted with permission from the 1963 edition of Desclée & Co., Tournai-Doornik, Belgium.

Considerably more freedom is provided by the third form of free organum. Oblique, contrary, and parallel motion are all used. Both perfect and imperfect consonances occur, and dissonances appear occasionally. The perfect consonances are the unison, fourth, fifth, and octave. Major and minor thirds, and in the thirteenth century, major sixths, were the accepted imperfect consonances. Dissonances included the minor sixth (!), tritone, large and small sevenths, and in the thirteenth century, the perfect fourth (considered to be a mild dissonance).

It should be noted that in the two earlier forms of free organum the vox principalis is in the upper voice whereas in this form the term *cantus* replaces the vox principalis and it is found in the lower voice. As a result, the vox organalis begins to assume more melodic importance. It is characteristic of this style that one part (either one at any given moment) always moves by step. The only exception seems to be in parallel motion, e.g., a pair of fifths. The various characteristics of this form of free organum are demonstrated in Example 4.7.

Melismatic Organum

The several refinements in the three preceding forms of free organum represent developments in polyphony over approximately three centuries. The final type of organum departs rather sharply from those that precede it: the style is no longer note-against-note but is one sustained line accompanied by a florid melismatic line. Although this type of organum was conceived as an unmeasured form of music, one of its significant features is that it enabled the composer to create two independent lines containing different lengths of note

O   ra

Example 4.8. Melismatic Organum. London, British Museum. Add. 36881, fol. 22ro.

value within the unmeasured context and yet to retain control over principal vertical moments in the music (at the point of syllable or word change).

In this type of organum the lower voice is sung as a series of sustained pitches and may be but an extract from a plainsong melody. This voice, originally called vox principalis and later cantus, now assumes a new name, *tenor* (from Latin *tenere*, to hold). The upper line is normally florid as indicated and in its purest form is an embellishment of the vowel of the syllable being sung in the lower voice. Formerly called the vox organalis, this voice is now termed *duplum*.

The controlling element that coordinates the two voices is the strict practice of changing syllables simultaneously in both parts. Any interval is acceptable between the points of change, but only perfect consonances may be used at these critical locations. Likewise, the piece must begin and end on perfect consonances. See Example 4.8.

This melismatic style of composition was used by Leonin, a composer associated with the Notre Dame Cathedral in Paris during the twelfth century, in extended compositions that combined simple, unadorned plainsong melodies, unmeasured melismatic organum, and measured discant passages. Leonin's mixed style suggests that he was an early precursor of the multimovement concept which was to flower at a much later date. The premise that led him to this mode of organization may have evolved from textual and liturgical considerations rather than from the more abstract musical concerns of the later composer.

It should be noted that other forms of organum existed and were practiced. These included organum at intervals other than those specified earlier (e.g., parallel organum at the third). Also, there developed in the thirteenth and fourteenth centuries a form of three-part largely parallel music in England, English discant, and in France, Fauxbourdon. The melody was in the lowest part in the English discant and in the top part in the Fauxbourdon. The vertical intervals in the two forms were the same, however, with a third between the lowest part and the one above, and a sixth between the lowest part and the top part. See Example 4.9.

To gain a more practical understanding of the performance of organum and to engage in an invaluable exercise for ear training, it is recommended that students work in teams and practice singing in two to four parts. Given the pitch of the original plainsong, each student should be able to locate his or her starting pitch and to "improvise" a part appropriate to the particular form of organum decided upon in advance. This practice should not be limited to any single form but should include all. Free improvisation of melismatic duplum parts, in addition to being considerable fun, can be extremely valuable in training the ear and increasing its sensitivity to the style.

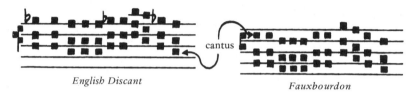

English Discant   Fauxbourdon

Example 4.9. English Discant and Fauxbourdon. *Liber Usualis*, p. 81. Cantus from Kyrie III. Reprinted with permission from the 1963 edition of Desclee & Co., Tournai-Doornik, Belgium.

Summary

The beginnings of controlled polyphony are the earliest indications of the directions and characteristics that were to evolve as some of the most distinctive features of Occidental music. The simple note-against-note parallel writing that characterized the first somewhat tentative steps toward independent lines rapidly gave way to greater freedom of interval and directional choice.

The new freedom was compatible with the aesthetic spirit of the period, and it opened up new sound possibilities, offered judgments about relative degrees of dissonance and consonance, and allowed for new compositional freedoms that provided the composer with considerably more opportunity for personal self-expression.

Three basic types of organum developed: a note-against-note parallel form of singing in two to four parts; three degrees of note-against-note free organum, the third form of which relegated the source line (the original plainsong) to the lower voice and a subordinate position; and melismatic organum in which the upper voice became highly florid and independent of the lower, sustained tenor line. Somewhat wider ranges became the norm, and more variety in melodic intervals was employed. Together, these developments demonstrate the extension of the composer's musical vocabulary and the gradual unfolding of the premises for the subsequent evolution of an abstract musical art form.

chapter 5

aRs nova notation

The fourteenth century in music history is characterized as the *Ars Nova* (new art). The name was taken from the title of a treatise by the composer-theorist Phillipe de Vitri (c. 1290-1361). It was used by theorists of the day to distinguish from the preceding period (the *Ars Antiqua*) this time of vigorous activity, significant development, and considerable refinement in both the notational system and compositional practice.

As we have seen, each stage in the evolution of notation is a further refinement of the devices and symbols used in preceding periods, with the addition of relatively few new ones. Although the Ars Nova was no exception to this phenomenon in its early stages, during the approximately 150 years in which this notation prevailed, there were introduced a fairly large number of modifications of old symbols and many new symbols. This resulted in an extensive, distinctive, and extremely flexible resource for composers and provided the principal components of our present notation.

A new value, the *minima* (a diamond-shaped note with a vertical stem from the top point of the diamond), was introduced early in the period and was followed soon after by the *semiminima* (the minima with a flag added to the top of the stem). Even smaller values made their appearance later in the period (the *fusa* and *semifusa*), but these will not be discussed here.

Essentially two different forms of notation — the French and the Italian — evolved from the basic principles of the Ars Nova during the fourteenth century. The Italian was relatively short-lived and had less of a lasting impact on

61

notational developments. Consequently, although our discussion will be primarily concerned with the basic principles of Ars Nova notation, when a choice must be made, the French practices will guide our decisions.

It has been suggested in preceding chapters that over a period of several hundred years, increasingly smaller note values assumed the unit-of-measure function. This phenomenon resulted from the gradual introduction of smaller values, clearly defined, into the notational spectrum. In the Franconian system, the breve became the unit of measure as a result of the introduction of the semibreve; in the Ars Nova system, the appearance of the minima caused the semibreve to usurp the role held by the breve.

During the period that led to the development and use of the Ars Nova notations, there was a rather rapid dissolution of the influence of the rhythmic modes. Time values were increasingly more sharply defined, and signatures began to appear which identified the various possible combinations and relationships that had been evolving between the several note values and metrical patterns. Example 5.1 provides a summary of the note values being used and their respective relationships to each other. The terms *modus*, *tempus*, and *prolatio* which appear in this example refer to the divisions of the longa, breve, and semibreve, respectively.

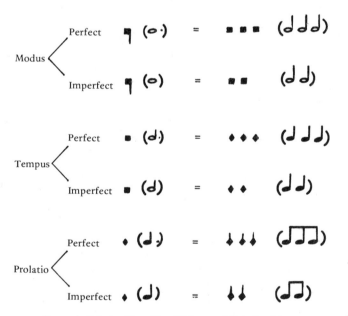

Example 5.1. Ars Nova Note Values and Relationships.

The Four Prolations

Phillipe de Vitri is credited with having identified the four principal relationships that prevailed during this period. These are termed the *four prolations* because they reflect four groupings of minima (or, more accurately, divided semibreves). The four prolations are shown in Example 5.2.

Note that reference to the tempus in Example 5.2 defines the division of the breve into two or three semibreves, and prolations refer to the division of the semibreve into two or three minima. The resulting group of patterns is referred to as the four prolations, which are equivalent to modern metrical signatures as delineated in this example. Students should also note that because of the new role of the semibreve, it, rather than the breve, is transcribed as a quarter note, which accounts for the meter signatures shown.

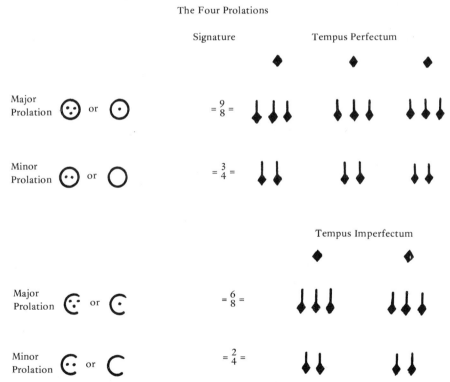

Example 5.2. The Four Prolations. In the meter signature, the circles and half circles relate to the tempus, and the number of dots defines the prolation.

Rests

Rests in the Ars Nova period were almost identical to those introduced in the Franconian period. The only differences were those that naturally resulted from the addition of the new note values (i.e., the need for equivalent rests) and the abandonment of the major-minor distinction for the semibreve. Ars Nova rests are shown in Example 5.3 with their modern equivalents (the semibreve is considered a quarter note).

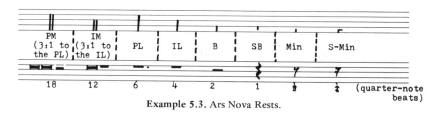

Example 5.3. Ars Nova Rests.

PM = Perfect Maxima	B = Breve
IM = Imperfect Maxima	SB = Semibreve
PL = Perfect Longa	Min = Minima
IL = Imperfect Longa	S-Min = Semiminima

Composers were quick to capitalize on the significant increase in flexibility provided by the notational innovations, and a wide array of new compositional devices rapidly gained favor. Many of these will be discussed in the chapters that follow, but of particular interest here, because specific notational symbols are employed for its compositional use, is the device of *syncopation*.

Syncopation (Dotted and Colored Notes)

Syncopation, or the displacement of anticipated beats, was achieved by a variety of means. The first and most familiar to us is the use of a dot following a note. This dot (*punctus additionis*), which is still used today, represented the addition of half the value of the preceding note to the note following it (e.g., a dotted semibreve equals the value of a semibreve followed by a minima). This is one of the many uses of the dot and the only one with which we shall be concerned in this discussion. Example 5.4 demonstrates the punctus additionis in several possible rhythmic figures.

The use of syncopation was quite widespread during this period and may justifiably be considered a characteristic technique in the music of the time.

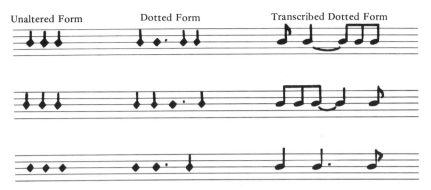

Example 5.4. Three Uses of the Punctus Additionis.

Another device that had a wide variety of uses (among them, rhythmic displacement) was the red note. These notes were introduced shortly before the Ars Nova and appeared in manuscripts for approximately 100 years. An important contribution of the use of coloration was the introduction of the concept *hemiola* ("one and one-half") or the replacement of two equal values by three equal values. In multiple-part writing, this would occasionally produce a three-against-two relationship between two voices. In early usage, red notes never appeared in imperfect meters, but later they were used as freely in those as they were in perfect meters. Red notes had at least a half-dozen different uses during this period. We shall limit our discussion to their use as rhythmic displacement, described above and demonstrated in Example 5.5.

Example 5.5. Coloration for Rhythmic Displacement. Red notes are represented here as open notes.

Analytical Considerations

A wide range of devices was developed during the fourteenth century to accommodate the rapidly evolving compositional techniques. These included means for identifying passages to be performed in augmentation and diminution of varying degrees; complicated rhythms; and puzzle canons. The black, white, and red notes discussed earlier were used as well as such new devices as hollow red notes, half red and white notes, half red and black notes, and a wide variety of attachments to the noteheads or stems. In his consideration of the notation of this period, Willi Apel states:

Musicians, no longer satisfied with the rhythmic subtleties of the *Ars Nova*, began to indulge in complicated rhythmic tricks and in the invention of highly involved methods of notating them. It is in this period that musical notation far exceeds its natural limitations as a servant to music, but rather becomes its master, a goal in itself and an arena for intellectual sophistries.[1]

In light of Apel's remarks and the nature of our concern in this study, we shall not involve ourselves in the complexities of what he refers to as "mannered" notation. But to understand more adequately the basic Ars Nova notation, we shall consider a monophonic virelai by Guillaume de Machaut, c. 1300-1377 (see Example 5.6).

The manuscript from which this diplomatic facsimile was taken indicates no tempus or prolation marking. Consequently, it is necessary to determine these from the context of the music. Usually this may be accomplished by sketching out the perfect and imperfect interpretations of the note and rest values in the piece. Understanding the flow of the text is frequently of great value in making these judgments, but the music will generally reveal its nature apart from the text. However, it is unlikely that an authoritative interpretation of this literature will result without a thorough understanding of the natural flow of the language. In Example 5.7 the first line of the piece has been sketched out rhythmically according to a perfect and and imperfect interpretation.

In the imperfect setting, the note and rest values are quite specific and leave no room for interpretation. But in the perfect setting other arrangements of the quarter and dotted quarter notes (imperfect and perfect semibreves) are possible. Problems arise if we attempt to carry the perfect or the imperfect through the piece. In the imperfect form we have a series of syncopated phrases (unlikely), a missing rest (possible), or an annacrusis (most likely). In the perfect form, aside from the fact that the text would be awkwardly underlaid (at best), by the time we reach the cadence in the middle of the third stave it is virtually impossible to make the values of the notes and rests conform to any reasonable rhythmic setting. Consequently, our decision here must be that we are working with an imperfect (minor) prolation.

If we scan the note/rest patterns in the greater portion of the piece and accept the minor prolation, we shall quickly see that these patterns fall into
groups of four (semibreve) beats and there is little difficulty in carrying these
through the piece (allowing for an annacrusis, as suggested above). Although
several annacrusis possibilities seem to exist, the natural flow of the French

Example 5.6. Virelai: *Tuit mi penser*, Guillaume de Machaut. Paris, Bibliothèque
Nationale, fr. 9221, fol. 161, as corrected by Carl Parrish, *The Notation of Medieval Music*, W. W. Norton, New York, 1957, p. 151.

text results in a minima followed by two semibreves. It should be noted that the rest at the end of the piece (or of a section) will not compensate for the missing beats at the beginning, as we are used to finding in notational practices of more recent vintage. No further difficulty should be encountered in transcribing the piece.

On the basis of the preceding discussion, Example 5.8 demonstrates the first line of the virelai transcribed into modern notation.

Example 5.7. Perfect and Imperfect Interpretations of *Tuit mi penser.*

Example 5.8. *Tuit mi penser* in Modern Notation.

Accidentals begin to be fairly widely used during this period both as key signatures (several different ones appear) and as momentary alterations. The flat was used, from the very beginnings of square notation, to lower the pitch a semitone. The natural sign was not used, which resulted in two interpretations of the sharp sign: cancelation of an earlier flat and raising a semitone the pitch before which it appeared. Signatures employed only flats (sharps do not appear in signatures until several centuries later), and pieces might have two different signatures for separate parts (e.g., no flats in one part and one flat in another). These multiple signatures may be found throughout the literature of the modal period and into the sixteenth century (and once again in recent years).

It should be noted that the scribes who prepared these manuscripts often did not place the accidental immediately before the note it affected. This was true in earlier notations, going back to plainsong, and the practice seems to have been to place the accidental in the most convenient position not too far before the note it affected. This might have resulted from taking into account the space available in relation to both the underlaying of the text and the amount of accessible parchment. The latter consideration may seem strange to us who live in a time when paper is abundant. During this period scarceness of paper was, at times, a severe limitation, to the extent that it actually influenced the handwriting of the period (especially in the early Middle Ages).

The Machaut example we have been considering is quite straightforward and has no complicating devices such as dots or red notes. Considering the widespread use of these devices in the period during which this notation flourished, we would be remiss in not examining the simple uses of these elements.

Two different uses of the dot are presented in Examples 5.9 and 5.10 — the *punctus additionis* and the *punctus divisionis*. The former, demonstrated in Example 5.9, is used to extend the value of a note by one-half, in exactly the same manner as in modern notation. In this example the dots following the semibreves and later the minima are punctus additionis that appear in exactly the same position and have exactly the same function in the resulting transcription (Example 5.10).

Example 5.9. Use of the Punctus Additionis. London, British Museum, Egerton 3307, fol. 72v. Note the presence of the meter signature in this manuscript.

Example 5.10. Transcription of **Example 5.9.** The open minima, which appear in the original in a lighter (brown-tone) ink, have been interpreted here as semiminima.

Example 5.11 demonstrates the punctus divisionis as it was commonly used in Italian notation of the period. In this example the dots function as our contemporary bar line does and do not affect the individual note values.

Two factors contribute to the interpretation of the dot in this example as a punctus divisionis rather than as a punctus additionis. First, even a cursory glance at the excerpt reveals the regular recurrence of the dot, suggesting the regular division of the piece into smaller convenient groupings. Second, any attempt to employ the dots in the example as punctus additionis produces in-

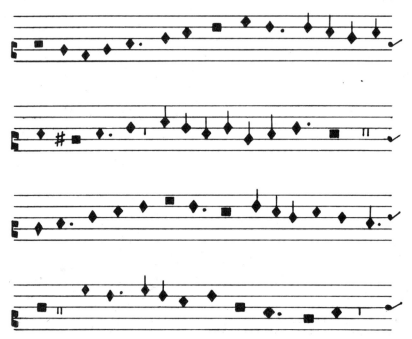

Example 5.11. Use of the Punctus Divisionis. London, British Museum, Add. 29987, fol. 32v. This example is presented according to the notational practices presented in this text rather than as a diplomatic facsimile of the original because the peculiarities of Italian notation that it encompasses are beyond the purview of this study.

congruous and frustrating results rhythmically. In Example 5.12 a modern transcription of the preceding example is provided for comparison.

In Example 5.13 the use of red notes is demonstrated. The meter (given in the manuscript) is an imperfect tempus with a major prolation ($\frac{6}{8}$), and the natural values of each of the black notes should be interpreted in accordance with Example 5.1. The red notes, on the other hand, are to be transcribed by reversing the metrical interpretation to read perfect tempus and imperfect prolation ($\frac{3}{4}$). Therefore, the first note in the upper voice of this excerpt (a breve) should be transcribed as a half note with the two following minima interpreted as equal eighth notes on the final beat of a three-beat measure. The black notes that follow are then interpreted in terms of their respective $\frac{6}{8}$ values.

The middle voice presents no problem if the value of the black notes is strictly interpreted in terms of the prevailing tempus and prolation. In the same manner, the first four notes of the lower score should present no problem when the simple procedures are followed. The three red notes (numbers five, six, and seven in that line) conform to the approach outlined above and produce a $\frac{3}{4}$ measure consisting of three equal semibreves.

The reverse procedure is followed when one is confronted with a perfect tempus and a minor prolation, which occurs in mild form in this piece a few measures following the excerpt provided in Example 5.13. Once again, the change of meter is clearly denoted in each voice part. In this instance (Exam-

Example 5.12. Transcription of Example 5.11.

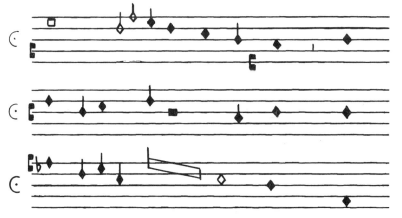

Example 5.13. One Use of Red Notes. London, British Museum, Egerton 3307, fol. 9r. Red notes appear as open notes. Punctus perfectionis have been omitted because they do not affect the meter and therefore do not concern us.

ple 5.14), the first note in each part is a red breve which, in this tempus/pro-
lation setting, must be interpreted as the equivalent of a breve in the reverse
metrical situation, i.e., a dotted half note in transcription. Both this homophonic passage and the one shown in Example 5.13 are small excerpts from a
much longer and more complicated piece included in a substantial manuscript
of the mid-fifteenth century.

Example 5.14. Second Use of Red Notes. London, British Museum, Egerton 3307,
fol. 9r. The large circle is a change of tempus/prolation sign.

The red-note technique demonstrated in Examples 5.13 and 5.14 is relatively simple to work with if the values of the respective tempus/prolation relationships are interpreted strictly. As indicated earlier, however, there are a
variety of uses for red notes that can introduce complexities not considered
in this discussion, and students should understand that further study is essential before they can confidently attempt to transcribe an unfamiliar manuscript. The use of this device presented here should be explored fully in student compositions.

Example 5.15. Transcription of Examples 5.13 and 5.14.

Summary

In the fourteenth century, notation evolved to a very high degree of exactness, enabling the composer to achieve clarity, individuality, and technical sophistication. Two distinctive forms of notation developed — French and Italian. The latter was relatively short-lived and contributed little to the further development of musical graphics. The former, however, clearly evolved from preceding notations and provided the foundation for the developments that were to produce the notation still in use in the twentieth century.

The notation of the Ars Nova is characterized by: the introduction of several smaller note values throughout the course of the period; a clear set of shapes defining each note and rest value; the use of red notes (and other gradations of coloration in the Italian "mannered" notation); and the definition of value relationships to each other through the four prolations. It should be noted that whereas earlier music was predicated on the perfection (3:1 relationships) and tolerated little use of the duple relationships, the Ars Nova used both with freedom. This provided the basis for heated disputation between adherents of "the art of Master Franco" (the Ars Antiqua) and those who advocated the new art.

During this period, as in no other preceding it, composers could be identified with compositions and personal styles. Also, composers permitted themselves the freedom of writing both sacred and secular forms of music, a practice not true of earlier periods and quite indicative of the rapidly evolving spirit that gradually elevated music to the level of an art form independent of extramusical dictates. This freer spirit that characterized the composers of the period must be attributed, in part, to the new expressive freedom that naturally resulted from the more refined and flexible notational developments.

Interest in notation during the period became almost an end in itself, to the extent that composers explored the visual appearance of the manuscript with about the same fervor as they pursued compositional possibilities. This interest is represented in the extreme by the compositions by Baude Cordier laid out in circles and in the shape of a heart.

The significance of notational developments during this period cannot be underestimated, for they provided the premises for the notation of the following six hundred years and, in large measure, enabled composers to think as creative artists, unencumbered by the inherent clumsiness of the tools of their art. Clarity and flexibility, albeit often in a context of considerable complexity, are appropriate descriptors for the notation of this period in music history.

chapteR 6

eaRly contRapuntal
concepts and devices

The gradual sophistication of notational practices during the thirteenth and
fourteenth centuries, which we have considered in several of the preceding
chapters, enabled composers to express their compositional intentions with
considerable accuracy. This allowed for increasingly refined evaluation of vertical relationships between parts, permitted greater exploration of the independence of the voices, and opened up the possibility of new compositional
techniques which could not have evolved to the extent they did (in some
cases not at all) within the limitations of earlier notational systems. These developments occur gradually throughout the periods of notational evolution
and must be understood in that context.

In this chapter and the next, we shall consider these contrapuntal devices
in an approximately historical order of development. However, examples will
be selected from any portion of the contrapuntal period we are considering to
clearly convey the concept irrespective of the date of origin of the particular
example. Examples will be presented within the limitations of our previous
notational study regardless of what their original notation may have been (although every effort will be made to remain as true to the original as is reasonably possible).

We have already studied the concepts of consonance and dissonance as
they had evolved in the practice of organum. These remained essentially unchanged throughout the period; although in some respects composers had
greater freedom, certain conventions became more defined. The fifth, octave,

75

and unison remained the perfect consonances throughout. However, some difference of attitude was reflected in compositional practices regarding the effect of the perfect fourth. For our purposes, even though examples can be cited to demonstrate otherwise, we shall not include the fourth as a perfect consonance.

The increasing abundance of compositions in three parts during the thirteenth and fourteenth centuries reveals that composers used complete triads extensively. However, the perfect consonance was retained on principal musical positions (e.g., the beginnings and endings of both sections and complete pieces). A peculiarity of the earlier contrapuntal (organum) practices, which seems to have fallen into disfavor by the fourteenth century, is the use of a strong dissonant tone resolving into a perfect consonance to begin a composition (see Example 6.1). Later practice demanded a much more discreet use of such sharp dissonances — normally on weak rhythmic positions.

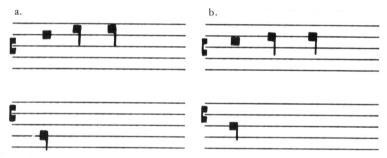

Example 6.1. Use of Sharp Opening Dissonances. Wolfenbüttel, Herzog August Bibliothek, 677: a. fol. 35ro; b. fol. 18vo.

With the exception of such dissonances and similar moments in the flow of the music, vertical intervals on important positions (either rhythmically or by virtue of text changes) were primarily perfect consonances. Imperfect consonances were used, as were many passing dissonances, in this early stage of contrapuntal development in rhythmically weaker positions.

The linear concept in the twelfth century was strongly conjunct, with few large skips and a heavy predominance of seconds and thirds. As notations became more definitive and musical styles achieved greater sophistication, more use was made of larger melodic intervals, a point we shall return to later in our discussion.

One of the earliest purely contrapuntal devices that enabled a composer to do more than simply string long lines of notes together or place a simple sustained line in juxtaposition to another more melismatic line was known as *Stimmtausch*. This technique requires the immediately adjacent alteration between two voices of two brief melodic phrases. That is, one voice sings a two-measure phrase accompanied by a second voice. In the next two measures the lower voice sings what the upper voice just completed, and the upper sings what the lower voice just completed. Both versions are sung in the same range in their inverted repetitions which in effect but not in fact produces repeat. This technique is demonstrated in Example 6.2.

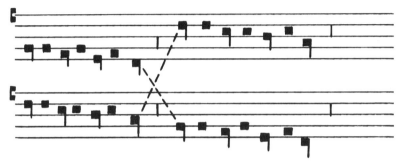

Example 6.2. Stimmtausch. Wolfenbüttel, Herzog August Bibliothek, 677, fol. 127.

When attempting to write a Stimmtausch passage, students should keep a few simple principles in mind. The two lines should be contrasting to enhance the sense of independence which contributes to the effect sought when this technique is used. The rhythms employed should be stylistic; if they are to relate to the twelfth century, they should be compatible with the rhythmic modes and both voices should be in the same mode. However, if they are to relate to a later period, they must draw upon the natural rhythmic concepts suitable to that style. The passage should be short — approximately two modern measures is a good limit within which to work. Finally, perfect vertical intervals should be employed at the beginning and the ending of the passage; usually a predominance of these should be maintained throughout. Coloring by means of imperfect consonances and dissonances should be included in relatively weaker positions with discretion. A passage of all perfect intervals would be exceedingly dry at best.

Examples 6.3a. and b. are very similar in many ways: there are mostly seconds and thirds in the lines; both are in the same rhythmic mode (Trochaic); both begin and end with perfect consonances; and the lines of both have relatively narrow ranges (under an octave). It is the critical differences between the two passages which lead us to prefer the second over the first. In passage a. we find a pair of unstylistic skips (the fifth, sixth, and seventh tones in the upper voice part outline a triad in a quasitonal cadence). Also, the general sense of motion between the two parts is parallel (if we consider each of the longer values, strict parallel fifths prevail throughout). This latter factor takes strong precedence over the superficial sense of contrary motion seen in the note-to-note relationship.

In the simple lines of the b. passage, a clear sense of contrary motion is apparent, helping to establish the individuality of the respective lines. The vertical relationships are more interesting (no strict recurrence of a single interval such as the perfect fifths in the a. passage) which, together with the variety of contrary, oblique, and parallel note-to-note motion, provide a much more interesting musical passage.

Some qualification must be offered to the remarks in the preceding paragraphs if we consider that Stimmtausch passages normally occur in the middle of a piece and can appear, theoretically, anywhere (although cadential sections employing this technique are highly improbable). Therefore, it is entirely possible that this portion of a piece might begin or end on an imperfect consonance and need not have a sense of formally beginning or ending at all.

The Stimmtausch technique pointed the way for the rapid development of canonic writing, early examples of which can also be seen in the compositions of the Notre Dame composers. Canonic writing evolved from Stimmtausch when the two voices did not begin together and continued the literal duplication beyond the initial Stimmtausch pattern. A large number of canonic possibilities exist, some of which were used in this early period and all of which are still used in the twentieth century.

Example 6.3. Problems in Stimmtausch.

Canon

Canon is simply a single melodic line which has been superimposed upon itself by one or another (sometimes several) of the possible means to be discussed below. This melody may begin at any time-displacement from the starting note of its original statement and may be initiated at any interval distance from that note. It may also be presented in augmentation, diminution, retrograde (also called *cancrizans*), or mirrored forms. It is quite possible to use more than one of these forms of canon in the same piece when more than two voice parts are used. These techniques of canonic writing may be found in all styles of counterpoint throughout history as long as the nature and spirit of the lines and their relationship to each other are recognized as being compatible with the particular style being attempted.

Two well-known examples of canonic writing from the Middle Ages are *Sumer is icumen in* (an anonymous thirteenth-century *rota*) and *Ma fin est mon commencement* (Machaut). *Sumer* is in four canonic parts accompanied by two parts in a continuously repeating Stimmtausch pattern. *Ma fin est* is in three voice parts; the top and middle parts are in retrograde with each other and the low voice is composed to the middle of the piece and backward from the middle to the end. This is in effect what happens in the Machaut piece, but it is accomplished by the top and middle parts actually reversing their respective roles at the middle of the piece. These two examples are provided in the workbook for further study.

It is recommended that, in addition to providing excellent bases for the study of canonic writing, these two canon examples be put to good use for class singing. This activity will assist the ear in gaining greater familiarity with the respective styles, provide a reading challenge, and prove to be quite a delight to perform.

The process of writing simple canon is relatively straightforward if students follow a few basic procedures. Inasmuch as the head of the canon (the first few measures) is the only portion that normally stands alone and must establish the mood and spirit of the ensuing piece, it is of the utmost importance that the material chosen to initiate the line be interesting and create a good sense of forward motion. The particular type of canon to be composed may lessen the importance of these considerations somewhat to accommodate any special needs or characteristics embodied in the less common forms (e.g., cancrizans canon). At this point in the discussion our concern is limited to simple canonic writing.

After the opening material is selected, the rhythmic displacement must be chosen as well as the interval at which the canon is to be written. In Example 6.4 several different types of rhythmic and intervallic beginnings are demonstrated. The first begins at the interval of an octave and on the third semibreve following the first tone of the initiating voice. The second begins a fifth below and on the fifth semibreve of the upper voice. The last example begins seven semibreves after and a third below the starting tone of the piece. These are only three of the many possibilities which may be employed and should be explored by students.

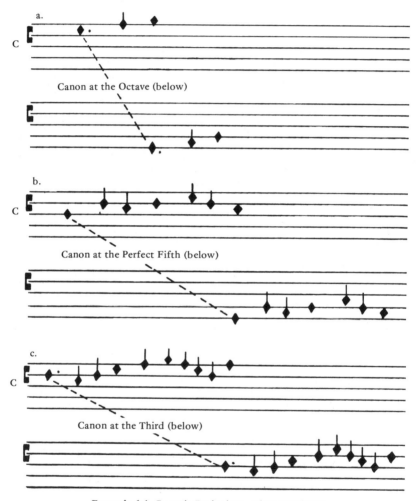

Example 6.4. Canonic Beginnings—Three Possibilities.

In each of these examples the primary step in writing simple canon is demonstrated, i.e., copy the opening passage at the desired interval and rhythmic position before proceeding to extend the first line. This first step is continuously repeated throughout the piece as long as a strict canonic setting is to be maintained. That is, as each bit of new material is added to the first voice, it is simultaneously added to the voice that follows.

Following these preliminary decisions and while retaining the basic layout, the first line must be extended over (or under) the second (depending upon the position of the lead line). In doing so, it is essential that the part maintain its own identity, both rhythmically and linearly. The vertical relationships must be compatible with the style, and the two voices must complement as well as contrast with each other. Contrary and oblique motion should be favored over parallel motion, although this should not rule out use of the latter. Perfect intervals should normally predominate. However, variety is an integral part of good musical conception in any style and, in this spirit, dissonance and consonance should be used with taste according to the limitations of the particular style being explored.

As the two lines grow, it is important that each produces a good sense of direction and follows all the principles of good line writing. Students should beware that in the additive process one may become overly concerned with the fragments that are being welded together to the neglect of the broader linear and contrapuntal conception. It is essential in any compositional process to "step back from the canvas" occasionally to gain a better perspective of the unfolding composition. In Example 6.5 a more extended canonic passage is shown. The numbers that appear above each of the lines indicate the order of procedure followed in constructing the passage.

Students should note several features about this canon. During the period under consideration it was entirely permissible to cross voices freely, a practice reflected in this piece. Because it is canon at the unison, it is reasonable to expect this voice crossing. The phrase flow of the lines is interesting because the lines do not coincide. That is, the phrase of the upper line ends with the breve, several semibreves after the entry of the lower part. The beginning of the second phrase of the upper part relates well to the beginning of the piece and dovetails with the end of the first phrase of the lower line. This figure recurs four times (as a natural result of the give and take between the two lines) and provides a slightly varying sense of unity to the unfolding canon.

Rhythmically the lines complement each other because while one is active the other is relatively less active, which strongly asserts the individuality of the respective lines. This is further enhanced by the subtle oblique and contrary-motion undulation that persists between the lines. These features should not be limited to good canonic writing but should extend to all contrapuntal efforts to achieve more successful musical results.

As suggested earlier, this example is an excerpt from a canon, not a complete piece. Performance of the passage would quickly make this evident. Canons often appear as complete pieces in various forms during this period (and in others) but they need not be. The canon is a contrapuntal device which may appear in any contrapuntal composition and frequently does. This should immediately suggest that a canon need not produce a sense of finality in cadence but may merely dissolve into free counterpoint; this practice is, in fact, not uncommon. However, should a canon be presented as a complete piece, it is not necessary to retain the strict imitation to the final note although this is often possible and successful. In other words, the last several notes of either or both voice parts may be treated freely to produce a successful cadence. This is neither to the disadvantage nor to the advantage of the canon and should be predicated upon achieving the most musical results possible.

The procedures outlined above apply with equal validity to several other forms of canon including mirror, augmentation, and diminution. The begin-

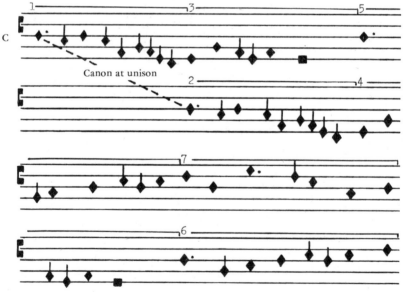

Example 6.5. Unfolding Canon.

nings of examples in each of these canonic types are demonstrated in Example 6.6. In mirror canons the process is almost identical with the one already outlined, the only difference being that whatever goes up in the lead part goes down in the follower. A canon in augmentation may be constructed in a variety of ways; the differences result from the degree of augmentation (e.g., double, triple).

Canons in augmentation have a peculiarity which must be taken into consideration. That is, as the lead voice unfolds at a given pace, the follower voice

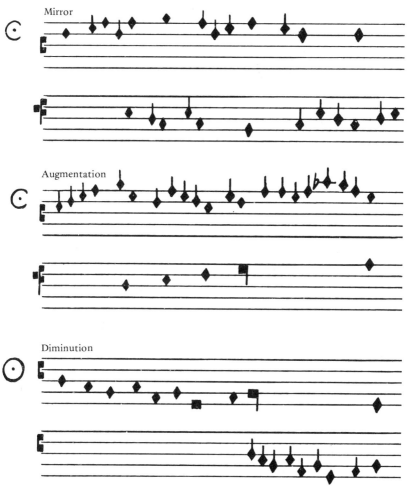

Example 6.6. Three Canonic Possibilities.

unfolds at the chosen augmentation pace (say twice as long). Therefore, for every addition made to the lead voice, the follower has twice that addition which, over a period of time, will project the follower voice far ahead of the lead voice. This will require one of two solutions to produce a meaningful musical conclusion to the passage. Either the voice in augmentation must be cut short to produce a cadence (another way of expressing the same idea is that the lead voice will continue in free counterpoint until the cadence is reached) or the two voices dissolve into free counterpoint which continues the piece beyond the confines of the canon. In the latter solution, it should be understood that the canon is conceived of as part of a more extended composition and not a compositional end in itself.

When composing a canon in diminution, the problem is reversed. That is, material from the lead voice must be consumed by the follower at a faster rate, which is defined by the degree of diminution. Unless the lead voice has a rather extended statement before the second voice enters, the two voice lines will coincide so quickly that the canonic intent will be rendered ineffective. It is possible in such a canon simply to permit the material to become free counterpoint from the moment the two voices coincide or to continue the follow-

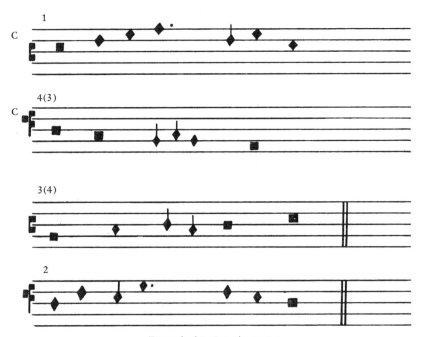

Example 6.7. Cancrizans Canon.

er voice as free counterpoint while the lead voice presents a new statement which can subsequently be taken up again by the diminution voice.

These several canonic possibilities may be used quite freely within pieces or as independent pieces, or they may be woven together in a multiform canon in a single piece. The one factor students must always keep in mind is that they should remain true to and consistently in the style within which they are working. We shall return to these questions in a later chapter when we study the musical forms of the period.

The approach to retrograde canon must be somewhat different from the approach to the canons discussed in preceding paragraphs. In cancrizans canon it is necessary to write the piece from the beginning and the ending simultaneously. What appears in the upper voice in the beginning will be in the lower at the end and vice versa. Therefore, the first several notes and rhythms of the piece (in both voices) must, when performed in reverse, produce a good final cadence. As students compose the upper part at the beginning, they should write that same line backward in the lower voice, strictly maintaining the retrograde rhythmic relationships. Likewise, when composing the lower voice for the beginning, the same process should be followed for the upper voice at the end. This process is demonstrated in Example 6.7.

As in earlier examples, the numbers indicate the order of composition for the several passages. This procedure should be followed until the middle of the composition is reached (the point where the two halves, in the opinion of the composer, constitute the desired length). The composer must, at that point, attempt to achieve a good connection between the two halves (see Example 6.8).

It is quite apparent that a retrograde canon, by its very nature, is in a completely symmetrical form. Thus it is especially important that the composer

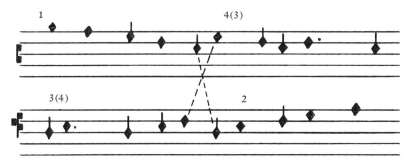

Example 6.8. Middle of Cancrizans Canon.

plan the contours of his lines with extra caution so that a good broad sense of musical direction can be created and sustained. The development of this technique (or any compositional technique) is meaningless unless the omnipresent goal and concern is the achievement of *musical* results. No formulas can be offered for this, but it is certain that writing a "correct" canon does not ensure that it will be a musical canon. Students must strive to attain good balance, proportion, rhythmic flow, linear contour, unity, variety, and ease of unfolding continuity — all within the spirit of the style.

Summary

With the development of the earliest functional notations which enabled composers to breathe independent life into separate lines came the earliest developments of imitative contrapuntal technique — Stimmtausch and canon. Early examples of these can be found in the twelfth-century Notre Dame composers' works. Although Stimmtausch was relatively short-lived, it contributed to the development of canon as a technique and could be remotely considered a very early precursor of the significantly more sophisticated contrapuntal technique of the Baroque period, invertible counterpoint.

Both Stimmtausch and canon are techniques which can appear almost anywhere in a composition, but unlike Stimmtausch, canon has sufficient variety and developmental possibilities to be a composition unto itself. Canon holds the unique position of having survived all periods and styles of compositional change and evolution and having remained an integral part of the technique of composers in every era including the present.

Several different types of canon have been explored throughout history, and many of these were employed during the Middle Ages. Basic canonic possibilities include simple canon in two voices, canon in mirror, retrograde, augmentation, and diminution. These canonic types may appear at any interval and at any rhythmic distance. They may also be used in three or more parts and can be combined in a variety of ways (e.g., a three-voice canon with each of the two follower voices at different intervals from the lead voice while, at the same time, one appears in mirror and the other appears in augmentation). As will be discussed in a later chapter, canons can also be written to be performed with accompanying free parts (a combination of canon and Stimmtausch in a single piece using separate voice parts is provided in the workbook — *Sumer is icumen in*).

In the earlier portion of the historical period with which we are concerned (through the beginning of the thirteenth century), perfect consonances appeared with greater frequency and on stronger musical positions than in the later portion. Imperfect consonances gradually became more important and were used more freely. Dissonances were used widely throughout the period but almost always in subordinate rhythmic positions and for purposes of variety and interest. The rhythmic content of a particular piece of music is largely dependent upon the limitations and freedoms inherent in the notations, with greater variety being possible in the latter portion of the period (the fourteenth century).

late contrapuntal
concepts and devices

The division of the contrapuntal portion of the Middle Ages into early and late must to a certain extent be arbitrary. However, it is a convenient reference which is, in large part, accurate. The contrapuntal practices that resist such designation at least permit enough flexibility of historical placement so as not to be blatantly incorrect. The evolution of technique in many areas of human endeavor may be obscured by anonymity, but any reasonable delineation within the confines of the knowledge available for the purpose of elucidating the nature and relationships of those techniques is justified.

In the last chapter we considered Stimmtausch and canon, two early contrapuntal devices which provided initial techniques by which composers could inject self-contained logic into compositions, freeing them from extramusical dictates. These techniques provided the premise for almost all contrapuntal styles in the entire history of music — some form of imitation. In another sense it would not seem unreasonable to surmise that they suggest, perhaps in only primitive form, the basic concepts of musical development which, in almost infinite variety, pervade the entire art of music. The simple fact that composers were prompted to look at the material of their music to see what inherent potential it had which might be used later in a composition should be a sufficient basis for this judgment.

Before continuing our discussion of other contrapuntal devices that evolved during this period, there is one other element, not unrelated, that must be considered. In the earliest stages of plainsong and the ensuing early polyphony, the use of an altered tone (Bb) was an integral part of the system. However, as indicated in some examples presented in earlier chapters, other alterations gradually appeared in the music. These were referred to as *musica falsa* and later as *musica ficta*.

Musica ficta was the alteration of a tone either up or down by a semitone. Through the thirteenth and fourteenth centuries several alterations were added to the original Bb. These included F, C, and G sharps and Eb with a rare Ab. These new accidentals were needed because of the more frequent transposition of the modes and the increased interest in the leading-tone function of the seventh degree of the scale. In addition to the early rules governing the use of the Bb, the new accidentals were treated in accordance with the following three basic guidelines:

1. Fifths, octaves, and twelfths had to be perfect;
2. A third opening by step to a fifth or a sixth opening by step to an octave had to be major;
3. A third closing by step to a unison had to be minor.

Example 7.1. Musica Ficta.

Musica Ficta is demonstrated in Example 7.1. All necessary alterations in Example 7.1 were made to accommodate the rules for the use of musica ficta. In the early stages of these developments the alterations were often not noted but were understood. This fact and the warning from theorists against the use of musica ficta too frequently make it difficult to ascertain when it should or should not be used, except in the instances noted above (it should be understood that it was not restricted to these instances).

The leading tone began to appear in the form of a lower neighboring tone (e.g., G-F#-G; D-C#-D; and A-G#-A). However, in a relatively short period of time composers seemed to recognize its strong harmonic implications, and it assumed a more significant role in the musical conception of the time. Example 7.2 demonstrates the use of the leading tone. Two forms of the same note (e.g., B and Bb) never appeared in adjacent positions in the same voice to produce chromatic motion (degree inflection).

Mention has already been made of the use of signatures during the period (see Chapter 5, p. 68) and in particular the peculiarity of conflicting signatures which do not appear again until the twentieth century. In manuscripts using signatures the signature is often presented only at the beginning of the piece even though it applies throughout. Inconsistent practice seems to be the rule in this as in so many aspects of the musical notation of the period, so that care and good musical judgment (sympathetic to the spirit of the music) is essential when the literature is studied.

Example 7.2. Raised Leading Tone.

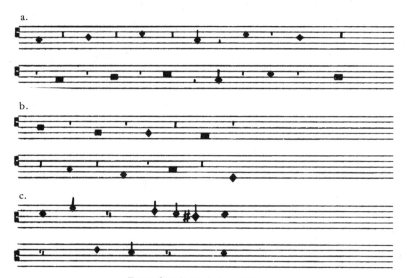

Example 7.3. Varieties of Hocket.

Hocket

Hocket is a contrapuntal technique described by the early fourteenth-century theorist Walter Odington as "A truncation . . . made over the tenor . . . in such a way that one voice is always silent while another sings."[1] That is, two voices will produce the effect of an alteration of sound and silence between them in several different ways. These include: (a) repetition of each melody note of the lead line by the follower line with or without the same rhythm; (b) alternation of the notes of the melody without repetition; (c) alternation between groups of notes rather than single notes. All of these tend to produce something of a hiccough effect which we know as hocket and which Reese suggests has a long history dating back to the use of primitive instruments.[2] The three different types of hocket described above are demonstrated in Example 7.3.

Hocket was usually employed in popular compositions as a portion of a piece, but a number of examples could be cited of complete hocket pieces. They appeared in either two or three voices; in the latter, the two upper voices were in hocket against a continuing tenor voice line. The tenor remained consonant with each voice as it entered whether on adjacent notes or in more extended groups.

When attempting to compose hocket, students should be certain that the spirit of the piece is compatible with this technique — generally gay and playful, corresponding "to the taste of rural and young people."[3] A suitable text should be selected unless the work is intended for instruments (see HAM, No. 32e), and the linear truncation for the two hocket voices should be planned to produce the most effective statement of the textual idea. Lines between the truncated parts (when simple repetition is not used) should be conceived so that one voice leads comfortably into the next (e.g., ending on an adjacent or the same melodic pitch). The rhythm must be compatible with the spirit of the style of the piece, but this device is likely to be more active than passive. As with all special techniques, especially those that are quite distinctive in sound, hocket should be used with discretion.

Isorhythm

Isorhythm (same rhythm) was an important contrapuntal technique which developed in the thirteenth century and was used widely into the fifteenth. It has returned in the works of twentieth century composers such as *Music for Violin, Cello and Piano* by Earle Brown. In a sense it was an extension of the basic concept of the rhythmic modes — a rhythmic pattern (in this case an extended one requiring the equivalent of several modern measures) that was continuously repeated throughout the piece or a major section thereof.

The isorhythmic pattern normally appeared in the tenor voice part, but later examples show that the technique was used in upper parts (although these generally reflect a somewhat freer treatment). Each statement of the isorhythmic pattern was referred to as a *talea*, and a piece could have many taleae. The line placed on this pattern could be through-composed or it could consist of its own melodic repetitive pattern. In the latter, the repeated line was termed *color*. This repeating melodic pattern could coincide with the talea of the isorhythm or it could unfold independent of it. That is, it was possible to have three taleae set to two colores, which simply indicates that the rhythmic pattern was stated three times and the melodic pattern was stated twice. See Example 7.4.

Some compositions have variations of the rhythmic patterns after the first two or three taleae, but these normally vary according to some logical scheme (e.g., augmentation). Isorhythm was quite widely used during the thirteenth

Example 7.4. Isorhythm. Motet: Machaut, *Qui es promesses—Ha! Fortune—Et Non Est*. Friedrich Ludwig and H. Besseler, eds., *Guillaume de Machaut, Musikalische Werke*, Vol. III, Breitkopf and Härtel, Wiesbaden, 1954.

and fourteenth centuries in the motet form (to be discussed in a later chapter). The isorhythmic motet was unquestionably one of the most important forms of the period and was remarkably well represented in the works of Guillaume de Machaut (only three of his motets are not isorhythmic). The motet from which Example 7.4 was taken consists of twelve taleae (two of which are shown in the example) and three colores.

When composing an isorhythmic piece, students must understand the nature and necessary approach of isorhythmic writing. Isorhythm is clearly intended to provide a subtle internal unity in a composition. The line itself may be derived from another source (e.g., plainsong) or it may be composed; normally it consists of larger note value because it is in the tenor voice (when used in the upper voices, this is not necessarily true).

We shall use the tune from three opening incises of the Sequence *Veni*

Sancte Spiritus for the isorhythmic tenor voice of a piece we shall construct. This simple tune (see Example 7.5) will be used in such a way that each incise coincides with a single talea and each of the two colores employed in the piece will consequently consist of three taleae. By the nature of the Sequence, this means that the first six incises of the plainsong are used (see *Liber Usualis*, p. 880). In Example 7.6 we may observe this tune set in the selected isorhythmic pattern, reflecting the three taleae of the first half of the piece.

Example 7.5. *Veni Sancte Spiritus* (excerpt). *Liber Usualis*, p. 880. Reprinted with permission from the 1963 edition of Desclee & Co., Tournai-Doornik, Belgium.

Example 7.6. Isorhythmic Setting of *Veni Sancte Spiritus*.

Brief consideration of Example 7.6 will reveal the basically slow rhythmic motion used, the rhythmic variety achieved within a very simple setting, and the rest that separates the taleae from each other. Although this last device is not essential, it is quite common practice in the spirit of this style.

The next step is to add two upper voices that are suitable to the given tenor. In doing so, several characteristics of the general late thirteenth-century and early fourteenth-century style should be kept in mind. These may be outlined as follows:

1. Pieces generally begin and end with perfect consonances;
2. Internal cadences may be perfect consonances, imperfect consonances, or triads;
3. Voices may cross freely, although the tenor voice is crossed less frequently than are the upper two;
4. Upper voices are normally considerably more active than the tenor;
5. Similar motion to all consonant intervals is widely used, but contrary motion seems to be preferred;
6. Upper voices tend to complement each other rhythmically, i.e., one is more active while the other is less so;
7. Upper lines tend to be through-composed, although occasional references

may be found to the characteristics of the tenor to which they have been set;

8. Owing to the different degrees of activity in the upper parts and the tenor, the latter is occasionally in a different meter;

9. Other contrapuntal devices (e.g., hocket) may be used in the upper two voices over the isorhythmic tenor;

10. Cadences commonly use the raised leading tone in the upper voice against a descending second in the lower — this will be considered at greater length later.

Continuing with the construction of an isorhythmic piece within the context of these guidelines (not defining a form or working with a text but confining ourselves to the musical problems of putting lines together), it would be helpful as our next step to define the vertical structures at the beginning and ending of each section. We may quickly note that the end of each phrase in the tenor is an ascending second which will, of course, not allow for the raised leading-tone cadence suggested in our list of ten principles. Although this figure is perhaps less common in the literature, it is not unusual. The resolve associated with this ascending tenor line is usually a descending stepwise motion to the octave or fifth. In Example 7.7 we may see the results of these decisions. It should be understood that these are not the only possibilities.

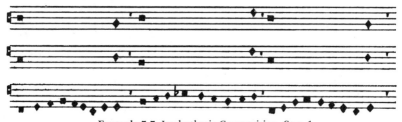

Example 7.7. Isorhythmic Composition. Step 1.

As we proceed to compose lines over the isorhythmic tenor, it should be understood that the particular cadence tones we have sketched in may have to give way to one of the other possibilities that exist in order to produce sensible and musically linear results. This kind of flexibility must be omnipresent in all compositional processes since in many situations a number of alternatives exist and obstinate adherence to one one when circumstances require another will only lead to unmusical results.

Beginning with the open fifth-octave structure shown in Example 7.7, one possible first step is to sketch in pitch choices for each of the tones in the tenor. Irrespective of their location or rhythmic value, these points are of critical concern for the vertical relationship decisions. In selecting the pitches for the upper voices, one of the primary concerns (in addition to its vertical acceptability) must be the creation of a good sense of melodic line and the contour relationship between the three lines. Example 7.8 shows one possible set of choices for the first talea.

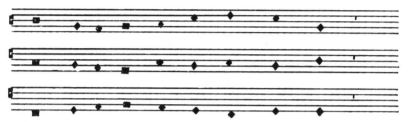

Example 7.8. Isorhythmic Composition. Step 2.

With the single exception of the third to fourth notes, the two outside voices are in contrary motion throughout. The middle voice, which of course must either parallel the other two voices or remain static, parallels the upper voice in all but three moves in this passage. Greater contrast can be achieved by introducing additional motion in the upper voices. The resulting skeleton of a passage employs imperfect consonances or triads on every important position with the exception of the beginning and ending of the passage, as determined earlier. The ranges of the respective voices are relatively narrow (a sixth in the upper and a fifth in the middle). Although this is not an essential characteristic, it is probably typical of the style and worthy of note, for the lines are later embellished as more activity is added.

The final step for this passage is to provide greater interest within and between the respective lines. Our concern is now to produce independent, stylistic, and musical lines that complement and contrast with each other. Example 7.9 demonstrates one possible solution. It should be noted that the five notes preceding the final one in the middle voice, which initially produced a very stagnant line, have been brought to life and given a sense of direction by discreet selection of additional melodic tones. The amount of activity in the two upper voices is almost identical but, by distribution of the activity in the respective voices, an attractive general sense of motion is conveyed.

The procedure for the second talea is exactly the same. Before beginning, students should note that the line for this portion of the tenor is almost identical with that of the first section, but it is set a perfect fourth higher. This is likely to raise the tessitura of the upper two voices or create more crossing of parts. Although an almost identical line arrangement could be composed for this section, it is wise to seek a different one. Example 7.10 offers a possible

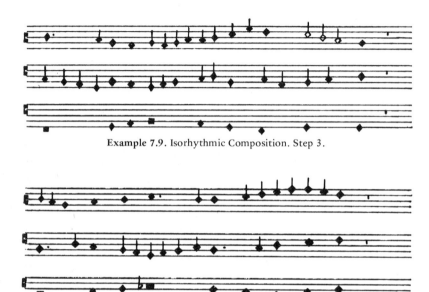

Example 7.9. Isorhythmic Composition. Step 3.

Example 7.10. Isorhythmic Composition. Step 4.

solution to this section. Once again the outer parts are primarily in contrary motion, and the upper line is quite similar in contour to its preceding counterpart. The middle line has the most significant changes but is not totally dissimilar from the preceding passage. The ranges of the two upper lines have been expanded upward (both lines in this passage have a range of a seventh) and rhythmically the respective lines are quite different from their earlier treatment.

Other elements contribute to the variety in this section. Whereas the predominant vertical sound in the first passage was minor triad or imperfect consonance (other than the perfect consonances at the beginning and ending of that passage), the principal sound in this section is major triad or imperfect consonance. A significant change at the end is the use of a minor triad at the cadence in place of the perfect consonance. Thus a degree of unity has been achieved by virtue of the similar linear contour in the upper line and the isorhythmic treatment of the tenor (which presents a particularly strong sense of unity in its almost total duplication of the shape of the first talea tenor). The other compositional elements join to produce the needed variety.

The final talea must be approached in the same manner as those considered up to this point. Completing this color and the additional color suggested earlier in our discussion should prove a worthwhile project for students.

Each tenor selected for an isorhythmic piece will have its own potential, limitations, and peculiarities. Students should consistently study each line carefully to gain proficiency in evaluating these elements. The weaknesses and successes of compositional pursuits will finally be determined by the sharpness of these judgments and the ability to capitalize on them.

Cadences

Although our discussion has been esentially confined to contrapuntal practices in recognition of the fact that the concept and spirit of the music of this period was principally contrapuntal, there is one vitally important area we must consider before closing our discussion. It has been and will continue to be an integral part of all our contrapuntal considerations, but in the final analysis it may be more accurately considered the precursor of the entire harmonic system that subsequently evolved a few centuries after the close of the Middle Ages. I am speaking of the cadence.

We have seen, in our discussion of plainsong, that the early monophonic cadence consisted of patterns peculiar to the particular mode in which the piece was composed. This was true throughout the Church literature and to some degree in the secular literature. The latter was freer, however, requiring a further look at cadential practices in the monophonic literature. Normally, the final tone was approached by step from above or below. Less often, but still with reasonable frequency, it was approached by the skip of a third from above or below. The penultimate tone, when moving by step to the final, may be approached by step or skip of a third from above or below. But when it resolves by skip of the third to the final, it is approached by step from either above or below.

Although these monophonic cadential practices in secular music may have coincided with the modal patterns associated with sacred music, considerably more freedom existed for a natural musical expression of the text. Attitudes toward the monophonic cadence were carried clearly and directly into polyphonic cadential practices.

Throughout the period, irrespective of the number of parts, the final resolve in polyphony was to a perfect consonance. Greater freedom was exercised in the composition of internal cadences after the earliest developmental stages. Imperfect consonances or triads became common in these lesser cadential positions throughout the greater part of the fourteenth century.

In early polyphony at least one voice in the final cadence resolves by step, and more often all voices do so (either ascending or descending). With two voices, contrary motion to the final tone(s) is the norm. In three-voiced compositions, the outer voices generally move by contrary motion while the inner voice parallels one of the others to its respective final tone. These penultimate tones are, as in the monophonic literature, normally approached by step and rarely by a skip more than a third. These points are demonstrated in Example 7.11.

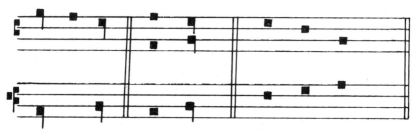

Example 7.11. Early Polyphonic Final Cadences.

In the fourteenth century, as suggested earlier, the final resolve was still to a perfect consonance. The approach to that final basic set of relationships suggests that composers had a new awareness of the concept of tension and resolve. A sense of harmonic motion began to make its presence felt in the increasing importance of the leading tone (the raised seventh degree of the scale) and more harmonically functional cadential patterns. Two widely used formulas gained favor during this period, and a number of variants on them can be identified. The two principal cadential patterns continued to be used well into the fifteenth century.

The first of the patterns is the *double leading-tone cadence*. In this approach to the final perfect consonance, the upper two voices are set one-half step below their respective tones-of-resolve (musica ficta may be employed to achieve this relationship), and the lower voice descends by whole step to its final (see Example 7.12). This cadential type was used in the late fourteenth century, extensively in the works of Machaut and his contemporaries.

The second cadential type is commonly known as the *Landini cadence* but is perhaps more accurately described by another widely used name — *under-*

third cadence. It occurred frequently in the works of the Italian composer Francesco Landini (1325-1397) and his contemporaries, and it was used well into the fifteenth century. This cadence could be considered a variant on the double leading-tone cadence, but it is distinctive enough both because it was used extensively and because of its individual character to be classified as a separate entity.

The motion of the three voices in the under-third cadence is identical with their respective equivalents in the double leading-tone cadence with the single exception of the upper voice which descends from the leading tone by step to the sixth degree of the scale and resolves directly to the root by the skip of a third. An example of this cadential form appears in Example 7.13.

Example 7.12. Double Leading-Tone Cadence.

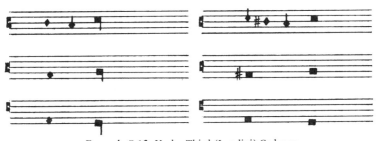

Example 7.13. Under-Third (Landini) Cadence.

A variety of other cadential types may be distinguished during this period. Consistency of practice is not apparent, and they seem to be more a result of the natural flow of the line to a stopping point than a distinctive cadential formula. One form, which is a variation on the double leading-tone cadence, is identical with that cadence but is distinguished by the whole-step ascending resolve of the middle voice. It is reasonable to question whether these may have been performed as double leading-tone types with the raised middle voice understood. However, a sufficient number of theorists have transcribed works in the altered form to justify consideration of this cadential type as an acceptable form. Another form of cadence is one in which the outer voices reverse their respective directions. The middle voice can move in either direction; usually it moves to the tone a fifth above the lower voice (as in the other cadential forms discussed). Finally, there is the type of cadence in which the outer voices move in parallel direction to either the fifth or the octave and the inner voice moves by contrary motion to an appropriate cadential tone. These several cadential forms are demonstrated in Example 7.14.

Important internal cadences were treated in the monophonic and polyphonic literature of the period in essentially the same manner as the final cadence. However, they were free because they often resolved to other tones of the mode and in the polyphonic literature to complete triads. The monophonic literature seemed to favor internal cadences on either the same tone as the final or a fifth above. Other pitch levels were used with a predominance of those pitches a third above or below the final tone. The polyphonic literature tended to favor the same tone in the early stages and a second above the final in the later stages, although other possibilities existed and were used.

The internal cadences often reflected more activity than is normally associated with final cadences and not infrequently revealed a dovetailing of phrases between the different lines at these cadential points. There was some use of alternate cadences (first and second endings) which become more apparent in later works. The treatment of each of these alternatives depended entirely upon the function of the cadence in relationship to the passage that was to follow it. The second of the two often appeared as a final cadence in treatment and the first as an internal, although no strict rule can be offered.

The cadences of a piece represent some of the most critical points in the flow of music, and every effort should be made to thoroughly understand the manner by which they relate to the balance of the music. This can best be accomplished by extensive study and analysis of works of the period and through practical efforts at composition.

Summary

The rapid expansion of the contrapuntal vocabulary of the composer during the thirteenth and fourteenth centuries produced a varied and rich literature which made it possible to distinguish individual musical styles and provided the premises for musical judgment and evolution through the centuries that followed.

Inherent in any compositional system at its early developmental stages are the ingredients that eventually lead to its dissolution and demise. The need for and use of the Bb in the early modal system clearly represents this pro-

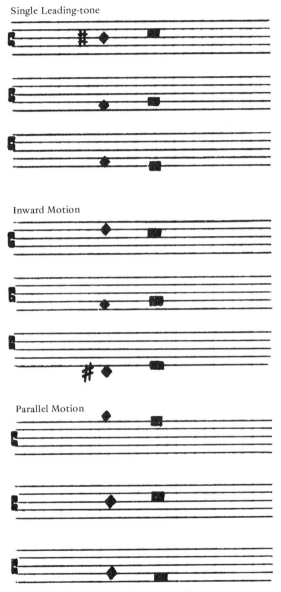

Example 7.14. Various Cadences.

cess. During the Middle Ages and later in the Renaissance the range was gradually extended, transposed forms of modes were used, and internal modal motion was introduced to vary the music. All of these developments created a
demand for additional chromatic alterations which subsequently provided the
foundation of the tonal system. The introduction of the new chromatic tones
which were more and more frequently employed as key signatures (sometimes producing mixed signatures between parts) was termed musica ficta and
rapidly became an integral part of the compositional framework.

Freedom of expression increased as the composer's musical vocabulary was
greatly enriched by such techniques as the hocket and isorhythm. The extensive use of these techniques (especially the latter), together with those discussed in the previous chapter, demonstrates the impelling desire of composers of the period to exploit sound as an artistic vehicle and to project their
own personalities into their music. The refinement and mastery of these devices enabled them to do this.

From the outset we have seen that the conclusion of a passage or a piece
required special consideration. This becomes especially apparent in the refinement of contrapuntal techniques and the resulting cadential formulas, and it
begins to suggest the increasing importance that homophonic considerations
would assume in the following centuries. The principal cadential patterns discussed, the double leading-tone and the under-third types, have many alternative possibilities that are clearly derived from them. All of these may be seen
in the literature for approximately two centuries, after which they are supplanted by clearly homophonic cadences which become an integral part of
the later tonal system.

chapter 8

sacred polyphonic forms

Musical forms during the Middle Ages were largely dependent upon the structure of the text. Repetitions of portions of a given text resulted in parallel musical repetitions, but a free unfolding of textual material was not often paralleled by through-composed musical treatment. This was especially apparent in secular music in which musical treatment of the poetic forms simply adopted the name of the particular form and the varying textual phrases were usually set to two distinctive musical ideas. In the sacred literature the textual forms were not as clearly defined and a more melismatic and through-composed style resulted.

Three principal sacred forms developed and were widely exploited in the thirteenth and fourteenth centuries: (a) the several organum styles; (b) conductus; (c) motet.[1] The term organum was applied to all polyphonic compositions during the early stages of the development of polyphony. However, during the period when Notre Dame in Paris was the center of musical activity (the late twelfth century and the early half of the thirteenth), it was restricted to sacred works. Gradually the conductus and motet became recognized as independent forms.

The general concepts and specific problems concerning the composition of organum have been discussed in Chapter 3. In that chapter reference was made to the three styles of organum employed by Leonin, which leaves us only to expand on the specifics of these styles.

Leonin's unmeasured melismatic style of organum was characterized by a free unmeasured melismatic upper voice which was composed over a sustained unmeasured lower voice; the melody for the lower voice was excerpted from the plainsong literature. This form of organum is thought to have been derived from the twelfth-century practices of the St. Martial school of composition. See Example 4.8.

The discant employed by Leonin was a note-against-note style. In it both of the voices used the rhythmic modes and rhythmically paralleled each other closely. See Example 8.1.

Example 8.1. Leonin's Discant Style Organum. Transcribed from William Waite, *The Rhythm of Twelfth Century Polyphony*, Yale University Press, New Haven, 1954, p. 212. Not notated as the original but in single notes for clarity. The brackets indicate original ligature groupings.

The third of Leonin's three styles of organum is referred to as a mixed style because the upper voice employs the rhythmic modes producing a rhythmically measured line against a sustained unmeasured lower voice. See Example 8.2.

Example 8.2. Leonin's Mixed Style Organum. Transcribed from William Waite, *The Rhythm of Twelfth Century Polyphony*, Yale University Press, New Haven, 1954, p. 50. Not notated as the original but in single notes for clarity. The brackets indicate original ligature groupings.

Although the above three examples do not reflect musical form in the traditional sense — the broad architectural concept of a piece — it is from these that later forms evolved. However, it should be remembered that these styles were used in a formal setting. The characteristic divisions of the church service and the traditional divisions of its subsections into solo and congregational singing (e.g., graduals and responses) contributed to an implicit formal sense. It is understood that when polyphony was used in the service in its early stages of development, the polyphonic sections were reserved for a small choir (perhaps two or three on a part) of trained singers whereas the monophonic passages were sung by the large choir or congregation. These alternations from one style to another were referred to as *clausulae*.

Conductus are pieces which, in the monophonic style of composition were set to Latin lyrics and were used in liturgical dramas of the twelfth century to accompany the entrances and exits of the participants. The later polyphonic conductus were free-composed compositions and are the earliest such works

Example 8.3. Conductus: *Veri floris* and transcription. The Conductus is from Madrid, Biblioteca Nacionale, 20486, fol. 129v, and the transcription is from Carl Parrish, *The Notation of Medieval Music*, W. W. Norton, New York, 1957, p. 96, Fig. 43, m. 1-3. Reprinted with permission of W. W. Norton & Company, Inc.

known. According to instructions of Franco of Cologne, the composer was to compose his own tenor, "as beautiful as he can," after which he was to add the second and (possibly) third voices.[2]

The conductus style was essentially a note-against-note style in which each voice was original (i.e., not based on an earlier plainsong). The most common forms of thirteenth-century conductus were in two voices although some were composed for three voices. All voices used the same rhythm (one of the rhythmic modes). When a third voice was included, it was expected to be consonant with *one* of the other two voices. These were composed from the bottom up (i.e., tenor, duplum, triplum) rather than all voices together. A single metrical Latin text (either secular or sacred) was used for all voices. The note-against-note style was retained throughout the composition. In some later conductus, cadenzalike passages (*caudae*) were inserted for one of the voices (normally at the end but possibly at other points). Finally these compositions were notated in score from, i.e., one voice directly on top of the other with the pitches that are sounded together over each other.

The style of this literature was highly conjunct, as has been suggested in earlier chapters. Few skips larger than a third were used. The treatment of the text was essentially syllabic with the exception of the caudae which were melismatic. The perfect consonances were used estensively with some imperfect consonances in less important rhythmic positions. Some dissonant intervals (seconds and sevenths) were used in weak rhythmic positions. See Example 8.3.

The motet was widely explored by composers from the early thirteenth century through the late fourteenth. It was so extensively used that it has come to be referred to as "the Symphony of the Thirteenth Century." Representing a more sophisticated level of compositional technique and having clearly evolved from earlier contrapuntal practices,[3] the motet almost supplanted the conductus by the middle of the thirteenth century.

The principal characteristics associated with the motet are:

1. It was composed in two, three, or four voice parts but three was the most representative;
2. The tenor was usually taken from a plainsong (often a melismatic passage from a Gregorian chant);
3. The tenor part probably was frequently performed on an instrument rather than sung;
4. Each of the vocal parts had a different text (at first only Latin was

used, but later it was not unusual to find a mixture of languages in the same composition);

5. Independent modal rhythms were used in each part (typical choices were the Trochaic, Iambic, or Tribrachic in the upper lines and Dactylic or Spondaic in the tenor);

6. The ordines of the rhythmic modes in the later forms of the motet were extended into longer and more independent patterns which, by frequent use in a repetitive fashion, created the technique discussed in Chapter 7 — isorhythm;

7. The music was written in part from a single page or on two facing pages with the tenor across the bottom, the motetus on the upper right, and the triplum on the upper left positions on the page(s). Other layouts were also used but this appears to have been the most widely accepted;

8. A gradual process of secularization occurred as tenor parts were taken from secular songs and dances rather than from the sacred literature.

Probably the most unique and distinguishing characteristic of the motet was the use of different texts for different voices. In the early motets, the upper voices were used to paraphrase the text of the tenor which had been excerpted from the monophonic literature. However, with the increasing secularization of the motet, the upper voices were often settings of love songs with no relationship to the Latin tenor. It should also be noted that it has become common practice to identify motets by the opening few words of *each* voice part (e.g., *Styrps regia-Armonizans cantica-Amen*).

This motet is a brief work, written in simple, clear modal notation. Example 8.4 provides the typical format described above. The transcription of the piece (see Example 8.5) clearly reveals that although there is a moderate degree of linear independence, the rhythmic construction is quite straightforward with two of the parts almost always duplicating each other rhythmically in a manner similar to the earlier conductus. The first pulse of each of the transcribed measures (except the third from the last) reflects a perfect consonance relationship between all three voices. The single exception is a first-inversion triad. The cadence is a form of the double leading-tone type discussed in the last chapter. A few sharp dissonances can be noted (e.g., the second half of measure 7 and the end of measure 9) but always in relatively weaker positions. The one in measure 7 conforms to the practice associated with the conductus of having at least two of the voices in consonance with each other. The same treatment is apparent in the second half of measure 11.

The fourteenth century witnessed the relative decline in the importance of the motet form, although many were composed and these represent important portions of the productivity of the composers of the period. During this closing century of the Middle Ages, the motet gained greater rhythmic freedom and adopted the isorhythmic technique as an integral part of its concept (although it would be incorrect to imply universal application of this technique to the motets of the period). As mentioned earlier, one of the two principal composers of the fourteenth century, Machaut, used the isorhythmic technique in all but three of his twenty-three works in this form. Careful study of the motet *Martyrum gemma* (provided in the workbook) and comparison of it with the earlier type in modal notation (Example 8.4) will help in understanding motet development.

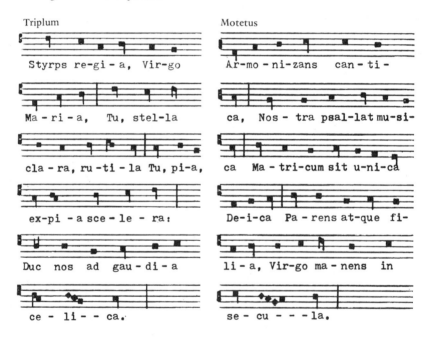

Example 8.4. Motet: *Styrps regia—Armonizans cantica—Amen*. Bamberg, Staatsbibliothek, Ed. IV 6, fol. 5ro.

Example 8.5. Transcription of **Example 8.4.** Pierre Aubry, *Cent motets du XIIIe siècle*, Rouart and Lerolle, Paris, 1908, Vol. II, p. 19.

Messe de Nostre Dame

In our discussion of the monophonic sacred forms in Chapter 3 the Mass was cited as being of major importance in the musical productivity of the period. It is interesting that polyphonic treatment of the Mass was quite slow to gain favor. The early polyphonic Mass movements were in the organum styles and were more frequently composed for the Proper until about 1300 when the Ordinary gained favor (apparently because it could be performed throughout the year rather than being limited to a single occasion). Many single movements in two and three parts were composed, but there was no complete Mass by one composer until Machaut's *Messe de Nostre Dame* in the middle of the fourteenth century. And it was not until almost one hundred years later that his example was followed.

Were it not for this work, little attention would be focused on the contrapuntal treatment of the Mass during this period. However, the technical achievements of this work necessitate that we consider it in greater detail. In addition to its being the first such work by a single composer, other important factors are: its imposing size; the composer's obvious concern with motivic unity; and the sophistication of his contrapuntal techniques (including imitation, repetition, and fugaltype entries).

The Mass is composed in four voice parts and has six sections: Kyrie; Gloria; Credo; Sanctus; Agnus Dei; and Ite, Missa Est. The four voice parts are (from the top down): triplum, motetus, tenor, and contratenor. Tempus and prolation were not indicated and had to be interpreted by modern editors from the note values. Also, accidentals appeared very sparingly in the score, and much discretion must be employed in determining when, where, and how they are to be used.

Three basic motives pervade the entire work. One of the three is presented in each large section of the Kyrie movement. There are numerous modifications of the motives as the movements unfold, but they are always distinctive. The three motives and one alternate form for each are shown in Example 8.6. One other melodic figure recurs throughout the work and could possibly be

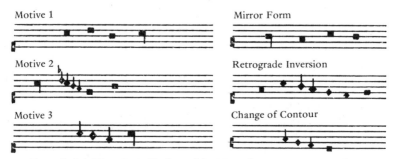

Example 8.6. Three Basic Motives of the *Messe de Nostre Dame*, Machaut.

Example 8.7. Motive 1a.

distinguished as an independent motive. However, the relationship of this figure to Motive 1 is so close, in my opinion, that here it will be considered a variant of that motive and for convenience will be termed Motive 1a. See Example 8.7.

The tenor of the Kyrie movement was taken from the Kyrie of Mass IV in the *Liber Usualis* (p. 25) and is presented in isorhythm. The form of this movement is the form of its source (aaa, bbb ccd). The opening Kyrie section has seven strict taleae in the tenor voice while the contratenor is in free isorhythm.

In the Christe section, both the tenor and the contratenor are strictly isorhythmic. They each have three taleae, and the two isorhythmic patterns coincide throughout. The same type of paralleling isorhythmic writing between the two lower voices is carried through the two Kyrie sections (*c* and *d*) which follow each voice in each section having two taleae. See Example 8.8.

First Kyrie Section (Tenor)

Christe Section (Tenor)

Christe Section (Contratenor)

Second Kyrie Section (Tenor)

Second Kyrie Section (Contratenor)

Final Kyrie Section (Tenor)

Final Kyrie Section (Contratenor)

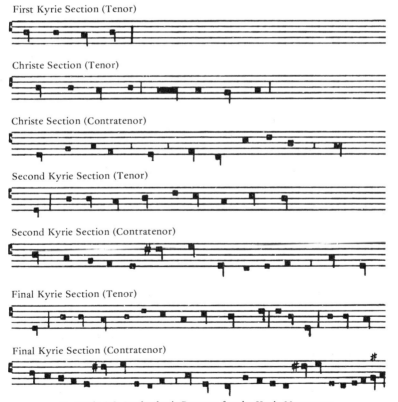

Example 8.8. Isorhythmic Patterns for the Kyrie Movement.

The rhythm and melody of each of the three large sections of the Kyrie movement, as was suggested by the distinctive motives associated with each, are quite independent although material from an earlier section does recur in a less distinctive form in later sections. However, the subdivided large Kyrie section is tightly unified by a literal restatement of the first four measures[4] of the *c* Kyrie portion at the beginning of the *d* Kyrie.

The cadences at the end of the Kyrie section are all double leading-tone types. The cadence that closes the Christe section follows the identical voice motion associated with the double leading-tone cadence, but the tones ascending to the final fifth and octave above the lowest voice are not raised. By using the musica ficta, these tones probably could be raised to produce the double leading-tone cadence, but this approach does not seem to be favored by modern editors. See Example 8.9.

There are some suggestions of the hocket treatment in this movement, but clearer examples occur later in the work and will be discussed at the appropriate time. Both imitation and sequence are employed in this movement and

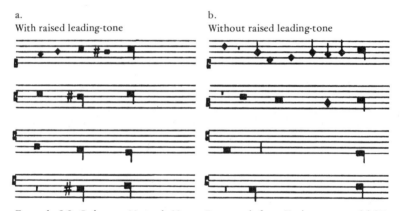

a.
With raised leading-tone

b.
Without raised leading-tone

Example 8.9. Cadences. *Messe de Nostre Dame:* a. is from Kyrie, measures 26-27; b. from Kyrie, measures 48-49.

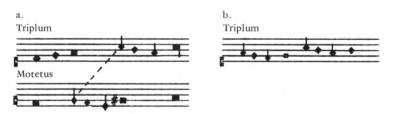

a.
Triplum

b.
Triplum

Motetus

Example 8.10. Imitation and Sequence. *Messe de Nostre Dame:* a. is from measures 51-52; b. from Kyrie, measures 75-80.

are demonstrated in Example 8.10. Although the lines throughout the movement are largely conjunct, there are some notable and unlikely large skips, which appear almost exclusively in the contratenor. It is especially interesting to note the several instances of the skip of an ascending major seventh. The principal vocal range for each of the voices is kept within an octave although a few extensions to a ninth (and in one instance a tenth) can be noted. Although not typical of the style, several occurrences of triadic outlining can be noted in this movement and in later movements.

Rhythmically a great deal of variety is introduced, with a considerable use of syncopation. Yet a clear sense of unity is maintained by a recurring rhythmic pattern which may or may not actually be associated with the motives mentioned earlier. The patterns in the first Kyrie statement, in the Christe section, and in the final Kyrie statement exemplify the characteristic and distinctive rhythmic figures used throughout the Mass to produce a broad unified work.

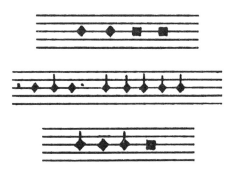

The great majority of primary pulses (i.e., the first beats in the transcribed measures) are perfect consonances, and all sectional cadences end on perfect consonances. Some internal cadences do end on complete triads in root position, and a fair sampling of first inversion and root position triads as well as some imperfect consonances may be found throughout the piece. A sprinkling of cross-relationships can also be noted (see Example 8.11), and their interpretation can be the subject for good debate.

The Gloria employs no isorhythm and is treated like a conductus. All the motives from the Kyrie movement reappear in the Gloria, but in some instances they are slightly modified. The opening phrase, *Gloria in excelsis Deo*, is sung by a soloist, the four-voice treatment begins with *Et in terra pax*.

No new motives appear in the Gloria movement, but a "rhythmically stereotyped" pattern recurs throughout the Gloria and Credo sections. The editor of the score used for this analysis believes they were "without doubt intended for instruments." The four appearances of this textless figure in the Gloria are identical. However, in the Credo section each entry of the presumably instrumental passage is different.

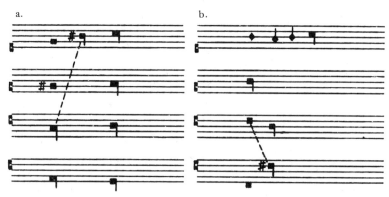

Example 8.11. Cross-Relations. *Messe de Nostre Dame*: a. is from Kyrie, measures 94-95; b. from Kyrie, measure 76.

Occasional appearances of sharp dissonances may be noted, although it does not appear that they were used for any special text-emphasis effect. See Example 8.12. Imitation is used in this (Gloria) movement, one notable example being between the two upper voices; the lead tones of each of the figures together produce a triad. See Example 8.13. A fine example of hocket occurs between the upper two voices near the end of the Gloria (in the *Amen* portion). An excerpt from this passage is shown in Example 8.14.

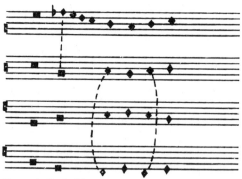

Example 8.12. Dissonances. *Messe de Nostre Dame*, Gloria, measures 10-11.

Example 8.13. Imitation. *Messe de Nostre Dame*, Gloria, measures 84-86.

Example 8.14. Hocket. *Messe de Nostre Dame*, Gloria, measures 120-124.

A new variation of the double leading-tone cadence, which has not yet been considered, appears in the Gloria. In this form, the two outer voices move by half steps up to the final tone; one of the remaining voices proceeds in the same manner in parallel octaves or unison with one of those already mentioned; and the final voice moves by whole step down to its final tone. In each case, the final tone is in the contratenor. See Example 8.15. It should be noted that all cadences in the Gloria, including the final cadence, are of this type. This cadence is again used extensively later in the Mass (the last three movements).

The Credo movement is treated much like the Gloria. There is no isorhythmic writing and its motion is highly chordal. All the motives introduced in the Kyrie are once again used freely throughout this movement, with a signifi-

Example 8.15. Inverted Double Leading-Tone Cadence. *Messe de Nostre Dame*, Gloria, measures 130-131.

cant reference to a modified form of Motive 1 at the rhythmic broadening of the passage *ex Maria Virgine*. Reese points out that "a broad treatment was destined to become standard for the whole *Et incarnatus est* in later Masses."[5] No new motives appear in this movement, but the brief instrumental passages referred to earlier in our discussion employ the rhythmic figure from the Kyrie section in various forms, which, after similar treatment in the Gloria, tends to reinforce the motivic significance of this element.

Imitative passages appear in various places throughout the Credo as they did in earlier movements. Some use is made of mirroring lines in various places in the work as a whole, but a particularly clear example occurs in this movement. See Example 8.16. This occurs between the upper two voices in measures 39 and 40 of the modern edition.

Example 8.16. Mirroring Lines. *Messe de Nostre Dame*, Credo, measures 39-40.

Double leading-tone cadences appear throughout this movement at important sectional endings. Slight variations of this type of cadence may be seen at less important stopping points.

The concluding *Amen* of the Credo section is set apart from the body of the movement by distinctive treatment (as the *Amen* of the Gloria section was set apart by the use of hocket). The two lower voices are in isorhythm with three taleae each. However, the voices switch parts for their respective final taleae. The upper two voices are set in rhythmic patterns distinctly reminiscent of the Kyrie portions of the first movement. A basic double leading-tone cadence brings the movement to a close.

The opening three statements of the word *Sanctus* in the fourth movement of this Mass are presented in an *aba* form. That is, the third Sanctus is a literal restatement of the first. Following this introductory passage, the two lower voices are presented in isorhythm, each having ten taleae which coincide throughout the rest of the movement.

The motives employed in the earlier movements appear in the Sanctus, but they are somewhat less important in terms of both frequency and position. Imitative and sequential writing can be noted, as well as hints of the use of hocket, but all of these are secondary to the isorhythm of the lower voices and the generally through-composed sense of the upper.

Following the opening Sanctus statements, there are two important internal cadences (before the Hosanna and the Benedictus); the first is a simple double leading-tone type and the second is an inverted form of the double leading-tone cadence. The final cadence, as has been noted earlier, is also an inverted form of the double leading-tone cadence.

The isorhythmic tenor is taken from the Sanctus of Mass XVII in the *Liber Usualis* (p. 61) and treats the plainsong source freely in that skips of a third are occasionally filled in with passing notes. The Agnus Dei portion of the same Mass was the source for the tenor of the Agnus Dei movement of the Machaut Mass.

The Agnus Dei movement begins without isorhythm, presents both lower voices in isorhythm (two taleae each) beginning with the *qui tollis* section, follows this with another brief passage on the words *Agnus Dei*, then concludes with an eighteen-measure (modern transcription) totally isorhythmic passage. All voices but the motetus actually include the nineteenth measure from the end in this totally isorhythmic section. The pattern is three measures long in all voices producing six taleae of four-voice isorhythmic writing. See Example 8.17.

Example 8.17. Four-Voice Isorhythm Pattern. *Messe de Nostre Dame*, Agnus Dei, measures 31-33.

All the motives that occurred in earlier movements are used in this movement but, as in the Sanctus, to a lesser extent. Each of the sectional cadences (including the final cadence) are of the inverted double leading-tone variety.

A brief Ite, missa est movement concludes the Mass. The lower two voices are isorhythmic and each has two coinciding taleae. Motives 1 and 2 are used extensively, but Motive 3 is only hinted at in a few places in the movement. A double leading-tone cadence brings the Mass to a close.

Phrasing throughout the Mass is asymmetrical, with an abundance of three- and five-measure phrases in all movements. Although there are varying degrees of modal drift within movements, the first three are in the Dorian and the final three are in the Lydian. This modal determination is made largely from the beginnings and the final cadences as well as, to a lesser degree, the linear behavior of the respective voice parts within the movements, especially near the beginnings and endings of each.

The *Messe de Nostre Dame* was the largest single work produced in the Middle Ages and clearly reflects the early concern of composers of multi-movement works with creating and maintaining unity by musical means. In this Mass we have observed the use of motivic unification — which in this work is a predominantly melodic device — as well as rhythmic unity achieved by extensive use of isorhythmic principles. To a lesser degree, unity is achieved by formal means. In latter movements reference is made to earlier sections (e.g., the literal repetitions in the Kyrie and Sanctus), thus producing a broader sense of musical organization.

Summary

Sacred polyphonic forms of the Middle Ages span a period of approximately three hundred years. They reflect the entire evolution of polyphony from organum to free and sophisticated composition in four-voice parts that developed and exploited a wide variety of contrapuntal devices.

The principal forms or styles were organum, conductus, and motet; each reflected a manner of writing rather than a broad architectural structure, which is implicit in the concept of "musical form." In fact, the broad structure of individual pieces was musically quite free and was defined more by poetic form than by musical techniques.

Three different types of organum associated with the Notre Dame composer Leonin were widely explored in early polyphony. These included melismatic, discant, and mixed styles, all of which were composed to a given plainsong melody. The first completely free form of polyphony, in which all material was original, was conductus. This style of composition was predominantly two-voiced — some written for three — and was always note-against-note, using either a sacred or a secular Latin text.

The motet was the most widely explored form of polyphony during the entire period. It evolved from earlier contrapuntal forms and gradually faded from favor in the fourteenth century as other forms gained prominence. It was used for both sacred and secular compositions and was most distinctly characterized by multiple texts for several voices, often in different languages. From its early repetitive use of the ordines of the rhythmic modes came the isorhythmic technique which served as one of the principal unifying forces in polyphonic compositions throughout the rest of the Middle Ages.

Although the Mass as a form is not a significant part of the musical output of this period, many individual movements were composed in the various polyphonic styles that prevailed. However, one complete setting of the Ordinary is known to have been composed by a single composer, and it stands as one of the most significant and remarkable single achievements of the period. This work, the *Messe de Nostre Dame* by Machaut, employed many of the compositional techniques that had evolved to that date, demonstrated the composer's clear concern for achieving broad musical unity, and set the model for many works subsequently composed during the Renaissance.

secular polyphonic forms

The secular monophonic forms that characterized the literature of the poet-musicians from the twelfth through the fourteenth centuries were adopted by the composers of polyphonic music during the late thirteenth and the four-teenth centuries. These forms included the lai, the rondeau, the ballade, and the virelai. The virelai was called *chanson balladées* by Machaut and *ballata* by the Italians.

Several new forms emerged during the fourteenth century. The most im-portant of these were the canonic forms of *chace* and *caccia*, the madrigal, and the secular motet. The secular motet differed from its sacred counterpart only in that the tenor was taken from the secular monophonic literature rath-er than from the sacred and the texts were concerned with secular subjects (e.g., love).

The various polyphonic techniques and principles we considered in our study of the sacred forms apply with equal validity to the secular. However, some important differences of practice should be noted which suggest a freer attitude in secular composition and a greater concern with the use of special effects or the exploration of a technique for its own sake. The canon, for example, was an extremely popular technique in secular compositions, and many entire works in varying forms were cast in a canonic setting. We have al-ready considered one of these, the rondeau *Ma fin est mon commencement* by Machaut. Another composition by Machaut, which is included for study in the workbook, *Dame, par vous — Amis dolens — Sans cuer*, demonstrates the use of canon for a complete secular form. The piece is a triple ballade, that is it is a three-part strict canon with three different texts (one for each voice) each in the form of a ballade.

A further strong indication that the canonic technique was popular is the fact that a pair of paralleling forms that are almost wholly dependent on canon became quite popular throughout much of Europe during this period. The first of these is the French chace; it typically was in two voice parts in canon throughout and used a text about hunting or "the chace." The Italian caccia was a development of the French chace and used three voice parts. The upper two voices were normally in canon and the lowest was free and tended to have longer note values. The canonic parts were usually separated by the modern equivalent of eight or more measures. Also, the caccia was normally divided into two parts: the first was usually longer and was always canonic and the second (*ritornello*) was homophonic or canonic. Because of the subject matter of the texts of these pieces, there was often an attempt to mimic the sounds of nature or the calls of the participants in the actions described. Very few examples of the French chace have been discovered, and Marrocco points out: "It is, however, surprising to note that of the several hundred known examples of secular music of the Italian *Ars Nova*, only twenty-six are in canon form."[1] He further points out that "these compositions were not intended for popular consumption, for the music was too refined, too florid, and rhythmically intricate, to be sung with any degree of competence by provincial or itinerant musicians."[2] A caccia by the leading Italian composer of the last half of the fourteenth century — *Chosi Pensoso* by Francesco Landini — is provided for study in the workbook.

The fourteenth-century madrigal usually had two sections, similar to the two parts of the caccia. The first had one to four stanzas, each of which had three lines of seven or eleven syllables. All stanzas were sung to the same music and all lines were usually in iambic pentameter. The second section was a ritornello, which always appeared at the end of the piece (it was not a refrain) and comprised two lines set in a rhythm that contrasted with the earlier portion of the piece. The texts were generally concerned with contemplative, pastoral subjects and were usually set in two (sometimes three) voice parts. The most common settings of the madrigal during this period were of eight (3+3+2) or eleven lines (3+3+3+2).

The madrigal of this period occasionally appeared in a canonic setting and was then very similar to the caccia. The sole distinction of the two forms in such a setting was the form of the text. The typical madrigal, however, was more closely akin to the conductus in the manner in which its lines related to each other than it was to other forms of the period (although architectural parallels can also be drawn with the ballade, especially for the eight-line madrigal). That is, the two (or three) lines of a madrigal tended to move in very close relationship to each other rhythmically, but the upper line was usually somewhat embellished. See Landini's *Somma felicita* in the workbook.

It has already been noted that the monophonic forms of secular music were adopted by composers of polyphony. However, the two examples of secular polyphonic forms that have been given (the rondeau *Ma fin est mon commencement* and the ballade *Dame, par vous — Amis, dolens — Sans cuer*) were presented in our discussion of a particular compositional technique (canon); this could be misconstrued to imply that canonic treatment of these forms was the rule rather than the exception. Although the basic forms are

Example 9.1. Virelai: *En mon cuer*, Machaut. Transcribed from Friedrich Ludwig and H. Besseler, eds., *Guillaume de Machaut, Musikalische Werke*, Vol. I, Breitkopf and Härtel, Wiesbaden, 1954, p. 83.

constant — being determined by the broad structure of the text — it is important that students be familiar with more typical examples of these forms.

The virelai retained much of its earlier identity as a song accompanying
dance when it was placed in a polyphonic setting. Also, it was widely adopted
in later forms of the fifteenth century (e.g., *frottole* and *bergerettes*). Machaut
wrote thirty-two virelai with music; most are in ternary meter and twenty-five
are monophonic. Example 9.1 typifies the polyphonic virelai in the relative
simplicity of its lines, the moderate use of syncopation, and the rhyming mu-

Example 9.2. Ballade: *Dame, comment qu'amez de vous ne soie*, Machaut. Transcribed from Friedrich Ludwig and H. Besseler, eds., *Guillaume de Machaut, Musikalische Werke*, Vol. I, Breitkopf and Härtel, Wiesbaden, 1954, p. 15.

Example 9.3. Rondeau: *Dix et sept. cinc. trese*, Machaut. Transcribed from Friedrich Ludwig and H. Besseler, eds., *Guillaume de Machaut, Musikalische Werke*, Vol. I, Breitkopf and Härtel, Wiesbaden, 1954, p. 66.

sical cadences (i.e., the melodic treatment of the cadences of the two sections is identical or very similar). See Example 9.1.

The rondeau and ballade gained a sophistication that changed their social role; apparently they were no longer used to accompany dance. The complexity of these forms has already been demonstrated (e.g., the rondeau *Ma fin est commencement*). A more typical example of the polyphonic ballade (which in Machaut's work ranges from two to four voices) is his two-voice ballade *Dame, comment qu'amez de vous ne soie* (See Example 9.2). In this piece the tenor is simple and slow moving, with a flowing, somewhat melismatic upper voice. The piece has rhyming cadences, as we saw in Example 9.1, and makes use of three different musica ficta signatures (no flats, one flat, and two flats).

Like Machaut's ballades, the rondeaux also appear in from two to four voices. They vary considerably in length, ranging from as few as twelve to as many as forty-two transcribed measures. Example 9.3 provides a characteristic Machaut rondeau in which the tenor is relatively less active than the upper voices. In this piece there is some imitation as well as some repetition of a melodic figure in several of the sections. As in so many examples of the literature of the period, there is also moderate use of syncopation.

Machaut's works seem to indicate that composers of the fourteenth century approached secular music somewhat differently from the way in which they approached sacred music. A greater variety of cadences is immediately apparent in secular music, and the most significant feature of these cadences is a more extensive use of skips of a fourth or fifth into the cadential tone. This is not very far removed from the type of resolve expected in a tonal cadence of later centuries. See Example 9.4. In this excerpt we may observe the upper two voices resolving in a typical manner to the fifth and octave above the final by ascending motion of a step. The lower voice reflects the principal

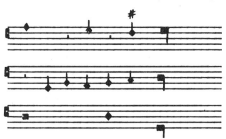

Example 9.4. Cadence from Rondeau: *Vo doulz resgars*, Machaut. Transcribed from Friedrich Ludwig and H. Besseler, eds., *Guillaume de Machaut, Musikalische Werke*, Vol. I, Breitkopf and Härtel, Wiesbaden, 1954, p. 57.

characteristic of this type of cadence, i.e., resolve of the penultimate tone to the ultimate by the descending skip of a fifth.

A second feature that appears to have been more widely exploited in the secular literature than in the sacred (although it is not peculiar to the secular) is the use of outlined triads and a wider use of disjunct motion. This type of linear writing is clearly more frequently found in the inner and lower voices than in the upper. It is believed that these lines were probably performed on instruments, which accounts for the freer attitude toward disjunct line. One excellent example of this type of writing has already been shown in the contratenor line of the rondeau *Ma fin est mon commencement* (presented in the workbook). More triadic forms are given in Example 9.5.

a.
Contratenor

b.
Contratenor

Example 9.5. Linear Triads in the Ballade: *Quant Theseus*, Machaut. Transcribed from Friedrich Ludwig and H. Besseler, eds., *Guillaume de Machaut, Musikalische Werke*, Vol. I, Breitkopf and Härtel, Wiesbaden, 1954, p. 40.

It should be noted and clearly understood that although the liberties described appear more widely in the secular than in the sacred literature, they should not be considered commonplace and must be used with restraint and discretion.

Instruments and Instrumental Forms

Reference has been made in a number of places in the earlier portion of this book to the use of instruments. Although any comprehensive consideration of the role of instruments during this period would stretch well beyond the scope and purpose of this volume, I would be remiss in not introducing the subject to the extent that it does pertain to our study.

Contrary to popular belief, instruments were widely used during the Middle Ages both in a solo capacity and for accompanying voices. Many different types of instruments were employed which enjoyed varying degrees of popularity. These included: bowed string instruments (e.g., rebecs and viols); plucked string instruments (e.g., harps and lutes); brass wind instruments (e.g., trumpets and sackbuts; wooden wind instruments (e.g., flutes and shawms); and a wide variety of percussive instruments (e.g., drums and cymbals). The organ developed considerably during this period, from the mammoth cathedral organs to the small portative organs. Keyboards developed in the latter part of the period (the fifteenth century) at approximately the same time as pedals, and together they provided the base for the further relatively rapid sophistication of this instrument.

Instruments were used as they were available, commonly producing heterogeneity of timbre in a performance and possibly significant timbral differences from one performance to another. Also, it was normal practice for only one instrument to perform each line.

Instruments were often used to accompany the songs of the troubadours and their counterparts. The instrument may have played the vocal line with the singer or it may have played one of the lower lines. Simple percussive accompaniments (e.g., small hand drums) were commonly employed as were heterophonic embellishments of vocal lines. In some works, the text would end, and for the equivalent of one or two modern measures the instruments would continue the line, providing momentary textural variety.

Instruments were also employed in the Church for processionals and liturgical dramas. The way in which they were used was essentially the same as elsewhere — availability first and function second. Again, scores were not written for the instruments, and instrumentalists basically used the vocal lines.

Instrumental notation is a separate study unto itself. It is assumed that in its earliest stages, the instrumentalist simply read from the vocal parts or improvised around the voices (as mentioned above). At a somewhat later date, a tablature form of notation developed with many variants appropriate for individual instruments and peculiar to geographical regions. The premise of tablature notation was that it provided a system of figures which was used to direct the player to the proper finger position on the particular instrument for the desired pitches. A form of tablature notation has been used in recent years to show chord positions for guitar music. These notations are beyond our purview. But for further information students are referred to the many sources listed in the bibliography.

The principal instrumental musical forms during this period were the *estampie* and the *ductia*. These were dance forms which, in their earliest stages of development, were monophonic. Some had texts written to them, but they were usually textless. The estampie scheme was closely related to the Sequence (see Chapter 3, p. 38), having a number of paired sections (usually from four to seven) each of which was termed *punctus*. These repeated puncti were often characterized by open and closed endings which could independently be carried throughout the piece, thus providing a degree of cadential unity. The ductia is usually represented as having essentially the same form as the estampie, but it was expected to be shorter (fewer than four pair of puncti). There is, however, some disagreement about the distinctions between these forms since there are examples of estampie with fewer than four pair of puncti (see HAM, no. 58).

The instrumental music literature of this period is clearly quite limited, although, as indicated earlier, instruments were widely used to accompany vocal compositions. Therefore students should employ appropriate instruments in the performance of their compositions for voices (such as replicas of early instruments when available or such substitutions as guitar, flute, oboe, tambourine, and any number of others), but they need not devote more than passing attention to the instrumental forms unless personal interest should so dictate.

Summary

There were no significant architectural changes in secular polyphonic forms over their monophonic counterparts. However, new forms were introduced which were derived from existing polyphonic forms, a departure from the earlier forms which were formally determined by the poetic scheme of their texts. These included the canonic forms of caccia and chace (and the canonic variants on the earlier monophonic forms) as well as the conductus and ballade-related madrigal.

Polyphony was exploited extensively for special effects that mimicked the sounds of nature, daily life, or specific events such as the hunt. This interest in musically depicting and interpreting human experience provided a further impetus toward the sophistication of compositional technique with artistic rather than solely functional purposes in mind. A freer compositional attitude seemed to prevail in the secular polyphonic literature than in the sacred — it appears to be less formula oriented. Consequently a greater variety of cadences and more triadic linear writing were employed. Both contributed to an early but unmistakable awareness of the basic forces of tonality (still two hundred years away from formal identification).

Although instruments were extensively used in both sacred and secular music, very few pieces were composed for instruments alone, and even these were restricted to the utilitarian role of accompanying dances. When used with voices, instruments either performed (one to a part) the lower voice lines while the upper were sung, or played the same lines being sung (with or without heterophonic embellishments).

the late fourteenth century

The end of the Middle Ages has been defined by some as the turn of the fifteenth century and by others as late as the middle of the sixteenth. A substantial number of arguments can be offered to support both of these points of view, but it is not our purpose to enter into such debate. One can, however, sympathize with the statement, "If there were such a thing as polyphony in prose, it would obviously be a godsend to the writer of history, whatever it might be to the reader."[1]

By ending Part I with a discussion of the final decades of the fourteenth century, it might be implicit that it is here that the Middle Ages end—and this may be so. However, implication is not our purpose. It is during this period that many of the compositional techniques of earlier periods reach heights of complexity, disintegrate into extramusical mannerisms, or tentatively begin to reveal new avenues for artistic development and expression. It is for these reasons that I end our discussion with the fourteenth century rather than continue into the fifteenth in which an entirely new fertile field of study would require explication.

Black mensural notation realized the fullest extent of its potential in the mannerisms of the late fourteenth century (especially in the manuscripts of Italian composers). Some composers became obviously concerned with the physical appearance of their music and with entirely extramusical notational devices such as writing on circular staves or, as in the famous Cordier rondeau *Belle bonne*, on a heart-shaped staff. Although not a large or significant

130

group, the composers who indulged in these frivolities did extend notation and its paralleling rhythmic complexity to such a degree that the following era produced a decisive reaction and a dramatic change in compositional attitude. Taken together, this combination of forces provided the foundation for the musical Renaissance of the fifteenth and sixteenth centuries.

In an attempt to define a wide range of rhythmic possibilities, Italian notation evolved a system of stems, tails, and dots.[2] As suggested earlier, because of its complexity and because it was used for only a brief period, this system must be considered beyond the purview of this volume. However, for the student's interest, some of these values are demonstrated in Example 10.1.

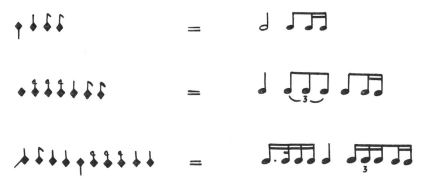

Example 10.1. Some Rhythmic Values of Italian Notation. Willi Apel, *Notation of Polyphonic Music 900-1600*, Fifth ed., The Mediaeval Academy of America, Cambridge, Mass., 1953, excerpted from pp. 372-373. Reprinted with permission of the publisher.

Probably the most unique feature of the music of the late fourteenth century is the height of rhythmic complexity achieved in some works. Cross rhythms, duplets, triplets, syncopations, and mixed meters were used to such an extent in some of these works that when they are presented in schematic form (see Example 10.2) they could reasonably represent some of the compositional efforts of composers of our own century.

Equally as pronounced is the incongruity between this rhythmic complexity and the relatively stable attitude toward vertical pitch relationships. Little or no change in the basic concept of dissonance or of the relative importance of the various consonances to each other is seen in this literature. Perfect consonances remain the principal vertical relationship at the beginnings and endings of compositions or of principal sections thereof, and there is a fair distribution of imperfect consonances and complete triads (in root position or first

Example 10.2. Willi Apel, *French Secular Music of the Late Fourteenth Century*, The Mediaeval Academy of America, Cambridge, Mass., 1950, p. 3*. Rhythms are lined up approximately as they sound.

inversion) on the primary pulses throughout the balance of the works. However, considerable freedom was exercised in the treatment of dissonance to the extent that "a musical style much more daringly and deliberately dissonant than ever before and, indeed, ever thereafter until the advent of the twentieth century"[3] evolved. The very extensive use of syncopation often produced sharp dissonances even on adjacent pulses (e.g., parallel seconds).

It should be understood that the vertical relationships are not the result of prevailing harmonic principles; as indicated earlier, they arise from the addition of one line to another, a practice that can be traced back to the very beginnings of polyphony. In this period, however, the composers began by relating the upper two lines to each other, the top line clearly being the most important, and then proceeded to add a third (lower) line in such manner that it was compatible with the lower of the two lines with which they started. Consequently, although the intervallic relationships between the middle and each of the outer lines were usually quite compatible, the relationship between the outermost parts could be in sharp contrast to what we normally associate with the general dissonant-consonant principles of the medieval period. An interesting example in which all the five principal beats following the first include such dissonances is presented in Example 10.3. It should be remembered that the lowest part is the lowest sounding voice not necessarily the lowest printed voice part.

This extension of the vertical possibilities did not produce any significant change of cadential concept. The cadences discussed earlier continued to be the most widely used. The irregular rhythmic treatment often produced some modest variations on these, but no major change in cadential concept can be postulated as having developed during this period. There are always exceptions to normal practice, and here we can point to the occasional appearance of other cadential types such as the one we today refer to as a *plagal* cadence, i.e., a harmonic move from a triad built on the fourth degree of a scale to a resolve on the scale tone (IV-I). Such a cadence is provided in Example 10.4.

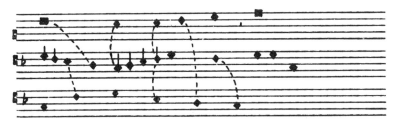

Example 10.3. Ballade: *Dame d'onour en qui.* Willi Apel, *French Secular Music of the Late Fourteenth Century*, The Mediaeval Academy of America, Cambridge, Mass., 1950, p. 33*.

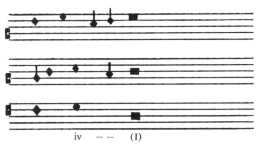

iv − −   (I)

Example 10.4. Early Use of a Plagal Cadence. A. T. Davidson and Willi Apel, *Historical Anthology of Music*, Vol. I, Harvard University Press, Cambridge, Mass., 1954, p. 50.

A slowly evolving interest in the interval of a third and in the triad may be observed during this period. This becomes increasingly apparent in vertical relationships and may also be seen in linear concept, especially in those instrumental parts that outline triads, as we have seen in Example 9.5. The linear concept reflects little change over what we have already considered in preceding chapters. The upper (vocal) lines remain essentially conjunct following the practices of the concurrent and preceding literature. The lower (instrumental) lines are considerably more disjunct.

Chromaticism increased in this period especially in the use of various forms of the double leading-tone cadence as part of the internal flow of music, i.e., what Apel refers to as "semi-tone progressions of triads."[4] There is, however, the persistent problem of the use of musica ficta, since composers

Example 10.5. Rondeau: *Fumeux fume.* Willi Apel, *French Secular Music of the Late Fourteenth Century*, The Mediaeval Academy of America, Cambridge, Mass., 1950, p. 64*.

left much to the performer and performance conventions. To compound the problem, some symbols seem to have been used in ways that are still not clearly understood. The passage in Example 10.5 reveals the extent to which composers felt free to employ chromatic alternations in their music.

Treatment of musical form during the latter half of the fourteenth century did not produce significant departures from preceding decades. The principal forms retained their identity although there was some preference for slightly modified versions of several forms. There was a distinct expansion of the musical concept, which led to some works growing to more than three times the length of like pieces in the preceding period.

The virelai treatment reflects the predilection for greater length which generally characterized the secular forms. However, this form, more light-hearted than the others, would have suffered by the increased length had the composers not made some modification in the three repetitions of the basic pattern. Apparently the great majority of virelai were composed with only one stanza of text, which sharply reduced the overall length of the piece. This modified form was termed the *bergerette*.

Most secular works during this period were in the ballade form. Although the ballade with refrain appeared earlier in the works of Machaut, the period we are presently considering adopted this version of the ballade as its standard. Other variants of the ballade included an eight-line (rather than the usual seven-line) form and the rounded ballade. The latter employed the same ending, often of considerable length, to each of the musical sections of the form. The rhythmic complexity that came to pervade this form was largely the result of the changed role of the ballade, when it became the central form of musical expression of the aristocratic society.

We can only understand and justify this *rhythme flamboyant* if we remember the very important social position of the *ballade* in these last days of chivalry. Music and society alike showed a positive aversion to all that was simple, natural, and reasonable. All this encouraged an exaggeration which led to the final exhaustion of the old traditions.[5]

The rondeau is the shortest of the forms and is often constructed in a symmetrical design, with all the musical sections of the same length. We have already witnessed this practice in the unique Machaut rondeau *Ma fin est mon commencement* (see this piece in the workbook). Other Machaut rondeaux

Example 10.6. Ballade: Jacob de Senleches, *Fuions de ci.* Reprinted with permission from Willi Apel, *French Secular Music of the Late Fourteenth Century*, The Mediaeval Academy of America, Cambridge, Mass., 1950, pp. 77* and 78*.

Example 10.6. *Fuions de ci.*

Example 10.6. *Fuions de ci.*

reflect this practice which assumed considerable importance during the period we are discussing. (However, it should be understood that the canonic technique employed in this Machaut work is unique and not, by any means, characteristic of other symmetrical rondeaux.)

The foregoing discussion can do little more than provide students with a brief overview of the style and techniques of the period.[6] To make possible a more comprehensive understanding, we shall proceed to a detailed consideration of a single composition.

The ballade *Fuions de ci* shown in Example 10.6 is presented in modern notation to avoid the severe complexities involved in attempting to read directly from an Ars Nova notational setting. Even in modern notation the rhythmic complexities are obvious. The Apel transcription used here is a remarkable achievement in providing clarity out of what might have been visual chaos had he tried to utilize the changing meters implied in the respective voices. In such an effort, the top line (*superius*) would have produced the series of meters shown in Example 10.7 for the first nine bars of the Apel transcription. An attempt to underlay the contratenor and tenor according to their respective sets of implied meters would produce a result that would make study or performance of the piece extremely difficult at best. It is an interesting experiment for students to attempt such a setting.

Example 10.7. Varying Meter Version of Superius Ballade: *Fuions de ci.* Willi Apel, *French Secular Music of the Late Fourteenth Century*, The Mediaeval Academy of America, Cambridge, Mass., 1950, p. 77*.

The fluidity resulting from the delicate interweaving of the rhythmically independent lines is the most immediately striking feature of the piece. At no point is there a rhythmic coincidence of all three parts for more than a fleeting moment. The two lower parts parallel each other rhythmically at only two points in the piece, and the second of these is a literal restatement of the first (compare measures 17-19 with 48-50). This rhythmic independence joins with extensive use of syncopation to produce an almost omnipresent sense of color and textural change.

An extensive use of suspension dissonances can be observed, in which there are sharp dissonances (seconds, sevenths, and ninths). In every instance, the resolve of this tension is produced by stepwise motion or embellished stepwise motion (e.g., a skip of a third down from the dissonant suspension tone resolving up by step to the expected tone of resolve). Although it would be inaccurate to suggest this procedure as a rule for the period, it does appear to have been the preferred resolve for suspension dissonances. In most instances these dissonances fall on strong beats of the transcribed measures, but examples can be noted on weak rhythmic positions (e.g., measure 27, between the tenor and the contratenor).

This particular composition is not characterized by extensive use of dissonances, but there is a moderate array of types. Passing tones, neighboring (auxiliary) tones, and free tones (dissonances entered and left by skip) all make an appearance. An especially interesting and sharp dissonance at the interval of a cross-relation unison (i.e., B and Bb) can be seen in measure 30. The Bb is essential, coming as it does from the octave skip and unison in the preceding measure. At the same time, the natural is indicated in the score from which Apel made his transcription. He does note, however, that two other manuscripts in which this piece appears do not have accidentals.[7]

Perfect consonances are employed at the beginning and the ending of the piece and may be seen in moderate numbers throughout. However, the principal harmonic texture is triadic, with chords appearing in both root position and first inversion. It is interesting to note that all the suspension dissonances, regardless of the strength of the rhythmic position, resolve to complete triads. Internal cadences are of the II-I (modified) variety and all resolve to a root-position triad. The final cadence is of a type that has not been discussed. Essentially it is a III-I harmonic move (with a Landini Sixth included), the final resolve being to a perfect consonance rather than to the full triad.

The ballade we are considering is a rounded form, which can be seen by comparing measures 16-24b with measures 47-55. The ending of the first half of the piece (after the repeat of the passage) is identical with the ending of the final section. Although some characteristic rhythmic elements may suggest otherwise, it would not be accurate to say the piece has motivic unity as a formal element (beyond the cadential repetition described above).

The range demands on the three lines are almost identical (a ninth for the upper two and an octave for the lowest) and not unusual when compared with the other literature we have studied. The treatment of the respective lines does reflect some differences which should be noted. The superius has a basically low tessitura, and the prevailing sense of the line is conjunct, including only two skips of a fifth, one of an octave, and one of a seventh with a rest between the two members of the interval. The contratenor has a medium to high tessitura and employs numerous fifth and octave skips (also a skip of a seventh with the respective members in closer rhythmic proximity than in the superius seventh). The tenor has a medium to low tessitura and about the same degree of disjunctiveness as the contratenor, with numerous fifth and octave skips.

The treatment of the lines is essentially what one would expect, with the vocal line (superius) primarily conjunct in concept and the instrumental lines (contratenor and tenor) primarily or largely disjunct. Independence of line, both melodically and rhythmically, is the prevailing concept which produces the textural interest and variety as the piece unfolds.

Summary

Polyphonic composition during the Middle Ages is characterized by the addition of one line to another rather than the creation of several lines simultaneously. The development of notation by the end of the period permitted the composer to define extremely small and varied rhythmic components. These two factors interact to produce the unique literature of the late fourteenth and early fifteenth centuries.

Infused with a high degree of rhythmic freedom and extending the boundaries of dissonance toleration by the resulting rhythmic complexities, the interrelationship of these highly independent lines produced fabriclike textures in expansive versions of the secular forms which trace directly from the monophonic secular literature of early centuries of the period. The fundamental principles of the period, however, remain unchanged. Perfect consonances remain the structural pillars appearing at the beginnings and endings of compositions. Vocal lines tend to remain essentially conjunct while instrumental lines assume a more disjunctive construction and begin to reveal early signs of interest in the triad as both a linear and a harmonic entity. Only moderate use of musica ficta can be observed, although a few examples of fairly extensive chromaticism can be cited.

Throughout the entire medieval period, the stage of notational development reached at any given moment was critical in the establishment of musical style and technique. Consequently, some of the most distinctive characteristics of each of the subdivisions of the general period may be observed in the notational practices of that particular time. This becomes especially apparent during the closing decades of the Middle Ages when notational mannerisms that may suggest but do not in fact affect the intent of the music can be observed.

Polyphonic modal orientation deriving directly from the linear ecclesiastical modes prevailed throughout the Middle Ages. Some awareness of harmonic relationships is apparent in the literature and becomes increasingly so in the period that follows — the Renaissance.

part two

the renaissance

chapteR 11

tRansition

The designation of a change of historical period should not imply a sudden change in style. The evolutionary continuum is not interrupted by convenient reference dates selected long after the fact. There is much difference of opinion about when one might securely date the end of the Middle Ages and the beginning of the Renaissance. The styles of the earlier period gradually evolved into those of the later period. However, some of the practices of the late Middle Ages clearly provoked a strong reaction at the beginning of the Renaissance. The early fifteenth century is the most widely recognized reference point for the change of period. However, at least one scholar (Thurston Dart) says the Renaissance did not begin in England until the late sixteenth century.

Although the normal human evolutionary process (here reflected in an art form) may be apparent, there is always the danger that recognizing that prominent personages climaxed the end of one period or invoked a new set of premises for the beginning of a new one may diminish awareness of the long evolutionary process of which they are a part. Such change may seem sudden when viewed in this manner, but rarely is this an accurate representation. Probably the greatest danger inherent in dividing human artistic evolution into convenient referential blocks of time is that one will encounter difficulty when attempting to bridge the reference points with the same smoothness one recognizes in the evolution between the reference dates.

It is in full recognition of these potential pitfalls that I have adopted the most widely accepted division of these two historical periods and have divided this study at the early fifteenth century. Various medieval practices continue well into the fifteenth century, and some practices associated with the Renaissance anticipate the beginnings of that century. In other words, an uninterrupted continuum of compositional evolution pervades this and all other historical demarcation points, and our study is in fact continuous rather than compartmentalized.

One of the clearly unifying features that bridges the two periods is the notation. Even when medieval notation was modified about the middle of the fifteenth century, it was a modest change from a black to a white notation. This simply means that for a variety of reasons (not all musical) notes that were from their inception solid black were now written as outlined or white notes. This change affected all but the smallest values (some new ones were introduced since the Ars Nova notation, as discussed in Chapter 5). The semiminima and the fusa occasionally appeared in white form, but the semifusa was always black. The ligatures of the Ars Nova remained but were similarly outlined, and their values remained the same.

A variety of repeat signs gained general recognition as did signs for pause, correction of errors, and important points of coordination between parts. Samples of these notational devices and the white forms of the notes and ligatures that were employed are shown in Example 11.1.

Because notation became very flexible and no longer seriously limited composers' expressive desires, this discussion will not dwell on the notational characteristics of the music but will instead attend to the architectural and aesthetic components. New notational devices will be mentioned when they are relevant to this discussion, but it should be remembered that notation is a complex study and it would be inappropriate to pursue it in greater depth in this book. Several excellent volumes are listed in the bibliography for students who are interested in exploring this fascinating field further. All subsequent examples will be presented in modern notation. Two modern notational devices that were not available during the period we are considering are the bar line and the tie. We must not be misled by the metrical implications of the former as they appear in the examples, and we must understand that the latter was accommodated by the use of appropriate note values.

Analytical Considerations

The music of the fifteenth and sixteenth centuries reflects a gradual process of refinement and sophistication of attitudes and techniques. So that these may be clearly recognized as they unfold, analytical guidelines are pro-

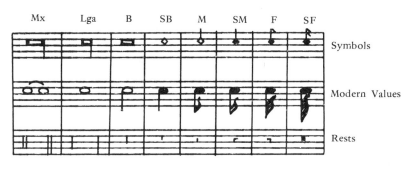

= repeat signs

= pause signs

= correction sign

Example 11.1. Some White Mensural Notational Symbols. Adapted from Willi Apel, *Notation of Polyphonic Music 900-1600*, Fifth ed., The Mediaeval Academy of America, Cambridge, Mass., 1953, pp. 87, 94-95. The modern values are presented in a four-to-one reduction.

vided which should be applied, as they are appropriate, to all works considered in the balance of this book.

The music of the Renaissance is largely contrapuntal which dictates that the first element to be studied in detail is *line*. Each line must be studied individually for a number of features. The range and tessitura (that part of the range where most of the line's activity and notes take place — the focal area of the line) must be defined and related to the general and specific features of the contour of the line. This leads to a consideration of the linear factors that contribute to the sense of motion which may be inherent in the particular line, e.g., altered tones and large skips and their locations. The presence of these altered tones and any pattern of usage should be noted. Phrase structure must be studied for the length, contour, motivic elements, and degree of symmetry that may be present. The importance of individual pitches should be noted by virtue of number of appearances, rhythmic importance, and melodic position or function. The size and characteristic use of skips, noting any that may be avoided, must be considered relative to the conjunctiveness or disjunctiveness of each individual line. Finally, the treatment of the text should be noted. To be considered are such factors as the importance of syllables in relationship to the pitches with which they are associated, the use of any musical means to reinforce the text (e.g., text painting — to be discussed later in our study), and the relationship of musical rhythm and textual rhythm.

A second factor of primary importance is *rhythm*. It must be studied in each independent line and then in terms of the totality — the effect of all lines working together. The meter employed and any changes of meter or cross meter (two different meters in two different parts) must be identified. The recurrence of rhythmic patterns or motives should be noted. The use of syncopation (a common device in this period) should be studied for location and the kinds of dissonances created as well as the resulting effect. The relative independence or dependence of lines and the special treatment that may be afforded significant sections of the piece (e.g., beginnings, endings, middle sections) must be taken into consideration. The rhythmic factors that contribute to a sense of phrase structure both within individual lines and in the broader phrases resulting from the combination of these lines are of primary importance if one is to understand the overall effect of the piece. Isorhythmic patterns (when present) should be noted. Dissonant tones are of major importance in creating the tension or forward motion of a piece and should be studied for their rhythmic location and the effect that one type of placement may have as compared with another. All these rhythmic factors must, of course, be viewed in terms of the general spirit, mood, and tempo of the composition.

The relationships that exist between voice parts, both horizontally and vertically, must be considered next. The amount of imitation, the imitative forms employed, the location and importance of this technique should all be noted with interest. The manner in which dissonances are approached and resolved and their musical or text-associated relationships must be identified. It is important to recognize the function of dissonance in the total effect of the piece, i.e., how it contributes to forward motion, tension and resolve, reinforcement of the idea of the text, the relationship between parts of the piece, and the importance and effect of cadential passages. When studying the dissonance concept of a piece, one must place it in perspective against the treatment and role of consonances. The location of consonances and the proportion of perfect consonances to imperfect ones, the number of imperfect consonances compared with the use of complete triads, and the positioning of all of these relative to each other and to their respective roles or impact in the piece must be noted. Triads must be studied from the point of view of their inversion (i.e., which member of the three-note chord is on the bottom — root position, first, and rarely second inversions are the three possibilities). Harmonic considerations become more and more important as we move closer to the next historical period (the Baroque), and the evolution of harmonic awareness and harmonic choice is an important and fascinating part of this study. These may be observed in the choice of altered tones, the use of inversions, the selection of patterns of chords for particular effects (especially at cadences), and the harmonic implications of the resolution of dissonances. It becomes more and more reasonable and valid to speak of dissonant tones as having a harmony-related role and to refer to them as *nonharmonic* tones.

Our study would be incomplete without a discussion of the broad architectural design of the piece — its *form*. In the first half of our study, the forms presented were largely text-determined. Some musically unifying elements could be discerned (e.g., isorhythm, repeated passages, and, to a much lesser degree, motivic relationships). Text continued to play a major role in form definition. However, there was increasing use of musical devices to convey the sense of broad organization and logic in a piece of music. Such devices as repetitions of or returns to distinguishable phrases in literal or modified form, increasing use of motivic elements, and major textural changes (e.g., a move from a polyphonic to a homophonic texture) became important factors in the creation and determination of the broad architectural design of a piece.

All of these many analytical tools will not apply to every piece. However, until students gain great facility in extracting the primary forces and distinguishing features of a given piece, it should become habit for them to work with these references at hand. They should attempt to apply all of them to every piece and to every part of each piece. This is a slow process requiring intense concentration and unrelenting devotion to detail.

Summary

This summary is given in outline form to assist students in their forthcom-coming analyses.

Notation
    a. White notation, essentially the same as the Ars Nova black notation;
    b. Greater use of smaller values such as the semiminima, fusa, and semifusa;
    c. No bar lines or ties, although they appear in modern transcriptions.

Line
    a. Range, tessitura, and contour (including factors that contribute to the sense of motion and direction, e.g., large skips and altered tones);
    b. Phrase structure within each line (including the contour of phrases, use of motives, degree of symmetry);
    c. Chromatic alterations (note any pattern of usage which may be apparent);
    d. Importance of individual pitches by virtue of number, rhythmic or melodic position, or special function;
    e. Skips (size, characteristic usage, numbers, and those avoided);
    f. Conjunctiveness or disjunctiveness of each line;
    g. Treatment of text as it relates to linear concept (e.g., the importance of syllables in relationship to pitches and the use of musical means to reinforce the meaning of the text).

Rhythm
    a. Metrical design (note changes);
    b. Degree of symmetry or lack of symmetry;
    c. Rhythmic motives;
    d. Rhythmic phrase structures (are linear and contrapuntal phrases paralleled?);
    e. Syncopation (including the locations employed and the dissonances which may result);
    f. Independence or dependence of lines;
    g. Special rhythmic treatment of the beginning, middle, or ending of the piece or sections thereof;
    h. Rhythmic treatment of the text;
    i. Presence and use of isorhythmic patterns;
    j. Rhythmic position and treatment of dissonant tones;

k. Proportional changes employed between sections or repetitions of a line.

Counterpoint   a. Imitation technique (literal or modified, amount used, location);

b. Treatment of dissonances (kinds, how approached, and how resolved);

c. Differences (if any) in the treatment of perfect and imperfect consonances;

d. Harmonic characteristics (if these appear definable as such, e.g., altered tones, triadic inversions, patterns of adjacent triads);

e. Mode delineation (determined by individual linear modes and their relationships to each other and the total tone orientation).

Form   a. Determine the function of the text in defining the form;

b. Musical elements contributing to the sense of form (e.g., phrase or period structures, literal or modified use of repetitions or returns);

c. Unifying elements (including the use of a cantus firmus motives);

d. Variety-producing elements (e.g., meter change, textural change, or variants on earlier material from the same piece).

early fifteenth century - dufay

A sharp reaction to the extremely complicated music of the late fourteenth century was apparent in the works of such composers as John Dunstable (c. 1370-1453), Gilles Binchois (c. 1400-1467), and Guillaume Dufay (c. 1400-1474). Although the stylistic changes are most obvious in the treatment of rhythm, a greater sense of restraint and clarity is revealed in a variety of other compositional practices.

Because there are many works from this period and the already large number of composers whose works are known and available is increasing, we cannot and will not attempt to survey the literature comprehensively. Indeed, it is not possible in a study such as this to cover the output or stylistic evolution of even a single composer. Therefore the discussions that follow will be directed toward in-depth study of a few selected pieces (or portions thereof); it should not be assumed that the pieces necessarily represent the finest product of the composer concerned or the most complete array of techniques characteristic of his style. Rather they were selected to demonstrate some of the techniques used during the period in order to help us gain a better perspective of the evolution of composition.

The largest and most important musical form of the fifteenth century (compared by Besseler to the symphony in the nineteenth century) was the Mass. One of the most prominent composers of this form was Guillaume Dufay. His four-voice *Missa Se la face ay pale* (c. 1450) is one of the most important of his Masses of the cantus firmus type and will be the focal point for our discussion.

The cantus firmus is usually a melody borrowed from an earlier work, presented, unadorned, in the tenor voice in relatively long note values; the remaining voices of the composition are constructed around it. Dufay's cantus firmus in the *Missa* is derived from the tenor of his own three-voice ballade, *Se la face ay pale*.

The cantus firmus is used in an interesting way by Dufay in this Mass. The rhythmic treatment of the line varies in the sections of the work, appearing in

Example 12.1. Cantus Firmus Proportions. Dufay, *Missa Se la face ay pale*. Original values—Credo, measures 125-142; 2:1—Kyrie, measures 1-35; 3:1—Gloria, measures 19-70. Reprinted with permission from Heinrich Besseler, Bärenreiter edition, 1964.

three proportionate relationships to the original values. In Example 12.1 these proportions are demonstrated: the original values (as they appear, transcribed, from the ballade), a 2:1, and then a 3:1 relationship.

The range of the lines in this Mass is: soprano, b'-e''; alto, e-a'; tenor, g-a'; and baritone, b-d'. Although in a large work like this the tessitura may vary from one section to another, the primary focus seems to be in the upper-middle portion of the voices. The three upper voices are predominantly conjunct but the lowest voice is reasonably well balanced between a conjunct and a disjunct conception. The latter has many fourths, fifths, and octaves. Linear tritones are rarely used; one does appear in measure 114 of the Sanctus in the

Example 12.2. Typical Phrase Contours. Dufay, *Missa Se la face ay pale*. Descending line: Kyrie, soprano, measures 1-3; Rising: Gloria, soprano, measures 34-39; Curving: Gloria, alto, measures 59-66. Reprinted with permission from Heinrich Besseler, Bärenreiter edition, 1964.

alto part. There is a small sprinkling of ascending sixths but no linear descending sixths. Very little use is made of musica ficta, *f* and *c* sharps are used exclusively as raised leading tones in internal cadences (neither appears at a final cadence), and a fair number of *b* flats are used for linear shaping throughout. In a number of instances *b* flats appear a few measures before a primary cadence on *f*, which may be an early anticipation of harmonic consciousness by composers of the period. This point will be developed more fully in a later discussion.

Linear phrase structures are asymmetrical and may vary in length from one measure to as many as eight or ten. In most instances a fairly clear contour can be defined (e.g., a simple arched line or a rising, a descending, or an undulating one). A few typical excerpts are given in Example 12.2.

Although motivic writing is not usually associated with composers of this period, it is quite apparent in this composition. The first phrase in Example

12.2 has two motives; the first the descending fourth from *c″* to *g′* and the second the final four tones — the three descending intervals of step, third, step. The third motive is a sequence of two descending thirds separated by an ascending second. The motives are melodic, not rhythmic, and they are modified variously throughout the piece. It is not uncommon to find two motives adjacent to each other or interlocked. The basic motives and some of the variants are given in Example 12.3.

Example 12.3. Basic Motives and Some Variants. Dufay, *Missa Se la face ay pale*. Reprinted with permission from Heinrich Besseler, Bärenreiter edition, 1964.

The principal tones throughout the Mass are *C* and *F*. Every section begins either with both tones between the several voices or with one (usually *C*) in octaves and unison. Every section ends with both tones present, forming a perfect fifth and octave. These tones have melodic importance in the internal passages of the lines.

Of secondary importance, but clearly with a greater role than the remaining tones, are the notes *G* and *D*. The prominence of these tones is apparent in their frequent appearance in important melodic positions (e.g., in large skips — especially in the lowest voice; also, longer values are frequently used with these tones).

An interesting linear feature of this work is the extensive use of the fourth. It appears as a simple skip between two notes; it may result from the scalelike motion from one member to another; or it may be subtly suggested by a weaving line which outlines the two member tones of the interval. The outer limits of two of the three motives constitute a perfect fourth and the third motive forms the interval of a perfect fifth (an inverted perfect fourth). But it is not only when the motives appear that the sense of this interval is felt; it pervades all lines a very large part of the time.

Although the Mass is in four voice parts, Dufay did exercise the freedom of a few divisi passages (e.g., Kyrie, measure 14 and Credo, measure 34).

In one prominent part of the cantus firmus an outlined triad is used fairly extensively. This is adopted for all voices principally in these same sections (i.e., the sections closest to the portion of the cantus firmus employing the outlined triad). However, the use of a linear triad is not limited to these sections but is used fairly extensively — a characteristic of Dufay's linear conception in this piece. At times the triadic linear concept can be directly related to the linear fourth, and in other instances these function as independent linear elements.

Rhythm

The opening of each section of the Mass for all voices except the tenor is in tempus perfectum and minor prolation, here interpreted as $\frac{3}{2}$. The tenor in these passages appears as either a double or a triple relationship (the latter in the Gloria and Credo, the former in the remaining sections) to the other parts. The duple relationship is represented in this modern transcription as $\frac{3}{1}$ and the triple as a $3 \times \frac{3}{2}$ meter signature. All sections of the Mass have proportions which are given in this transcription as $3 \times \frac{2}{4}$ meters, representing a broader metrical delineation of a modus perfectum, tempus imperfectum, and minor prolation. The modus perfectum is the only new element in our discussion. It represents the proportion by which the next larger value in the spectrum is identified. The interpretation of these passages, as Besseler points out, is accomplished by transferring the unit of measure from the half note to the quarter, maintaining a consistent pulse and flow throughout. The quarter note of the $3 \times \frac{2}{4}$ passage equals the half note of the preceding and following passages.

In general the upper two voice parts are most active, the lowest less active, and the tenor least active (except in the passages where it is in a 1:1 relationship to the other parts and is comparable to the lowest voice part). The smallest value is the eighth note (allowing for the meter adjustments described above); it appears infrequently and in one of three ways: in a dotted quarter/eighth pairing; in pairs of eighths; and in eighth/quarter/eighth syncopations. There are occasional exceptions to these basic groupings (e.g., the four descending eighth notes in measure 12 of the Kyrie or combinations of the groupings that may produce three consecutive eighth notes). These several possibilities are given in Example 12.4.

There are many examples of hemiola in this work. Isolated examples of linear and vertical hemiola can be distinguished. This juxtaposition of differ-

Example 12.4. Use of Eighth Notes. Dufay, *Missa Se la face ay pale*. Reprinted with permission from Heinrich Besseler, Bärenreiter edition, 1964.

Linear hemiola (measures 28-30, Kyrie)

Linear hemiola (measures 67-70, Agnus Dei)

Hemiola between voice parts (measure 97, Gloria)

Hemiola between voice parts (measures 97-98, Credo)

Example 12.5. Linear and Vertical Hemiola. Dufay, *Missa Se la face ay pale*. Reprinted with permission from Heinrich Besseler, Bärenreiter edition, 1964.

ent metrical elements in the composition is a subtle rhythmic force which contributes to a pervasive sense of fluidity. Typical use of hemiola in the Mass is shown in Example 12.5.

Dufay uses many syncopations. These usually appear in a quarter-half-quarter arrangement but can also be seen between half and whole notes and, as suggested earlier, between quarter and eighth values.

Phrases are asymmetrical both within lines and between lines. This lack of symmetry is a major contributing force to the sense of forward motion which pervades the piece. Phrases may vary from a measure or two up to eight or ten measures in a single line. By eliding cadences and overlapping lines, the phrases resulting from the combination of the lines may be very long (e.g., twenty to thirty measures). A cadential elision is demonstrated in Example 12.6.

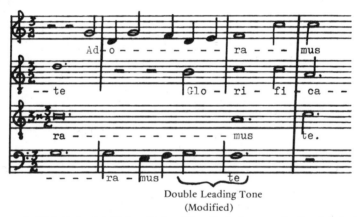

Double Leading Tone
(Modified)

Example 12.6. Cadential Elision. Dufay, *Missa Se la face ay pale*. Reprinted with permission from Heinrich Besseler, Bärenreiter edition, 1964.

Rhythmically the lines are quite independent of each other. Although moments of imitative melodic relationship can be found in moderate numbers (see Example 12.7), these linear imitations rarely retain the same rhythmic treatment.

The beginnings of almost every principal portion of the piece tend to move in slower rhythmic values which quickly give way to greater activity. With isolated exceptions where motion may momentarily stop in the middle of a section (e.g., measures 48-49 in the Sanctus), the established activity is maintained to the final cadential chord. Dufay uses a device in this piece (as he does in others, e.g., *Missa L'Homme armé*) which continues the motion even beyond the final chord of arrival at cadences. This device, i.e., resolving a third to a perfect consonance or embellishing the final triad to transform it into a perfect consonance, is demonstrated in Example 12.8.

Kyrie: measures 62-67

Example 12.7. Melodic Relationships between Lines. Dufay, *Missa Se la face ay pale*. Reprinted with permission from Heinrich Besseler, Bärenreiter edition, 1964. The highly triadic writing of the source material (the cantus firmus) is carried into all parts. Note the use of hemiola.

Example 12.8. Cadential Embellishment. Dufay, *Missa Se la face ay pale*. Reprinted with permission from Heinrich Besseler, Bärenreiter edition, 1964.

Counterpoint

The contrapuntal treatment of this Mass is, in large measure, freely conceived. Lines unfold for many measures without obvious melodic or rhythmic relationship. Subtle relationships often exist, such as the use of an intervallic pattern in the free voices which is derived from the cantus firmus in that general portion of the piece (e.g., the triadic treatment between the alto and the tenor in measures 152-153 in the Gloria — to a lesser degree this may also be seen in the soprano in the same measures).

A moderate amount of imitation does appear and, to a lesser extent, short canons are also used. Imitation ranges from the literal to various degrees of free imitation, e.g., the line imitating but not the rhythm, or the contour and rhythm imitating but not the literal note or interval relationships. Another form of imitation notable in this work is one that contributes to a strong sense of unity between the several movements. The opening four measures of all movements except the Kyrie are literal or almost literal statements of the same material in the same voice parts. That material is directly derived from the opening soprano part of the Kyrie. The opening Kyrie line appears in Example 12.2. For comparison, the opening of the Gloria is provided in Example 12.9. Note the imitative treatment (almost canonic) between the two voices. Canons are used infrequently; when they do occur they are brief and exclusively at the unison or octave. An example can be seen between the soprano and also in measures 100-102 in the Gloria.

Example 12.9. Opening of the Gloria. Dufay, *Missa Se la face ay pale*. Reprinted with permission from Heinrich Besseler, Bärenreiter edition, 1964. The line to the second *A* in the soprano is identical to the line to the second *A* in the alto. Only the rhythm is changed.

The principal dissonances used are passing tones and suspensions.[1] A number of anticipations (especially immediately before cadences) and escape tones may also be found. Such dissonances as appoggiaturas and neighboring tones are almost nonexistent in this work. Passing notes fall almost exclusively in weak rhythmic positions (weak beats or halves of beats). Suspensions naturally fall on the beat and most frequently on strong beats. A variety of these are used including 4-3 and 7-6 (these being, by far, the most frequent). In a few instances double suspensions may be observed such as the one shown in Example 12.10 (from measure 36 of the Gloria).

Other dissonant tones appear exclusively on weak rhythmic positions and

Example 12.10. Double Suspension. Dufay, *Missa Se la face ay pale*. Reprinted with permission from Heinrich Besseler, Bärenreiter edition, 1964.

are not widely used. However, one dissonance commonly used with a suspension preceding a cadence is the anticipation. Although the anticipation motion in the above example (the quarter-note *g* in the soprano) is not a dissonance, it is typical of the type of motion to which I am referring. If the bass in this example had an *a* instead of the *g*, this type of anticipation would be present. It should be noted, however, that such a change of line would not be possible in this example because it would create a descending sixth in the bass, an interval which is simply not used in this style.

All movements of the *Missa Se la face ay pale* begin with perfect consonances. Likewise all movements resolve to perfect consonances (every one from an initial complete triad). In addition to appearing in these primary positions, perfect consonances are used in numerous other locations in the piece. Most of the vertical relations are triads (in four-part textures) and imperfect consonances in three- and two-part textures. When triads occur, they are used exclusively in root position and first inversion. Second inversion triads are not used at all. The two triads most widely used (by a large margin) are *F* and *C*. These are followed by a fair sampling of *d*, *a*, *g*, and *G*. Others also appear much less frequently, e.g., *B* flat, *f-sharp* diminished, and *e*.

Although it would be inappropriate to impose a sense of harmonic relationships on these vertical motions (the implications of harmony develop much later), it is possible to suggest a few general guidelines. However, these can be considered only with a full recognition that linear factors were the commanding force in this period and vertical relationships were the result of linear decisions and wholly subservient to them. If one understands these phenomena, it is then possible to recognize that many triads move to other triads in a whole step removed (e.g., *a* to *G* to *F*), and that, especially at cadences, the ascending root relationship of triads is most frequently a perfect fourth. Almost any other root relationship is also possible except that of the tritone.

A number of different cadences are used in this Mass. They include those that were characteristic of the preceding period and also two principal cadences of the tonal period that follows. Representative of the former are the leading-tone and under-third cadences. Both appear most frequently in passages with two or three voice parts.

Example 12.11. Cadences. Dufay, *Missa Se la face ay pale*. Reprinted with permission from Heinrich Besseler, Bärenreiter edition, 1964.

Chords in which root relationships are a fourth above or a fourth below the final tone of a cadence create the two cadences later referred to as plagal and authentic (IV-I and V-I), respectively. Samples of each of the principal cadences used in this Mass are shown in Example 12.11.

Note the interesting treatment of the V-I cadence which appears in a number of important positions in the Mass. That is, the presence of the under-third before the final tone clearly demonstrates the evolutionary process from the under-third cadence, most commonly used in two- and three-part textures, to the V-I cadence, which rapidly becomes the principal cadence for four-part music.

The texture that pervades the largest portion of the piece is a four-part, horizontally conceived, polyphonic one. Parts cross freely and contrasting passages in two and three parts are scattered throughout. Almost no predominantly homophonic texture appears for more than a passing few chords, with the single exception of the final chorus of the Agnus Dei (measure 67ff), and even this is conceived horizontally.

Form

The architectural design of *Se la face ay pale* (the Mass) is largely determined by the text. The impact results from the traditional movement order and the proportions required by text length and traditional practice. Musical factors, however, play an important role in the broad design of this work. The most significant of these is, of course, the cantus firmus treatment discussed earlier. The characteristic three-part form of the Kyrie is created by a few devices: (a) the first and last sections are in four parts and the middle one in three; (b) the first half of the cantus firmus is in the first Kyrie section, it is omitted from the Christe, and the second half of the cantus firmus is in the final Kyrie section; (c) there is change from and return to the prolation structure of the Kyrie (as discussed earlier).

A strong cyclical impact is produced by two means: each section following the Kyrie opens with the same two-part texture and the same material; and motives are used throughout the Mass. This is reinforced by the subtle impact of the cantus firmus — both by its presence and by the effect it has on the material around it (the derivative nature of that material from the cantus firmus is quite often apparent). This is seen in exaggerated form in the passage at the end of the Gloria (measures 192-193) which literally returns at the end of the Credo (measures 192-193). These two movements are identical in length (198 measures), a phenomenon clearly resulting from the proportional use of the cantus firmus.

An intensive comparative study of the ballade which served as the source for the cantus firmus of this Mass, and which is included in the accompanying workbook/anthology, is strongly recommended.

Compositional Considerations

When attempting to simulate the style of a composer, one must try to achieve a balance between literally adopting each minute practice of the composer and the desirable goal of producing a piece of music with which one may feel a sense of personal identity. The latter is most difficult to achieve because most of us have been exposed to and conditioned by a musical vocabulary far exceeding that of the period in which we are working here. With these remarks as premises, we can now attempt to define the process of composing such a piece.

The first step is to select a cantus firmus. Our choice will be the tune that enjoyed so much popularity during the period and to which Dufay himself composed a Mass — *L'Homme armé*. Using the Mass just studied as a guide, we

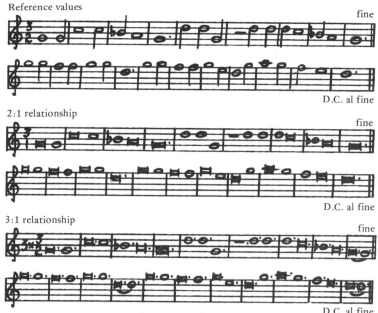

Example 12.12. *L'homme armé*, in Proportional Settings.

can lay out the *L'Homme armé* tune in the three proportions used: 1:1, 2:1, 3:1. See Example 12.12.

To demonstrate the simulating process, we shall write the first Kyrie section of a Mass using the Dufay work as our guide. His treatment of the cantus firmus in this movement was to use approximately the first half of the source tune for the first Kyrie section in a 2:1 prolation. Having made this decision and following a brief study of the tune to determine its mode as transposed Dorian, we can take the next step and lay out the score for the entire section with appropriate clefs, signatures (modal and metrical), and distribution of measures. These first few steps are demonstrated in Example 12.13.

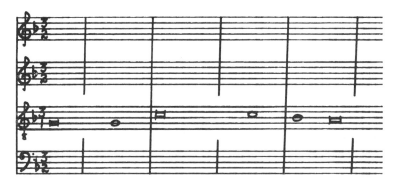

Example 12.13. *L'homme armé*. Kyrie layout.

Several possible choices exist for the next step, and students should proceed in the manner which they find most comfortable. Stylistically it is more appropriate to compose each line as a complete entity, adding each subsequent line to the completed ones. This may more successfully contribute to a sense of linear motion which, of course, is the nature of so much of this music. It is also possible to compose all lines simultaneously measure-by-measure, if one is continuously alert to the danger of homophonic rather than polyphonic factors playing the principal role in decision making. Both forces are evident and vertical considerations are of great importance in achieving a successful representation of the style. But foremost this music must be linear in conception and effect.

In this piece, we shall start by placing our first note choices for all parts to provide a point of departure for each of the lines. These simply produce the perfect intervals of fifth and octave which are the norm for this style. The fact that Dufay used only octaves and unisons at the beginning of *Missa Se la face ay pale* need not restrict us to those relationships, although we can easily begin in that manner.

Having made these first choices, we can proceed to compose a soprano line which will be compatible with the tenor's cantus firmus. We have noted that Dufay's free lines were often derived from the cantus firmus line at various points of the piece. With this in mind, we can design the beginning of the soprano line to suggest the contour of the opening portion of the *L'Homme armé* tune — an ascending fourth followed by a descending fourth. Following this, we can hint at the contour of the line and employ one of its characteristic rhythms — the short-long figure. The three measures which will have been completed by this process (see Example 12.14) can be followed by two measures that loosely invert the materials of the first two measures and that, in turn, can be followed by a freer treatment of the short-long figure immediately above where it appears in the tenor. A restatement of the opening figure with modest rhythmic modification followed by a typical cadential pattern will conclude a well-conceived line.

Example 12.14. Opening Soprano Line.

One could legitimately cite the presence of a problem at the cadence — the soprano does not end at a point in the tenor where one could reasonably expect a cadence. This is true, but as long as the sounding notes in the several voices are compatible, elision of cadences is common practice. One voice may be in the middle of its phrase or beginning a new phrase as others are ending their phrases.

Although we could continue to finish the soprano line considering the same types of factors as we have up to this point, for the sake of space we shall return to the beginning and work on the next line — the alto. As an inner line, the alto has some freedoms and some restrictions not characteristic of the others. For example, cadentially its motion is not as strongly dictated as is that of outer lines, and linearly it does not have quite the freedom of motion enjoyed by outer lines (even though it may cross parts freely). Beginning with the *d* chosen earlier, a line moving in slower motion than the soprano with some parallel and oblique motion to that reference line seems appropriate. As the soprano drops to the lowest part of its range in the fourth and fifth measures, it is possible for the alto to rise and descend in contrary motion and by crossing the soprano to spread the upper voices. Also, in the descending measure (measure 5) it is possible to use the very subtle, limited imitation one finds occasionally in the works of Dufay. In rhythmically designing the line, it is also possible to bring a sense of hemiola into the third measure. It is interesting to note that from measure 7 to the cadence, it is possible to approximate an inversion of the first several measures of the piece (loosely

Example 12.15. Three Upper Voices.

interpreted) as well as writing a compatible and effective line. The three lines completed to this point are shown in Example 12.15.

Example 12.16. Opening of Kyrie to Original *L'homme armé*.

Returning to the beginning of the piece again, we must now add the final line — the bass. The bass must be treated with special care because all vertical relationships are determined from the lowest sounding part. Consequently (except when resting or crossing upper parts), the bass serves as the foundation for dissonances and the final determination of the triad, imperfect, or perfect consonance structure. It must, of course, be treated with great care at the approach to cadences, for it plays a large role in determining the cadential type used and in successfully executing the critical point of the piece. Although there is no obligation for other voices to either imitate each other or directly or indirectly relate as melodic entities to the tenor, they occasionally do so. The bass performs these functions much less frequently.

One way to approach the writing of a bass line is to sketch the first note of each measure to produce a reasonable line and to write a sensible bass to the other voices at these important rhythmic points. Special attention must first be given to the cadence: then the line can be completed and refined. The completed first section of this short Kyrie is shown in Example 12.16.

The procedure for completing this Kyrie section and for writing the balance of the Mass will remain unchanged. The specific decisions will naturally vary, possibly significantly, as the musical demands change; but the process remains the same. Students should understand that as the lines unfold and new possibilities are identified, they should consider it a normal part of the routine to mold and shape the music to produce the most satisfying musical and stylistic result possible. Having devised a soprano line that is attractive and works well with a given cantus firmus does not mean that if as one works on the alto richer possibilities are revealed, they should be ignored rather than change the earlier written line — the contrary should forcefully be understood to prevail. At the same time, one must be cautious that a good line is not ruined by hasty change to accommodate a problem of interline relationship.

Summary

Dufay's style, represented by his *Missa Se la face ay pale*, reflected a clear reaction by Burgundian composers to the complexities of late fourteenth-century music. His style is presented concisely in outline form.

Line

1. Primarily a conjunct conception (seconds and thirds);
2. In disjunct passages, the perfect consonances (fourths, fifths, and octaves) predominate; there are a few minor sixths and isolated sevenths (they normally appear between phrases rather than within phrases);
3. Some use of triad outlining (at times fairly extensive);
4. Voice lines are normally within the range of a tenth;
5. The bottom line frequently assumes a somewhat "harmonic" function, with its contour reflecting relationships between chords by motion of fourths and fifths;
6. Adjacent skips in the same direction may follow each other freely, but rarely are more than two used in succession; these are always with the basic intervals of thirds, fourths, and fifths;
7. Musica ficta includes: F, C, and G sharps, and B and E flats. These are used in passing, as neighboring tones, and are occasionally in appoggiatura positions, as well as providing leading tones at cadences;

Rhythm

1. Sixteenth notes are not used when the breve equals a transcribed half note;
2. Much use of syncopation (♩ ♩ ♩), which is not necessarily dissonant but is frequently used with change of chord or chord position;
3. Moderate use of hemiola;
4. Many short, scattered rests, reflecting irregular phrasing in and between voices;
5. The first beat of the metrical pattern usually has longer value except when syncopated;
6. Active motion may begin in the first measure and vary freely with slower motion. Either (but most often the active) may appear immediately before a cadence;
7. A cantus firmus tenor normally moves in slower metrical values and, as in *Se la face ay pale*, may receive periodic ratio adjustments.

Counterpoint

1. Mostly a fluid, through-composed style of writing;
2. Much use of triads, which are most often in root position but often in first inversion. No use of second inversion triads except in the weakest possible rhythmic position;
3. Modest use of imitation, stretto, and canon;
4. Motives, when present, tend to be subtle and unobtrusive and dissolve in the general texture – they are more linear than rhythmic;
5. Spacing between voices is generally close but the bass and tenor may separate more frequently and by wider intervals than the other voices;
6. Free crossing of parts is used throughout;
7. Rare (and questionable) use of cross relations;
8. Musica ficta may be used in close proximity to the natural form of a note, but *never* do two of the same forms appear adjacent to each other in the same voice;
9. Frequent use of textural contrast within as well as between sections (i.e., contrast between two-, three-, or four-part textures);
10. Dissonances: seconds, sevenths, tritones, and fourths (when used between the lowest part and any other) appear fairly often and generally in weak rhythmic positions (except suspensions which normally fall on strong beats);
11. Although not used in *Se la face ay pale*, conflicting key signatures can be found in Dufay's works;
12. Cadences:
    a. Double leading-tone cadence is common in three-part textures;
    b. Under-third and double under-third are common in both three- and four-part textures;
    c. V-I cadences are common in four-part textures;
    d. Combination cadences (e.g., V-under-third-I) are occasionally used in three- and four-part textures;
    e. Internal cadences often have full triads or imperfect consonant resolutions;
    f. Final cadences always end on an open fifth and/or octave.

Form

1. Generally determined by the structure of the text (or its liturgical requirements) but reinforced by musical means;
2. Some references back to earlier sections as the piece unfolds;

3. Internal sectional structures established by use of different prolations, altered relationships between tenor and other voices, and sharp changes of texture (e.g., from chorus to solo or from two to three or four voice parts);

4. Phrases quite fluid with frequent occurrences of one ending as another begins and broad overlapping of voice parts with a high degree of assymetry.

chapter 13

middle and late fifteenth century - johannes ockeghem

Increasingly larger numbers of accomplished composers can be identified as the fifteenth century continued to unfold. Such men as Antoine Busnois (d. 1492), Jacob Obrecht (1430-1505), Loyset Compère (d. 1518), and Johannes Ockeghem (1430-1495) can be mentioned as some of the principal figures of the period. Ockeghem will serve as our subject for studying the continuing evolution of compositional technique through this period.

Styles of composition are very personal phenomena and therefore generalizations are dangerous. However, we are not attempting to discuss the stylistic characteristics representative of the period in general or even of the subject composer in particular. We are attempting to develop a working knowledge of compositional technique and to gain a sense of historical perspective for these practices.

Several general characteristics of Ockeghem's style, which, if kept in mind, will prove helpful in this study, include the following: a great sense of fluidity which tends to obscure internal cadences and lessen the importance of harmonic relationships; more independence of voice parts, with larger ranges and fewer crossings; increased use of imitation and limited but outstanding use of canon; and characteristic increase of motion at most cadential approaches by using dotted rhythms.

Fluidity is of particular interest and importance. It is of interest because of the means by which a fluid effect was achieved and it is important because it

171

had a pronounced influence on much of the music in the last century of the Renaissance.

One practice that contributed significantly to the often prevailing sense of fluidity was Ockeghem's treatment of line. Lines are generally asymmetrical in relationship to each other, i.e., the beginnings and endings of individual linear phrases do not coincide — they are of unequal length. Likewise, the phrases within each line are normally asymmetrical (of unequal length). Also, a phrase

Example 13.1. Ockeghem, *Missa Mi-Mi*, Gloria, measures 1-8. Reprinted with permission of Kalmus Music Publishing Co., Opa-locka, Florida, and Belwin-Mills Publishing Corp., New York, New York.

may begin in one line a moment before a phrase ends in another line, which tends to elide any sense of pause. These techniques can be clearly seen in the opening measures of the Gloria from Ockeghem's *Missa Mi-Mi.*

In Example 13.1, the long flowing soprano line, which rises a minor sixth and returns to its starting note through an undulating descent over approxi-

Example 13.2. Syncopation in Ockeghem, *Missa Mi-Mi.* The first part of the example: Kyrie, measures 22-24; the second: Gloria, measures 15-16. Reprinted with permission of Kalmus Music Publishing Co., Opa-locka, Florida, and Belwin-Mills Publishing Corp., New York, New York.

mately two-thirds of the passage shown, can be contrasted with the alto which has a total range of a perfect fourth during that same span of measures (and the note that extends the alto's range to the fourth appears only once near the end). Whereas the soprano is one long line which could possibly be divided once (in measure 5), the alto naturally divides itself three times into small fragments (the longest is three measures). During this same passage, the bass voice has one natural division (measure 4) and extends beyond the ending of both the soprano and the alto. The tenor is one long phrase which ends before the soprano's final tone and begins a new phrase as the soprano ends.

The elision in measures 7 and 8 is a characteristic treatment of a set of lines which creates a sense of continuous flow. This same practice can be found in large portions of this Mass as well as in numerous other works. It should be noted in passing that although the ranges in this particular passage are comparatively narrow, in this Gloria section of the Mass the bass range extends an octave and a sixth (from *E*-*c'*), the widest vocal range, and the tenor has the narrowest with a span of an octave.

Although it is peripheral to our primary interest, note that the head motive in the bass is used at the beginning of every section of the Mass and, in some instances, at the beginning of internal sections (e.g., the final Kyrie section in the tenor). Likewise, the opening soprano line of the Gloria is found in the tenor of the Kyrie and in a number of other locations in the Mass (not all confined to the beginnings of sections).

Example 13.3. Syncopation in Ockeghem, *Alma Redemptoris Mater*, measures 43-52. Reprinted with permission of Kalmus Music Publishing Co., Opa-locka, Florida, and Belwin-Mills Publishing Corp., New York, New York.

Just as asymmetrical treatment and relationship of lines contributes to fluidity, so extensive use of syncopation reinforces that effect. Ockeghem used large numbers of syncopations and juxtaposed various syncopated elements in different lines at the same time. Brief passages demonstrating this treatment are shown in Example 13.2.

Passages in which syncopation is used more extensively can be found throughout Ockeghem's, as well as others's music. A typical example of syncopation being used in some form in every measure for as many as nine consecutive measures is provided in the excerpt from Ockeghem's motet *Alma Redemptoris Mater* (Example 13.3). The music is very fluid.

Texture

· Interest and variety may be achieved by placing different textures next to each other. Types of textural variation may include: contrapuntal as opposed to homophonic; unaccompanied line as opposed to accompanied line; and differing thicknesses of effect created by varied numbers of lines and their relative proximity to each other.

An awareness of the possibilities of textural variation is reflected in the works of all composers to some degree. In Ockeghem's works contrapuntal textures far exceed homophonic. A brief example of the homophonic is provided in Example 13.4.

Example 13.4. Excerpt from Ockeghem, *Missa Mi-Mi*, Gloria, measures 64-66 (upper three voices — bass tacet). Reprinted with permission of Kalmus Music Publishing Co., Opa-locka, Florida, and Belwin-Mills Publishing Corp., New York, New York.

The opening of the Agnus Dei of the *Missa Mi-Mi* is a four-voice contrapuntal texture. With the exception of two and two-thirds measures when the bass drops out and another two-measure section where the alto is silent, the first part of the three-part Agnus Dei is entirely in four voice parts.

The middle Agnus statement opens in two voice parts (tenor and bass) and adds a third about half way through (the soprano). This is followed by the final Agnus statement which returns to a four-part texture throughout. With only a few brief and isolated exceptions, a polyphonic texture prevails in the Agnus Dei.

The same type of organization is used in the preceding Sanctus section; it is also divided into three principal parts, the first and last of which are in four voice parts. The middle section (Pleni sunt coeli) is in two or three voices as was the middle portion of the Agnus. However, the organization of these voices in the Pleni is somewhat different and more interesting. The passage opens in two voices (soprano and alto) which are imitated exactly by the lower two voices five measures later. As the soprano and alto end, the tenor and bass begin, creating the single four-voice chord in the entire section. The tenor imitates the soprano and the bass imitates the alto, producing what is known as *paired imitation*. This technique was used quite extensively by des Pres, who will be discussed in the next chapter. The example of paired imitation in Ockeghem appears only in the first measure and one-half, after which the voices are treated freely. Following the six-plus measures of tenor and bass, the bass drops out and the soprano and alto enter. The upper two voices remain to the end of the section while the tenor drops out four measures before the end.

In a passage such as this, another element is of concern to the composer. Together with the polyphonic texture and the changing voice texture, an awareness of the coloristic potential of different vocal qualities cannot be ignored. Different voices have different coloristic qualities. This is true whether we consider male voice as opposed to female voice or two different male or female voices, regardless of their respective ranges.

Canon

A moderate amount of varying degrees of imitative writing can be found in Ockeghem's works. We have observed the use of canon by earlier composers (e.g., Machaut) and in specifically canonic forms (e.g., caccia). In Ockeghem's music canonic treatment ranges from loose momentary suggestions of canon through increasingly greater formality and clarity to complete canonic works (e.g., *Prenez sur moi exemple amoureux*). An example of the first, in this instance canon of the pitches set in a free rhythmic treatment, is provided in Example 13.5. This canon is between the tenor and the soprano while the bass and alto are free-composed voices and are only remotely related to the others (although for a few notes the bass is canon with the head of the tenor).

The *Prenez sur moi* is a three-voice canon from beginning to end. The voices are set in canon one transcribed measure apart, and each of the following voices is at the interval of a perfect fourth above the one immediately preceding it. Characteristic of much of the music of the period, the piece has a fair number of suspensions (mostly 4-3). An unusual suspension occurs between the two lower voices in transcribed measure 28. A tritone between *b* and *f* appears as a result of an *f* suspension to the first beat. The *f* resolves in an ascending direction producing an interval of a sixth (*b-g*). See Example 13.6. It is possible that one of the two member tones could be altered in per-

Example 13.5. Free Canon. Ockeghem, *Missa Mi-Mi*, Sanctus, measures 61-62. Reprinted with permission of Kalmus Music Publishing Co., Opa-locka, Florida, and Belwin-Mills Publishing Corp., New York, New York.

Example 13.6. Tritone Suspension.

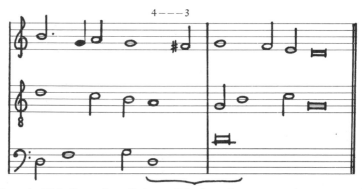

Example 13.7. Octave-Leap Cadence. Ockeghem, *Prenez sur moi vostre exemple amoureux*, measures 34-35. Reprinted with permission of Kalmus Music Publishing Co., Opa-locka, Florida, and Belwin-Mills Publishing Corp., New York, New York.

formance, eliminating the tritone. In such a treatment the suspension would no longer function as a dissonance (fifth to sixth relationships result), and this point would be negated. However, since this is a canon, it is possible to observe the composer's treatment of this same relationship when it appears in the other two voices. In both instances it is treated as a suspension (one a 4-3 and the other a 9-10), which provides a good basis for judging that the tritone-sixth treatment is, in fact, what the composer was expecting.

The final cadence of *Prenez sur moi* was fairly widely used during this period; we made only passing reference to it earlier. The *octave-leap cadence* is characterized by the crossing of two lower voices to their respective final notes. The lowest voice skips up an octave to the fifth above the final tone while the middle voice (of a three-voice texture) descends by step to become the lowest sounding voice at the end. See Example 13.7.

Compositional Considerations

In this chapter we have not devoted our attention to as many small details of practice as we did in some earlier chapters. Rather, we have concerned ourselves with more evasive and elusive phenomena. However well one masters the specifics of a technique, that mastery will have little import if more subtle aspects of style are not understood.

Students must develop sensitivity to texture and proficiency in the control of textural change. The ability to write a successful homophonic or polyphonic passage is not sufficient. It is necessary to develop a technique that will permit smooth motion from one kind of texture to another, to add or delete voices, and to compress and expand spacing between voices. Related to these considerations are those of vocal color and tessitura. A single voice may have a different coloristic impact in the lower portion of its range than it has in the upper, in the same manner that a low male voice will have a different coloristic impact than a high male voice — the distinction is one of degree.

Much writing and analysis focused on these problems is necessary to develop the desired proficiency. Such practice is an essential part of the mastery and understanding of all compositional practices, irrespective of style. However, a few suggestions, some of which are related directly to this period, can be helpful as points of departure for such compositional efforts.

Much of the music we are considering begins on a set of perfect intervals — a root and fifth with either or both doubled in unison or at the octave. The dominant texture is polyphonic, with voices crossing more or less freely (depending on the peculiarities of the individual composer or composition). In the asymmetrical writing we have considered, voices enter and leave from consonant positions only, on either strong or weak beats but always on a beat natural to the flow of the line in question. The momentary deletion of a voice line (a practice sprinkled through all voice parts) — whether for a beat or portion thereof as a breathing point, or for a measure or two for textural interest — is a healthy practice, producing variety, ease of performance, and interest to both performer and listener.

The most widely employed tessitura is the middle of the respective voice ranges. A variety of descriptive adjectives may be used, but the following are offered as a reference or point of departure. As one moves lower in a vocal range, the sound tends to become broader and darker. Movement toward the upper part of a vocal range will produce brighter, often thinner qualities. Extremely high and low tones are less secure in terms of intonation and clarity. Extremes of vocal range are not found in the period under consideration.

When different voices are used together, the respective qualities of each are affected. This is more pronounced when they are in relatively close proximity. The farther they move from each other, the more they are distinguishable from each other. Consequently, in this music wide spacing of voices is relatively rare. The relationships in the overtone series can remind us what the normal desirable distribution is — wider spacing between lower voices and progressively narrower gaps as one moves higher in the range.

Smooth motion between homophonic and polyphonic textures may be achieved by gradually changing the rhythmic motion of individual lines. In homophonic textures, the motion effect often seems to be slower because all voices are moving in the same rhythmic setting. The varying rhythm of polyphonic passages tends to create a sense of more rapid overall motion. On occasion these expectations may be reversed, and students should, as in all matters, remain flexible enough to accommodate these differences.

To move from a polyphonic to a homophonic passage, the motion effect of the respective passages should be kept in mind and the relative rhythmic values should be lengthened gradually in each of the voices, as appropriate, until they rhythmically coincide for the beginning of the homophonic passage. Clearly, the technique is reversed if the problem is reversed (i.e., homophonic to polyphonic). Specific assignments are provided in the workbook to assist students in gaining a greater understanding of and proficiency with these techniques.

It is not uncommon to find different textures combined with changes in meter to heighten a particular musical or textual effect. It may be the refrain of a secular song or a particularly important portion of a sacred text (e.g., Et resurrexit tertia die) which the composer is attempting to set apart from an earlier section. In such instances, the preceding section will simply cadence and the new section begin, thus set apart — as separate entities.

Canonic writing poses difficult problems of texture and color change. Such passages must be treated with extra care and awareness that an over-long section may become ineffective because it lacks variety in texture and color. Attempts must be made to direct lines into different tessituras, to vary the homophonic as opposed to the polyphonic effect of rhythmic motion, or to make discreet, brief departures from the strictness that may prevail (e.g., dropping a voice down a fifth rather than up a fourth).

There is an omnipresent danger that students will become so interested in or concerned with the intricacies of note-to-note relationships that they will be oblivious to the critically important broader architectural considerations of variety, balance, proportion, and unity. All analyses and compositional efforts must integrate these factors which are part of the multiplicity of phenomena which must be understood and to which students must be made sensitive if the study of stylistic evolution and the development of a creative writing technique are to be successful.

Summary

Johannes Ockeghem has been the reference composer for this chapter. The specifics of his personal style have not been our primary concern, but they have provided the opportunity to become acquainted with compositional factors that are more elusive and that require the understanding of substantial basic technique before they can be fully understood.

Compositional considerations such as texture variation, coloristic potential, tessitura of individual voice parts and their impact on other voices sounding at the same time, the influence of spacing, and the relationship of each of these to the others as well as the influence metrical or textual considerations may exert, are some of the areas that Ockeghem's style has provoked us to study. These are as critical to the understanding of music or the simulation of a particular style as the mastery of the basic techniques (e.g., good line, dissonance treatment, and sensible cadences).

Ockeghem's use of canon brought to our attention the degrees of freedom that may be associated with that technique and, at the same time, provided us the opportunity to investigate the limitations imposed on textural and coloristic concerns by extended use of canonic writing.

chapter 14

late fifteenth and early sixteenth
centuries - josquin des pres

One composer clearly stands out in the late fifteenth and early sixteenth centuries — Josquin des Pres (1450-1521). His many works, reflecting a mastery
of technique, are an important force in the continuing evolution of the art.
He used extensively paired imitation, sequential passages, a variety of canons,
literal repetitions, mixed meters, and numerous other devices, all of which
characterized his personal style and significantly influenced those who followed him.

Josquin's *Missa Pange Lingua* is a paraphrase Mass for which the source
material was derived from the hymn *Pange Lingua.*[1] The paraphrase technique antedates Josquin and is simply the elaboration and embellishment of
the original line. The Mass opens with the bass and tenor in imitation at the
interval of a fifth one $\frac{3}{1}$ measure apart. This imitation dissolves quickly into
free counterpoint which continues until the passage ends at the end of measure 6. In measures 5 and 6 the identical passage begins again, this time between the soprano and alto voices. The soprano sings the first four measures
(plus one note) of the original tenor part and the alto the first four measures
(plus one note) of the original bass part. The two female voices are a paired
imitation to the male voices.

In this instance the paired imitation is between two voices that are semi-
independent. That is, the paired voices are in imitation with each other to begin with but dissolve into free counterpoint after the first four notes. There
can also be paired imitation between pairs of voices that are in strict canon

182

with each other or pairs of voices that are totally independent of each other. The paired imitation passages may be very brief or quite lengthy. The technique is used extensively in this Mass as well as throughout the works of Josquin. A more abbreviated paired imitation passage (from the Gloria of the *Missa Pange Lingua*), treated in the same manner as the one described above, is provided for study in Example 14.1.

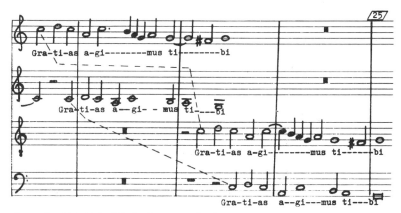

Example 14.1. Paired Imitation. Josquin des Pres, *Missa Pange Lingua*, Gloria, measures 21-25. Reprinted with permission from Friedrich Blume, ed., *Das Chorwerk, Josquin des Pres, Missa Pange Lingua*, Nr. 1, Möseler Verlag, Wolfenbüttel, 1938.

An interesting treatment of paired imitation occurs later in this Mass. At the beginning of the Osanna section of the Sanctus there is a three and one-half measure passage in the basses and tenors — two independent lines. At the start of the fourth measure, the soprano and alto restate these same lines at the interval of a perfect fourth higher. There is nothing atypical about the passage to this point. However, as the soprano and alto statement ends, the bass and tenor once again state the same passage (at the beginning of the seventh measure) a large second lower than the original statement.

Repetition is also used extensively in this work (as well as in others). Repetitions, whether or not on different pitch levels, occur both in single lines and in multipart passages. A passage in which all four voices repeat approximately every measure and one-half is in the Gloria section, measures 34-39. Three statements of an interlocked imitation between the tenor and the bass (at the interval of a sixth) are an integral part of this passage.

Another interesting passage demonstrating a variant on the repetition technique is given in Example 14.2. In this passage there are three statements of a two-measure phrase in the tenor voice. The first and last are identical. The middle statement is the same, except that the interval between the fourth and fifth notes has been expanded to a sixth from the original fourth and the entire passage is set a whole step lower than the statements that precede and follow it. It is also interesting to note that the soprano voice has two statements of this same material. The first, beginning a fourth higher than the tenor entry, suggests the beginning of a canon. However, this first soprano statement has the same intervallic structure as the second tenor statement and, in strict terms, begins a canon with the second tenor statement. This interpretation of the canon remains strict through the second entry of the tenor since the so-

Example 14.2. Varied Repetition and Canon. Josquin des Pres, *Missa Pange Lingua*, Agnus Dei, measures 17-24. Reprinted with permission from Friedrich Blume, ed., *Das Chorwerk, Josquin des Pres, Missa Pange Lingua*, Nr. 1, Möseler Verlag, Wolfenbüttel, 1938. Note the evolving imitation in the last three measures. At x there is a change of rhythm, at y the line is filled in, and at z the interval is expanded from a third to a fifth.

prano continues with the original form of the first tenor statement. See Example 14.2.

Invertible Counterpoint

A momentary, isolated instance of a device that was developed to a high degree of sophistication in the historical period that followed is a single measure of invertible counterpoint. A complete discussion of this technique must be left for the study of Baroque compositional practices. However, its presence in this work cannot be ignored.

In Example 14.3 the two measures in question may be compared. The alto voice in the *a* part of the example becomes the bass part in the *b* excerpt. It has been moved down a perfect fourth. The bass in the *a* excerpt becomes the alto in the *b* but has been moved up a seventh (a combined total of a tenth). Consequently, whereas the vertical interval between the two voices at the

Example 14.3. Invertible Counterpoint. Josquin des Pres, *Missa Pange Lingua*, Agnus Dei II, measures 32-34, 39-41. Reprinted with permission from Friedrich Blume, ed., *Das Chorwerk, Josquin des Pres, Missa Pange Lingua*, Nr. 1, Möseler Verlag, Wolfenbüttel, 1938.

start is a third (discounting the octave) in the *a* excerpt, it is a unison in the *b* excerpt. The voice that was the lowest sounding voice in the first becomes the highest sounding voice in the second. This change of parts at a different interval (the tenth in this instance) is termed invertible counterpoint (or double counterpoint) at the tenth.

As noted, it is premature to devote attention to the development of facility with invertible counterpoint, but since it is possible that students will encounter other instances of invertible counterpoint as their studies continue, it is desirable that they become aware of its characteristics and use.

One might ask whether Josquin used this technique consciously or inadvertently. We can only conjecture. Because Josquin was clearly very conscious of organization in both small and large dimensions and was a master of the many techniques necessary to achieve that kind of architectural logic, it is reasonable to assume that he did this consciously but perhaps did not fully realize the potential of the technique.

Sequence

Related to Josquin's use of paired imitation and repetition is his extensive use of sequence. His sequential writing ranges from brief melodic figures to extended entries of two or more parts. A brief linear sequence is given in Example 14.4.

Example 14.4. Linear Sequence. Josquin des Pres, *Missa Pange Lingua*, Gloria, measures 100-101. Reprinted with permission from Friedrich Blume, ed., *Das Chorwerk, Josquin des Pres, Missa Pange Lingua*, Nr. 1, Möseler Verlag, Wolfenbüttel, 1938.

A passage in which all four voice parts participate sequentially is in Josquin's *Missa de Beata Virgine*. Measures 20-26 constitute the total sequential passage. The bass and soprano begin together in sequence, but the alto and tenor enter one and one and one-half measures later, respectively. The soprano ends in the middle of measure 25, and the other three voices continue to the end of measure 26. The tenor is varied in this last measure by the rhythmic compression of the sequence figure, the omission of four notes. A total of four-plus measures are in strict four-voice sequence. See Example 14.5.

Another extended and interesting use of sequence is in the Benedictus section of Josquin's *Missa Pange Lingua* (measures 137-148 of the Sanctus). In

┐ = end of sequence for the voice part.

Example 14.5. Four-Voice Sequence. Josquin des Pres, *Missa de Beata Virgine*, Gloria, Cum Sancte Spiritu, Measures 20-26. Reprinted with permission of Kalmus Music Publishing Co., Opa-locka, Florida, and Belwin-Mills Publishing Corp., New York, New York. The half brackets mark the ends of sequences for voice parts.

this passage there are three alternating entries between the tenor and the bass, with the tenor statement always a perfect fifth above the bass. In the three entries, the bass moves from the initial tone (*A*) up a perfect fourth (to *D*) and finally up a whole step from the *D* (to *E*). The tenor follows the same pattern on the three notes *E*, *A*, and *B*, respectively. At no point do the two parts sound together except in the last tenor response when the bass has begun new material which is subsequently responded to by the tenor in a free canonic manner. This entire passage ends in measure 157 with a simple contrary-motion, stepwise cadence (leading-tone type).

In the following measure a series of canons begins which is also presented in this sequential fashion between the same two voices. Some freedoms are taken in a few instances, but the effect of the section is highly canonic and sequential. The section ends in measure 183. The entire sequential passage (measures 137-183) is worth in-depth study. The whole Sanctus section of this Mass is provided for further study in the workbook/anthology.

Other Devices

Even within this relatively limited study of Josquin, it has become increasingly apparent that he was clearly concerned with the design and organization of his musical materials from the smallest to the largest dimensions within which he worked. What we have discussed to this point can be reinforced by a wide variety of additional references with the concept of architectural logic in mind.

One of the smallest factors, in terms of representing but a given moment in the music, is the relationship of the text to the music employed as its vehicle. Not infrequently there is *text painting* in Josquin's music (as well as in the works of his contemporaries). With this device the meaning of the text lends itself to some form of musical representation. An example is in the *Missa Pange Lingua*, when the words *Hosanna in the highest* (*Osanna in excelsis*) are presented so that the word *highest* is sung on the highest notes of all the voices' ranges at that particular melodic moment. See Example 14.6.

Josquin's awareness of the text is also revealed in his handling of the most important part of the Mass — Et incarnatus est. In the *Pange Lingua* Mass, this section is set apart from those that precede and follow it by the dramatic change from a polyphonic to a homophonic texture, followed again by the basic polyphonic texture of the largest part of the work. The particularly polyphonic character of the section that immediately precedes the Et incarnatus passage is heightened by the introduction of a hemiola figure in the alto voice. This, combined with imitative writing in the other parts, heightens the sense of polyphony and increases the dramatic impact of the change that follows.

Example 14.6. Text Painting. Josquin des Pres, *Missa Pange Lingua*, Sanctus, soprano, measures 103-107. Reprinted with permission from Friedrich Blume, ed., *Das Chorwerk, Josquin des Pres, Missa Pange Lingua*, Nr. 1, Möseler Verlag, Wolfenbüttel, 1938.

The Et incarnatus est passage is twenty measures long and is exclusively homophonic. The rhythmic values are limited to whole notes and double whole notes, and the passage is divided into four distinct sections. The first is a four-measure phrase consisting of four distinct chords (a single passing note could be interpreted as implying another chord — it is also the only rhythmic departure in the entire passage). Two five-measure phrases follow, each consisting of six changes of chord quality. The final phrase is six measures long and is rhythmically the slowest moving part of the entire section.

Although it would be premature to become involved in a study of harmonic concepts as they are related to tonality and later become the principal force in the music of the Baroque and periods that follow, it must be noted that the progressions of chords used in each of these four phrases can logically be interpreted in terms of the principles that pervade the music of the periods that follow. For the benefit of those who may have some familiarity with the tonal harmonic system, the progressions for these four phrases are shown below (in terms of C major):

Phrase I	I vi ii (vii$^{o}_{6}$) I
Phrase II	vi ii vi ii I V
Phrase III	V I (V) ii V$_6$ vi
Phrase IV	vi IV ii V I

Although we have stopped to pay particular attention to this passage because of its liturgical importance and because it received special treatment from the composer, it should be understood that significant portions of the general output of the period would lend themselves as well to a harmonic analysis. However, consistent adherence to the specific progressions associated with tonal music is not likely to be found. These harmonic practices are the result of vertical consonant-dissonant decisions concerning the relationships between lines rather than decisions resulting from horizontal relationships between vertical combinations of sound. The latter is a complicated phenomenon which will require in-depth study later. It is, however, quite reasonable to assume that composers of the period had some awareness of the harmonic properties that create tension and relaxation and the sense of forward motion. The evolution of harmonic thinking through the Middle Ages and Renaissance will be considered in a later chapter.

In the last several pages we have seen architectural concern reflected in the smallest dimensions and in a single passage in a broad compositional setting.

The broad architectural design of the *Missa Pange Lingua* is not unlike other Masses of the period in its use of a unifying head-motive (an opening set of notes that is used at the beginning of each large section of the Mass). An awareness of the broad relationships in an architectural sense is revealed in Josquin's design of the Sanctus section of the Mass.

The Sanctus is designed as a five-part form; each of the parts is clearly distinguished from the others by the special treatment it receives and the obvious alteration between two- and four-voice subsections. The opening Sanctus section unfolds in paired imitation followed by a four-voice passage in which the bottom two voices remain in canon for all but the cadence and the others are in free (but not unrelated) counterpoint above.

The second section has two voice parts (soprano and alto) and is largely canonic, with several, brief repeated passages and frequent departures from the canonic sense. This is followed by a third section in four voice parts, which we have already, to an extent, discussed. An interesting alternation between the several voices of canonic material can be observed. The fourth section returns to the two-part texture and is highly sequential. This section was also discussed at some length earlier in this chapter. The final section of the movement is a literal repeat of section three — the four-part Osanna in excelsis. As suggested earlier, intense study of this movement can be very profitable, and the movement appears in the workbook/anthology.

Compositional Considerations

Although our discussion has been limited, the style of Josquin is interesting and challenging for students to attempt to simulate. Such a compositional problem can help students to refine their understanding of the techniques discussed and will contribute to the general development of compositional facility. In doing so there are several factors which must always be kept in mind. Some of these relate directly to things we have considered in earlier chapters, and others require attention because they are more important in this style, are used uniquely in this later style, or are simply new to the compositional vocabulary. These items follow in outline.

Line

a. Range is approximately a twelfth in each voice;

b. Principal melodic intervals are (in approximte order of importance) seconds, thirds, perfect fourths, perfect fifths, octaves, and ascending minor sixths;

c. The effect is highly conjunct, with a moderate use of large skips;

d. Some use of short sequential linear patterns;

e. Frequent use of repeating notes (half notes or longer) with a change of text or syllable in every instance. Anticipation-type repeated notes also appear frequently in smaller note values but do not require change of text or syllable;

f. The ascending step-skip (e.g., G-A-C) melodic pattern (and its inversion — skip-step descending) are used with half notes or larger;

g. Normally there is only one appearance of a high note in each phrase — some (few) exceptions can be noted;

h. Skips of a perfect fifth or larger normally return within the interval by step or skip — some exceptions can be noted;

i. The linear tritone is not used by skip but some examples can be found of a stepwise-produced tritone effect (departure and arrival tones on a strong beat in a stepwise line);

j. Free use of the lower neighboring tone (use of the upper neighbor is rare);

k. Frequent use of the cambiata figure;

l. The raised leading tone is used widely and is normally approached by step from above and returns to the same tone;

m. With the whole notes as the unit of measure, very few eighth notes are used and these always appear in pairs on the weak portion of a beat in a totally conjunct setting.

Rhythm

a. Long rhythmic values open and close sections, with greater activity in the middle of the sections;

b. Much use of triple meter (with the whole note as the unit of measure in the transcriptions employed);

c. Some use of changing meter within a single voice part and cross meters between voices;

d. With the whole note as the unit of measure, the motion is predominantly whole and half note values;

e. Descending quarter-note motion begins on the weak beat whereas ascending may begin on either the strong or the weak beats (mostly weak);

f. Two quarter notes do not stand alone in place of an accented half note;

g. Half notes or longer values may be tied to notes of equal value or half their value (long must precede short);

h. Twelve successive quarter notes is the largest number in the *Missa Pange Lingua* — the norm may be considered between 6 and 8 successive quarter notes;

i. Eighth notes (very few used) always appear on the weak quarter beat normally following a dotted half note.

A lovely line from the *Missa Pange Lingua* which reflects many of the features described above and which students can use as an effective model for their compositional efforts is provided in Example 14.7.

Example 14.7. Opening of the Credo. Josquin des Pres, *Missa Pange Lingua*, tenor, measures 1-15. Reprinted with permission from Friedrich Blume, ed., *Das Chorwerk, Josquin des Pres, Missa Pange Lingua*, Nr. 1, Möseler Verlag, Wolfenbüttel, 1938.

Contrapuntal Elements

Interrelationships between lines

a. Much use of imitation, often as strict canon;
b. Much use of paired imitation entries in a four-part texture;
c. Triadic relationships predominate in three- and four-part texture (these are mostly root position, but a moderate number of first inversions are used — second inversions are rare and occur only on weak beats);
d. Moderate use of short passages in parallel thirds, sixths, or tenths;
e. A few examples of weak vertical tritone and cross relations (two different forms of the same note, e.g., B and B^b, in close rhythmic proximity between two different voices);
f. Use of choralelike passages to create dramatic contrasts with the basic contrapuntal texture may be observed periodically;
g. Moderate use of literal repetition of short passages;

h. Noteworthy but extremely limited use of invertible counterpoint;

i. Cadences:

   1. Triad relationships of iv-i are the most widely used;

   2. Other cadential progressions include: V-I, ii-i, ^{b}VI-I (the latter two are relatively rare);

   3. Perfect consonances are used at the ends of principal sections or movements (the i or I used above does not refer to full triads but to the perfect consonances that produce the sense of tonic);

   4. Full triads are used cadentially at the ends of internal sections;

   5. Important cadential triads are always used in root position;

j. Nonharmonic tones: (dissonant tones that are not part of the chord being used)

   1. Wide use of suspensions (mostly 4-3 and 7-6 with some use of 9-10 and 2-3);

   2. Free use of lower neighbor;

   3. Frequent use of the cambiata figure;

   4. Many passing tones almost exclusively in relatively weak rhythmic positions;

Rhythmic relationships between lines

a. Moderate use of hemiola passages;

b. Some use of cross meters (e.g., $\frac{3}{1}$ vs. $\frac{4}{1}$);

c. Equal use of triple and duple meters;

d. Equal rhythmic importance of all voices.

The reasonably specific delineation of compositional practices reflected in Josquin's *Missa Pange Lingua* is indicative of the increasing sophistication of compositional control and judgment exercised by composers of this period and is a prelude to further refinements. To more comprehensively understand Josquin's style, it would be necessary to extend this detailed analysis to many other works which would refine the above specifications significantly and provide a truer representation of the composer's practices. However, this is not our purpose and the above outline will suffice.

Summary

Organization, small and large relationships, increasing sensitivity to harmonic considerations, and a growing awareness of the power of musical techniques for expressive purposes reflect the efforts and concerns of the composers of the late fifteenth and early sixteenth centuries. In this chapter, these phenomena have been somewhat narrowly presented and represented through the analysis of primarily one work by the leading composer of the period. Although the phenomena we have analyzed reflect Josquin's personal style, they are also indicative of the prevailing attitudes and interests of his contemporaries.

Devices such as a head motive for each section of the Mass, hemiola, imitation, and suspension are not new but may be handled in a personal fashion. Paired imitation, text painting, and significant texture changes for dramatic purposes are, although not entirely new, distinguishing trademarks which raise the craft to higher levels of artistic expression. What might be designated as new in this period certainly anticipates practices that came to fruition later. But, as with all things that are new, they clearly evolved from the techniques and practices of the past. Examples are the growing sense of harmonic relationships and the use of harmonically related progressions, and the tentative exploration of new areas of contrapuntal refinement and development (e.g., invertible counterpoint).

This is an incredibly rich period which students are strongly encouraged to explore beyond the confines of the theoretical considerations barely revealed here. It contains a wealth of beautiful literature for performance and extensive study.

sixteenth-century
secular forms

In the discussion of Renaissance music we confined our study almost exclusively to the sacred literature — selected works of a few representative composers. However, a secular literature flourished during this entire period. Examples could be cited in the work of those composers whose sacred music we considered in preceding chapters.

In the sixteenth century, secular music gained an added impetus from the growth of a new wealthy bourgeoisie which followed the example of royalty in their encouragement of the arts.[1] Although a variety of secular forms were used, two clearly attracted the finest composers and were produced in large numbers — the *chanson* and the *madrigal*.

Before discussing these forms, we should note two important developments in printing and notation. The French publisher Attaingnant is credited with being the first (c. 1528) to insist on accurate placement of the text beneath the music to which it was to be sung. Within a few years after that date (c. 1532), the first use of oval note heads can be seen in the printing of Jean de Chauncy of Avignon.[2]

Chanson

Thousands of chansons were composed during the period. One of the principal composers in this form, Clement Janequin (1485-c. 1560), is credited with over 280 such compositions. Janequin and Claudin de Sermisy (1490-

1552) are the two principal composers of a group collectively referred to as the Paris School.

In the chanson, four-voice writing is preferred. This is presented in a predominantly chordal style, reflecting a distinct reaction against the contrapuntal complexity of the preceding periods. Generally, few contrapuntal devices were used (e.g., the typical canonic and imitative writing that pervades earlier periods). With the rise of chordal thinking, phrases became more clearly defined and characteristic masculine and feminine endings may be seen to alternate in these pieces. In sacred music and in earlier secular styles, it was common practice to use melodies composed earlier as the point of departure or reference for composition. This practice was rejected by the chanson composers.

Rhythm becomes more sharply defined in chanson writing. A characteristic opening rhythmic figure is adopted (♩ ♩ ♩) and may be found in a large number of these compositions. Likewise, there is very little change of meter in this literature (contrary to earlier practice), and the predominant meter is *alle breve* (equivalent to $\frac{2}{2}$). Frequent use was made of rapid repeated notes.

The chansons typically employed freer texts and, as is typical of many of Janequin's, were quite long and descriptive. The text strongly influenced the character of the music resulting in much text painting. Also the setting of the text was generally highly syllabic.

Janequin's chanson *L'espoir confus*[3] demonstrates the basic form of the chanson — *ababcdEE*. Numerous variants on this format can be found, but this type clearly predominates. This particular piece embodies a number of the characteristics delineated above as well as some slight liberties.

The opening of *L'espoir confus* is entirely chordal and syllabic. The first two measures provide an augmentation of the typical chanson opening rhythm (which is found later in the piece in its natural form — as the beginning of two of the internal sections). In the fourth measure, we find the first suggestion of contrapuntal influence in this piece, i.e., the imitation of the descending eighth notes of the soprano and alto by the tenor. This contrapuntal influence is further revealed in the use of imitative entries and the rhythmic independence of lines at the beginning of the *c* section (*Amour le scait*). This latter passage is shown in Example 15.1.

In three of the voices in Example 15.1 students should note the half note followed by two quarter notes referred to earlier. The ascending eighth-note figure is an inverted form of the one in measures 4 and 5, as discussed above.

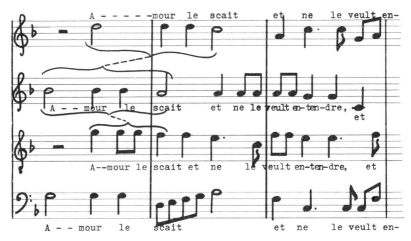

Example 15.1. Chanson: Janequin, *L'espoir confus*, beginning of section c. Reprinted with permission from A. Tillman Merrit and F. François Lesure, *Clement Janequin, Chansons Polyphoniques*, Vol. III, Editions de L'Oiseau-Lyre, Les Remparts, Monaco, 1965, p. 11.

The meter throughout the first portion of the piece remains clearly *alle breve* (from the beginning through the *d* section). The final (*E*) section makes a momentary change to a triple meter (two measures) and then concludes with a return to the alle breve. In this otherwise strongly duple piece, in addition to the two-measure triple-meter interruption mentioned, there is a change of metrical reference for two measures by the use of triplet half notes. See Example 15.2.

The linear style of this piece is considerably more disjunct than the style of most of the music we have studied to this point. In the soprano, melodic skips of a sixth and an octave ascending (both resolving down by step) are important components in the line. One unusual, large skip can be found in the *E* section where the soprano leaps a diminished seventh from an *F* sharp to an *E* flat. The lower note of this pair is approached by step from above and the upper note is left by step in a descending direction.

The disjunctiveness of the lowest sounding voice is somewhat different from that of the soprano. There are a significant number of fifths and fourths in this part, which are clearly harmonic in their relationship and function. During this period harmonic awareness was increasing. The close relationship of chords whose roots lay a fifth away from each other was clearly recognized and extensively exploited by the composers of this period. Many examples could be cited from almost endless numbers of compositions. One of sev-

Example 15.2. Janequin, *L'espoir confus*, measures 36-42. Reprinted with permission from A. Tillman Merritt and F. François Lesure, *Clement Janequin, Chansons Polyphoniques*, Vol. III, Editions de L'Oiseau-Lyre, Les Remparts, Monaco, 1965, p. 14.

eral examples that could be excerpted from the chanson we are considering is given in Example 15.3, with appropriate chord names and chord numbers as related to B flat major (the most convenient and appropriate referential tonality for this excerpt). In Example 15.3 every bass note serves as the root of a triad. When a skip of a fifth or a fourth takes place in this line, the relationship between the two triads in terms of the referential tonality is a perfect fifth (I-V, vi-iii, and iii-vii, although the latter may be debatable). The last two measures of this passage embody two different classifications. The upper continues the B flat major tonal interpretation and the lower has a modulated interpretation (i.e., the referential tonality changes in the middle of the passage from B flat major to G minor). Although the chord names change according

Example 15.3. Harmonic Function of a Disjunct Base Line. Janequin, *L'espoir confus*, measures 8-12. Reprinted with permission from A. Tillman Merritt and F. François Lesure, *Clement Janequin, Chansons Polyphoniques*, Vol. III, Editions de L'Oiseau-Lyre, Les Remparts, Monaco, 1965, pp. 10-11.

to the tonality in which they are placed, the relationships remain unchanged.

Students should note that a number of different dissonant tones are used in this passage. These are marked in the score with the following abbreviations:

$$PT = \text{Passing Tone}$$

$$\frac{9\text{-}8}{4\text{-}3} = \text{Suspensions (vertical intervals)}$$

$$Ant = \text{Anticipation}$$

$$APT = \text{Accented (as in APT = Accented Passing Tone)}$$

Dissonant tones such as these become increasingly important as tonality becomes a more dominant force in the following century. They were used in varying degrees in most earlier styles and are an integral part of linear embellishment, motion, and vertical tension. Mastery of the use of dissonant tones (later known as nonharmonic tones) is essential to any composer in any style. Students must try to develop the ability to use these tones with discretion and taste. Our discussion in many of the preceding chapters has indicated the location and manner of use of such tones in all styles studied. However, students must cultivate an awareness of and sensitivity to such detail in their performance and study of scores and then be able to intelligently and tastefully transfer these practices to their own writing.

Basically there are two forces in music — activity and repose. Dissonant tones can create the effect of a wide range of levels of activity, from the most subtle and gentle bend of a line to dramatic conflict and tension. Without these tones, music can be bland and uninteresting; with an overabundance, music can be offensive and inexpressive. But there is no formula to guide students in the selection of just the right number or distribution. It is in this context that the individual's growing musicality must be jealously pursued, cultivated, and finally depended upon.

Earlier in our discussion of the chanson it was suggested that there are numerous variants of the form. One such example is Janequin's *Il estoit une fillette* which has the form *aa,bb,cc,DD*. The *a,b,* and *c* sections are very short — four measures each and all groups are repeated. The final section (*D*) is twice that length (eight measures) and is also repeated. Although the form in this piece departs from the typical chanson form, the style of the piece is more decidedly homophonic than was that of *L'espoir confus*. The text treatment is entirely syllabic and almost no single line has independent rhythmic motion.

If we scan Janequin's other chansons, we find many variants of practice. *Une belle jeune espousée* opens with a half note followed by two quarter notes, the characteristic chanson rhythmic figure, in a chordal setting. Within a couple of measures, however, polyphonic writing appears, which is then sprinkled through the balance of the piece. A surprising number of meter changes (five) are used in this piece. *Une jour Robin* opens with a brief suggestion of canon which quickly dissolves into free writing which, sporadically throughout the piece, employs imitation but remains entirely syllabic.

Students are encouraged to peruse many of the chansons of the period (available in a variety of collections), to look for individuality and its constituent elements as well as universality in every piece studied.

A polyphonic type of chanson was favored by Franco-Netherlandic composers (e.g., Clemens non Papa, whose works were popular for over a century). In the early chansons of Adrian Willaert (c. 1485-1562), strict double canons were the rule (i.e., the two upper lines were in canon with each other and the two lower lines presented an independent canon with each other). However, even these canonic types retained a strong sense of syllabic and homophonic effect.

Madrigal

The sixteenth-century madrigal was a favored form of the Franco-Netherlandic composers, many of whom lived in Italy for extended periods of time.

Likewise it was a favored form of the Italian composers of the period.

Generalizations about the madrigal form are, at best, precarious since it had an extended evolution and varied significantly in its numerous stages. The single element of primary importance is the significance of the text on which the form is totally dependent. Musical representation of the text was the composer's principal goal and madrigals abound in text painting, both obvious and subtle. The only truly distinguishing element is the number of syllables per line. The norm is seven or eleven syllables (five-syllable forms are rare possibilities). The average number of lines is ten with a range of from six to sixteen.[4] The works of Willaert, with which we shall be principally concerned, are mostly fourteen lines since they employ the poetic sonnet form almost exclusively, which consists of two quatrains (four lines each) and two tercets (three lines each).

The madrigal texts chosen reflect a distinctly high level of taste. Willaert's are primarily from the poetry of Petrarch. Beyond the question of quality and the syllable structure mentioned, there are no formal criteria for the number of verses or the manner of rhythming. The function of the music was to express the content of the text. The voices were equal and were textually treated with equal care. In this same spirit the texture could be syllabic and chordal, polyphonic, and with or without imitation — whichever would best express the content of the text. Because of the sophistication and subtlety of these pieces, madrigals were often considered "performers' rather than listeners' music."[5]

Willaert, whose students included such prominent composers and theorists of the period as Cipriano de Rore; Andrea Gabrieli; Gioseffo Zarlino; and Nicolo Vicentino (who could be considered the avante-gardist of the period, having experimented with microtones and extreme chromaticism), produced many madrigals. His early works suggest interest in harmonic experimentation, occasional use of fauxbourdonlike parallel thirds and sixths, and color. In his later works, phrases were less clearly defined, and line was emphasized more than color (although the bass retains numerous large leaps which characterized Willaert's earlier work as well); imitative writing, expressive use of chordal passages, and moderate chromaticism within lines of equal importance all became stylistic elements.[6] Gerstenberg remarks of his attitude toward form, "Of Willaert's compositions it may probably be said that poetic detail, especially as projection of visual images, takes precedence over the preservation of poetical form, thus becoming independent of the latter."[7]

Because Willaert used the sonnet structure, his madrigals are divided into two parts which he clearly defines. Many of the cadences for the first parts of these pieces end on a triad that is a perfect fifth above the final triad for the second parts, i.e., a dominant-tonic relationship. Some have the subdominant-tonic relationship, but there are relatively few of these. The cadences are in most instances either dominant to tonic triads or subdominant to tonic triads, all treated in root position. A typical treatment is shown in Example 15.4.

Compositional Considerations

The principal difference between the chanson and the madrigal is in the text and the resulting form. The text of the madrigal, as discussed earlier, is more sharply defined for length and number of syllables per line and is universally associated with finer literature. The chanson enjoys a freer text within a relatively clearly defined musical form. The text of the chanson may be quite descriptive and, at times, quite long. The text of the madrigal is usually not long and is often concerned with the subject of romantic love.

Specific compositional practices in the chanson and madrigal, however, are quite similar in many respects, allowing, of course, for individual composers' stylistic differences. If understood in this context and accepted as a reasonable generalization (but, nonetheless, a generalization with inherent dangers), the following outline can prove extremely helpful to students.

Line

a. The content of the text strongly influences the contour of the line, particularly in the madrigal;
b. The treatment of the text is highly syllabic;
c. Lines are equal and independent but are clearly beginning to be influenced by the growing awareness of harmonic implications (especially apparent in the bass lines);
d. Intervals greater than a fifth must be approached from and resolved within the interval — there are exceptions (e.g., an effort to more effectively depict a text), but they must be treated with great discretion;
e. The range of any single line does not often exceed a tenth;
f. A linear tessitura may be selected for the expressive or coloristic possibilities it offers the requirements of a text;
g. The bass line is most often conceived in terms of its harmonic function (root-of-triad relationship) and may be quite harmonically disjunct (i.e.,

Example 15.4. Final Cadences in Willaert, *Amor, Fortuna—Né spero i dolci*. Reprinted with permission from H. Zenck and W. Gerstenberg, eds., *A. Willaert, Opera Omnia*, American Institute of Musicology, Dallas, Texas, 1966, p. 4. Armen Carapetyan is director of the Institute, which is now located in Rome.

move by means of many ascending fourths and descending fifths—the dominant-tonic relationship);

h. Chromatic alterations are present for coloristic effect as well as for tritone avoidance and strong cadential motion;

i. There is moderate use of repeated tones, generally with changes of syllable or word but occasionally without such change (no apparent pattern of these exceptions seems to be definable).

Rhythm

a. The majority of this music is set in an alle breve meter with infrequent changes of meter;

b. Rhythmic motion is generally quite straightforward with some mild syncopations;

c. Successive quarter notes (in $\frac{2}{2}$ meter) rarely appear in numbers greater than eight or ten, the principal motion being half-note motion;

d. The smallest values (eighth notes) appear in pairs infrequently and are always set in a totally conjunct fashion (i.e., stepwise motion between them, to approach and to leave) on the weak portion of a beat;

e. Beginnings and endings of principal sections tend to move with longer rhythmic values than the internal portions of the compositions (i.e., whole-note and double-whole-note values);

f. Although lines are conceived as independent and equal, their frequent rhythmic coincidence produces a highly chordal effect;

g. Because contrapuntal elements have secondary importance in the secular styles, the phrases become more clearly defined and coinciding phrase division between the several lines appears more frequently;

h. Half notes or longer values may be tied to notes of equal value or half their value (long values precede short).

Contrapuntal Elements

a. Independence and equality of lines, although distinctly an integral part of these styles, are influenced strongly by a growing awareness of harmonic relationships;

b. The music is consistently triadic, and final cadences (of sections or complete pieces) close with full triads — root position exclusively at cadences and mostly through the body of the compositions (some limited use of first inversion triads may be seen);

c. Moderate use of the cambiata figure and other basic dissonances which characterize earlier styles;

d. Parallel motion between two voices at the intervals of perfect fifths or octaves occur only when the upper voice moves by step and the lower by skip (no strict parallels are used), the only exceptions being when a third voice moves in contrary motion to an imperfect consonance between the voices that are moving in similar motion;

e. Cadences are almost exclusively IV-I and V-I;

f. Number of voices may vary from three to seven, with four the most popular in the chanson and five in the madrigal;

g. There is very little use of the traditional contrapuntal devices (e.g., canon, imitation, and melismatic writing) in the mature periods of these styles — more can be seen in the early stages;

h. Some use of patter text settings in multiple parts may be observed (especially in the chanson);

i. Cross relations may be seen in very close rhythmic proximity but never do two forms of the same note occur simultaneously (e.g., B flat and B natural);

j. In works with many independent parts (e.g., a seven-voice madrigal), the texture normally consists of less than the total number of parts available (e.g., four, five, or six) with frequent additions and deletions of individual lines for a variety of musical and textual effects;

k. When four or more parts are used, the basic members of triads (root and fifth) are doubled freely (normally more roots than fifths) with relatively little doubling of the third (the color tone) — practically no doubling of the third is seen in major triads.

In general, there is greater freedom of practice in the chanson literature than in the madrigal. This is especially true for rhythm; greater use is made of smaller values which are treated more freely as in the patterlike passages sprinkled through the works of Janequin.

Other Secular Forms

Many other forms enjoyed varying degrees of popularity during the fifteenth and sixteenth centuries. These include the *frottola*, the *villanesca*, and the *canzone*. The term frottola was actually used for a multitude of variants and subforms which included the canzone (a more serious version of the frottola which, in some respects, evolved into the madrigal), *odo, capitolo, strambotti*, and *villota*. These share some basic characteristics and were composed by commoners, churchmen, and nobles. They supplanted the earlier rondeau and bergerette.

In these pieces, many of which are quite inconsequential, a declamatory and syllabic style was favored. Gay, light-hearted melodies were somewhat burdened, however, by the prevailing thick, four-part texture which clearly reflected concern with harmonic relationships and employed patterns of chords. Lines had small ranges and employed numerous repeated notes with little or no contrapuntal devices. All voices began and ended together in relatively short, clearly defined phrases. The complete text was provided for many of the voices under the superius, with only incipit provided for the other voices. A common cadence pattern was the antiquated octave-leap cadence. These works were often performed as solo vocal pieces with instrumental accompaniment and, in some instances, as solo instrumental pieces. Many form variants were used; one popular type was the *abbc, abbc, abc, abc* (sonnet type).

The villanesca was a "... less polished, more folklike counterpart" of the madrigal.[8] It employed texts dealing with love and lovers' woes, some of which were obviously obscene. A typical rhythmic pattern associated with the villanesca is the following:

Its form was, most commonly, *ab* + refrain, *ab* + refrain, *ab* + refrain, *cc* (or *ab*) + refrain.[9]

Along with the secular vocal works, and partially as a result of the performance practices associated with them, instrumental forms began to attract the attention of composers as potential artistic, expressive media. They included the instrumental canzone (which came to be instrumental variants of already existing vocal pieces) and the *ricercare* which, by virtue of its sectional structure and contrapuntal concept, was most closely associated with the motet.

More than passing recognition and acknowledgment of these several forms is well beyond the purview of this study. However, interested students are encouraged to explore these forms more closely and to attempt to compose in these more light-hearted styles.

Summary

The secular forms of the fifteenth and sixteenth centuries are numerous and varied. They reflect a wide range of tastes, interests, social strata, and compositional sophistication. However, all of them demonstrate a lessening dependence on contrapuntal practices and an increasing interest in harmonic possibilities.

As a result of the decidedly triadic conception and the changing compositional interests and attitudes, relatively little use is made of contrapuntal devices (e.g., imitation and canon), phrases become more sharply defined and occur in the several parts simultaneously, the bass becomes a definitive force in harmonic determinations normally disjunct by fourth and fifth relationships, cadences are largely limited to the V-I and IV-I possibilities (the notable exception being the octave-leap cadence which continues to be employed in many frottole), musical forms change with changing poetic forms (there is significant interest in the sonnet structure), and instruments become increasingly important (from relatively innocuous accompanying responsibilities to the development of a substantial instrumental literature).

The two principal forms in this maze of secular musical activity were the chanson and the madrigal. The former was most closely associated with composers from France (e.g., the Paris School) and the latter was representative of the Franco-Netherlandic composers who resided in Italy and the native Italian composers. Both forms experienced an evolution that makes generalizations weak, at best, and virtually meaningless when individual styles are taken into consideration. To provide students with a basic reference and an opportunity to become familiar with and develop some facility in secular styles, examples of the works of two composers (one for each of the two principal forms) were discussed — Clement Janequin for the chanson and Adrian Willaert for the madrigal.

Binary meters characterize both types, with some metrical changes occurring in the chanson but the madrigal remaining quite firmly bound to the $\frac{2}{2}$ setting. Some minimal use was made of contrapuntal devices in both — especially in the early stages of development. Both employ a basically syllabic and homophonic style with the number of voices ranging from three to seven (the chanson favoring four and the madrigal five). Text painting and musical coloration of textual ideas may be seen in both (harmonically and by means of vocal tessitura in addition to the linear text painting). Although numerous variants may be found for each, basic forms can be identified: in the chanson *ab*, *ab*, *cd*, *EE* was frequently employed and in the madrigal the sonnet form of two quatrains and two tercets was often used. One of the most distinctive and important characteristics of the madrigal is the text. The texts were of the highest literary quality, which combined with the music to produce a refined, sophisticated body of vocal literature.

palestrina: part one

Giovanni Pierluigi Palestrina (c. 1524-1594), a composer of sacred music, was one of two major figures at the end of the Renaissance (the other was Orlando de Lassus). His work has gained greater notoriety than most other composers of this period largely as the result of the work of the late Baroque theorist Johann J. Fux. Almost 150 years after Palestrina flourished, Fux retrospectively delineated a set of rules for Palestrina's style which defined one of the most restrictive and sophisticated compositional practices of all time (including even the total serialists of the mid-twentieth century).

The Fux approach to the study of Palestrina is often referred to as *species counterpoint*, suggesting a pedagogical set of five gradually more involved species of counterpoint, ranging from a two-part note-against-note style to a multiple-part (four or five) free style. Although there are some distinct advantages in this approach to a complicated style of composition, I shall attempt to remain consistent with the analytical approach employed to this point. For just as there are advantages to the species approach, so there are strong offsetting disadvantages (e.g., memorizing a set of rules out of context and often for contrived examples that do not typify the composer's music).

Our study of Palestrina's style will be divided into two parts. The first concerns all the important elements of line, related rhythmic factors, and the manner in which the composer set text to the line. The second deals with the process of putting lines together — the harmonic and contrapuntal implications (including dissonant tones).

To begin with, the general aesthetic considerations that dictate the compositional decisions made in this style should be fully understood. This will help students grasp the rationale underlying the specific guidelines which will be presented for each step in the unfolding of the style. Four premises provide the basis for all that follows:

1. The music is a vehicle to reinforce the meaning of the text, which is of primary importance; the meaning of the text must not be lost.
2. A smooth, fluid effect characterizes this composer's works and maintaining this effect should be a factor in all decisions.
3. Stiff and abrupt effects must be avoided for they cause the music to assume a greater importance than the text.
4. Extremes of the vocal range should be avoided, and voices should not be spread more than a tenth, with the upper sounding voices remaining closer to each other (following the basic principles reflected in the overtone series). Rarely are there intervals of more than an octave between the soprano and alto in a four-voice texture.

The guidelines that follow are strict enough in practice to be considered rules, although there are some notable departures in Palestrina's own works.

Contour of Line and Use of Intervals

Fourths, fifths, octaves, seconds, and both major and minor thirds may be used, either ascending or descending. Minor sixths occur only in ascending motion and then only when preceded and followed by descending motion. Major sixths are not used. A melodic tritone is not acceptable when used either as a skip in any rhythmic relationship or in stepwise motion where the tritone members fall on strong beats creating a clear sense of the interval.

Conjunct motion must predominate in this style, although skips should be used to create variety and interest. It is normal to begin a phrase on the mode final or fifth above, to emphasize the reciting tone somewhat, and to end on the mode final on an accented beat. Upper and lower neighboring tones may be used when returning to a half note, but only lower neighbors are acceptable when quarter-note motion continues. Sequential writing should be avoided with the exception of the sequences shown in Example 16.1.

Bb is used to avoid a melodic tritone with F and is also used between two A's in the untransposed forms of the Dorian, Mixolydian, and Ionian modes

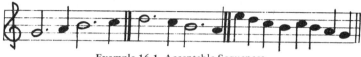

Example 16.1. Acceptable Sequences.

(it is used less often in the Aeolian). In the untransposed Lydian mode, B is almost always altered to Bb. In transposed forms of these modes (e.g., when a Bb key signature is used), the equivalent tone (Eb) is similarly used. Motion from a tone to an altered form of that tone (e.g., F to F#) is called degree inflection and is not permitted in this style. The leading tone is raised at cadences in the Dorian, Mixolydian, and Aeolian modes. All augmented and diminished linear intervals are unacceptable in this style (e.g., motion from F to G# in the Aeolian cadence where the F must be altered to F# or the G# approached from another note above it).

No line should have a range exceeding the natural range of the voice for which it is written, and normally it should not extend beyond the combined ranges of the authentic and plagal modes in which it is set. In each line there is usually only one high note for each moderately short melody or phrase. This high note appears most frequently about two-thirds through the phrase (never at the end) and is occasionally repeated in an embellished setting (where the importance of that note is heightened by the embellishment).

Symmetrical writing is not characteristic of this style. A variety of phrase lengths should be employed, and it is common for many of these to be of irregular length (e.g., three or five measures).

Stylistic practice dictates that limitations imposed on skips are interpreted strictly when used with rapid note values and are considered more as tendencies as values get longer. However, the rhythmic relationship of the line to other lines has an important influence on this limitation. If prevailing values are long in the several lines, more restraint is required. If at least one of the other lines utilizes more rapid values, greater freedom in the use of skips is acceptable in the slower moving lines.

Skips of a fifth or larger must be approached and left within the interval. Ascending skips must be treated with care and are usually followed by descending motion.

More than two successive skips in the same direction are not acceptable. Two such skips may not cumulatively create an interval of a seventh or one greater than an octave. Adjacent skips in the same direction must have the larger interval on the bottom. This limitation does not apply to major and minor thirds in triadic motion. The leading tone may be approached by a skip only from above.

Ascending skips are normally followed by descending stepwise motion, but descending skips are often followed by smaller skips or ascending stepwise motion. Descending skips do not always have to be followed by ascending motion unless the skip is a fifth or octave.

Rhythmic Characteristics

The composite rhythmic effect (i.e., the rhythm resulting from all lines considered together) is normally characterized by a slow start, an increase of motion through the body of the piece (or a large division thereof), and a reduction of motion as the cadence is approached. To a lesser degree this may also occur throughout individual phrases.

The transcribed unit of measure is the half note, which is most frequently found in binary meter but which may appear in ternary. Half notes should dominate the sense of motion, but variety should be sought by the use of slower and faster values. It would not be unusual for approximately one-quarter of the values used in any single phrase to be quarter notes with some (relatively few) pairs of eighth notes.

Ties connecting notes of the same value may only be used with half notes or larger values. Quarter notes may not be tied to each other but may be tied to a preceding half note. Notes may be tied only to notes of equal value or to notes of half their value. The longer of a pair of tied notes must always appear first except at a cadence where the shorter note may appear first (in such cases the notes used are normally half notes or longer values).

The use of syncopation is common. Syncopated notes are frequently approached by notes of shorter value. A syncopated, dotted half note is frequently followed by a pair of eighth notes. Quarter notes may not be syncopated.

Descending motion normally begins with longer values on a strong beat but may begin with quarter notes on a weak beat or portion of a beat. Ascending motion may begin with quarter notes on either strong or weak beats. However, ascending, stepwise quarter-note motion is best preceded by a descending skip.

Ascending skips from accented quarter notes are not acceptable and are usually avoided from accented half notes. Ascending skips from unaccented quarter notes may be used if the initiating quarter note is approached from above, if the skip arrives on a weak beat, and if the quarter note is not the last

of four or more consecutive quarter values. Descending skips from two successive accented quarter notes are not considered desirable.

Quarter notes may not be employed as participating members of two adjacent skips in the same direction. Two successive quarter note skips in the
same direction are not acceptable.

Nine consecutive quarter notes are generally considered to be the maxi-
mum, and such extended passages of quarter values are infrequent.

Half notes or longer values may be repeated freely if there is a change of
word or syllable. Quarter notes may be repeated only when used as anticipations. As such, they must be approached from above on an unaccented quarter position.

Two quarter notes may not be used in place of an accented half note except when they are followed by a half note that is suspended.

It is best to continue upward from an unaccented quarter note in stepwise motion although a descending skip of a third may be used. It is best if
an extended ascending quarter-note line ends on an accented note of greater
value or an unaccented, syncopated half note. Unaccented upper neighboring
tones are rarely used and, when used, must be followed by a half note or longer value.

Eighth notes occur only in pairs in a totally conjunct setting (approached,
joined, and left by step). They may be used only in place of an unaccented
quarter note and must be preceded by a quarter note or dotted half note.
Eighth notes should be used sparingly.

Text Treatment

A natural, smooth-flowing, and unobscured treatment of the text is of paramount importance. Strong syllables are normally placed in strong rhythmic/
melodic positions (i.e., on strong beats or striking syncopations). Weak syllables and less important words are placed in relatively weaker rhythmic/melodic
positions. Repeated notes of half note or larger values require a change of syllable, but quarter notes sung as anticipations may be sung with their note of
arrival without a change of syllable (the only repeated note having this liberty).

Words are fragmented according to their natural syllable divisions and may
change on half-note values or larger. Syllable or word changes may take place
on a single quarter note when it follows a dotted half note. Otherwise quarter
notes may not accommodate syllable changes. Following a group of quarter
notes, syllables are expected to change on the second longer value to occur

(not before). Changes of syllable may take place on the first of a group of quarter notes following a longer value. Syllables may not change on or after eighth notes.

Normally, imitative melodic lines employ the same text treated in the same manner in subsequent entries. The last syllable at a cadence is always sung with the last note articulated. Words are occasionally run together when the last syllable of one is the same as the first syllable of the other (within the same phrase), e.g., *Kyrie eleison*. Musical and textual phrases should complement each other, e.g., a new and often distinctive musical idea is presented with each new phrase of the text (often as imitative entries). No strict pattern of text repetition is followed, e.g., *Kyrie eleison* may appear three times in one voice and more or fewer times in another.

General Observations

The preceding guidelines to Palestrina's style reflect the intensive analyses to which his music has been subjected by Fux and numerous other theorists. Strict adherence to these guidelines is essential to simulate Palestrina's mature style, but it is equally important that students bring refined musical judgment to the note-to-note decisions they must ultimately make. Example 16.2 is a typical Palestrina line, demonstrating many of the preceding principles. However, some discreet liberties were taken for what may have been conscious or intuitive responses to the function of this line musically (i.e., it is a cadential soprano line to the Kyrie section, which, when set against the other voices, produces syncopations and suspensions which strengthen the cadential effect. The slight freedoms are the step/skip ascending motion from measures 2 to 3

Example 16.2. Cadential Soprano Line. Palestrina, *Missa Sine Nomine*, Kyrie eleison, measures 34-38. Reprinted with permission from L. Bianchi, *Le Opere Complete, di Giovanni Pierluigi da Palestrina*, Vol. XXI, Edizioni Istituto Italiano per la Storia della Musica, Rome, 1956, p. 53.

and the ascending skip from an unaccented half note at the beginning of measure 3.

In the example, the composer's departures from the retrospective definition of his mature style are neither significant nor difficult to justify musically. However, an earlier work that provides a wide variety of significant departures from his defined style is his *Missa de Beata Virgine*. The brief excerpt in Example 16.3 from the alto line of the Gloria of this work shows a most unusual line for Palestrina. Note the ascending motion continuing from an ascending skip of an octave in the middle of a phrase.

Example 16.3. An Atypical Palestrina Line. *Missa de Beata Virgine*, Gloria, alto, measures 21-23. Reprinted with permission from R. Casimiri, *Le Opere Complete, di Giovanni Pierluigi da Palestrina*, Vol. IV, Edizioni Istituto Italiano per la Storia della Musica, Rome, 1939, p. 4.

Numerous other departures from the typical Palestrina linear concept can be found in this work. Such devices as sequences (Gloria, tenor, measures 42-44), highly disjunct line (Credo, tenor, measures 124-126), and a sprinkling of ascending sixths must be considered in this context. However, in this compos-

Example 16.4. A Typical Palestrina Line. *Missa Sine Nomine*, Credo, tenor, measures 79-93. Reprinted with permission from L. Bianchi, *Le Opere Complete, di Giovanni Pierluigi da Palestrina*, Vol. XXI, Edizioni Istituto Italiano per la Storia della Musica, Rome, 1956, p. 62.

er's mature style, these rather sharp departures simply do not appear and must be considered foreign to the style and technique we are attempting to understand.

The line in Example 16.4 demonstrates many of Palestrina's characteristic approaches to linear writing. It starts in a relatively high tessitura, eases down, moves up — a little higher than the starting point — momentarily eases down again, and then, with a clear example of text painting (*Et ascendit in caelum*), ascends to the high point of the line, this top tone having the longest value of the entire passage.

A more detailed analysis of this line using the guidelines provided will prove fruitful. The line opens with three repeated half notes, each of which has a change of word or syllable. These are followed by a whole note and a half note descending by stepwise motion. The half note is left by an ascending minor-third skip to a syncopated whole note, followed respectively by a descending step and a minor third. Each of these notes is accompanied by a change of syllable. This is followed by an ascending step to another syncopated whole note which presents the first syllable of *die*. This syllable (*di*) is sustained through the next two measures while the line moves more rapidly. The syncopated whole note already mentioned is followed by two descending, stepwise quarter notes on the weak second beat of the measure which return by step to a half note. The half note, in turn, moves up by step to a syncopated, dotted half note over the bar line. It descends by step to a quarter-note anticipation of a quarter note which is followed by two descending, stepwise eighth notes. These resolve by step upward to a whole note and the final syllable of the word occurs on the following note a step below that whole note.

The passage continues a third above the last note, moves up by step and a third in the form of an ascending, embellished scale by resolving to a step below the high note of the third, is followed by a series of three ascending quarter notes and one descending conjunct quarter note, and reaches the high point of this stage of the unfolding line by a skip from an unaccented quarter note up a minor third to a syncopated, dotted half note. Three conjunct notes of increasing value (quarter, half, and whole) descend a perfect fourth for a momentary repose.

The climax of this passage is reached by using text painting, which begins following a half rest with three repeated half notes (all with a separate word or syllable) which are followed by ascending, stepwise motion to the highest note of the entire tenor line (A) — a double whole note. It resolves down by step to a whole note. Conjunct motion prevails throughout.

It took ten measures for the composer to weave his line up to its high point and, characteristic of his style, a little more than one-third of that time (four measures) to settle the line down. These measures (90-93) begin with a half-note rest followed by five half notes. The first three of these ascend by step to lightly touch the top note of the line on the weak fourth beat of the measure and then proceed down a third and a step from that note (a departure from the skip/step guideline). Continuing in stepwise motion down, a dotted half note, a quarter note, and two additional half notes appear before the line changes direction. Stepwise motion up to a whole note is followed by another step up to a double whole note to end the line.

In noting the several departures from the skip/step guideline, students must remember the qualifying footnote regarding the degree of strictness of interpretation appropriate to the relative values being employed. Likewise students should recognize that it is possible to subdivide this passage into smaller components (i.e., measures 79-86, 87-89, and 90-93). Each of these can be studied as separate entities and can be expected to produce equally rational conclusions. However, the total textual/musical passage we have just scrutinized is so integrally conceived that for the fullest understanding of Palestrina's linear compositional thinking one segment should not be divorced from another.

The example we have examined demonstrates many of the specific guidelines that have been presented. It is not unique. However, each line has its own life, its own requirements, its own limitations, and its own beauties. Students should analyze many Palestrina lines in the manner just demonstrated and should attempt to compose their own lines, always striving to achieve the essential stylistic integrity of the style while aspiring to create beautiful lines.

Summary

The mastery of Palestrina's style is largely dependent upon understanding the significance of the text to which the music is composed and the relationship of the music to it. It is a style in which the music is secondary to the text but in which the music achieves the most refined and polished technique and artistry. As a result, every nuance and detail is designed with extreme care in the context of an omnipresent awareness of the totality. The music must flow with grace and remain unobtrusive while avoiding abruptness of any kind. Any attention-commanding device should be avoided. The first requirement is a beautiful, finely wrought line.

It is possible to speak of Palestrina's lines in general terms as having something of an arch concept. This means that the linear high point frequently comes between the middle and two-thirds of the way through a passage with relative lows before and after. However, this should not imply that the line resembles a sine wave, for this is rarely so literally. The lines always have an undulating quality and are rarely disjunct to any significant degree. The arch concept can be extended to Palestrina's rhythmic design because phrases (as entire movements) usually begin with slower values, are more active in the internal sections, and resolve with slower values at the end. The smaller the value, the more strictly one must interpret the guiding principles. In a setting where relatively long values (e.g., half notes) are the smallest values present, they must be treated with greater care.

Text underlay is of critical importance because of the basic premise for this music. Its meaning and impact must never be lost but, rather, must be enhanced by the musical setting. Consequently the rhythmic placement of the text is of paramount importance. Each syllable or word must always be heard distinctly.

Line, rhythm, and text treatment must be mastered before success can be attained with the contrapuntal practices of this sophisticated and intricate compositional style. Students should not proceed to the next chapter until they can confidently deal with the problems posed in this chapter.

palestrina: part two

Palestrina's polyphonic style is subject to the same principles delineated in the last chapter as primary considerations in the design of line, the use of rhythm, and the setting of texts. Lines must be combined to produce the smoothest possible effect. Unclear, abrupt, awkward, or overly dramatic effects must be avoided. The rhythmic effect of the total motion of the lines must be as carefully wrought as the rhythm of any single moment in any individual line.

Placing two or more parts together requires a clear understanding of consonance and dissonance. This is not new to our study but because of the strict adherence to certain practices in Palestrina's style it is extremely important here. These practices (in the same reference of consonance and dissonance with which we have worked) are spelled out in the guidelines that follow. Students are alerted to their importance and advised to learn them well.

Two-Voice Counterpoint

It is the practice in two-voice counterpoint to begin and end on perfect consonances. When a cantus firmus is used in the upper voice, the perfect fifth should not be used to begin or end.

Contrary motion is generally preferred, but both oblique and parallel motion are used with care and discretion. However, special attention should be paid to the fact that parallel motion between unisons, perfect fifths, or perfect octaves is strictly forbidden. This practice holds true in many styles, most notably in Johann Sebastian Bach's chorale style. It has frequently bemused the author that this one practice seems persistently to cause more students more trouble than any other aspect of the styles of Palestrina and Bach. It is hoped that if students are alerted to the problem, the road may be a little smoother if the problem and the rationale for its adoption by two giants in the field of contrapuntal composition are fully understood.

Parallel motion, as described above and demonstrated in Example 17.1, tends to destroy the sense of linear independence because of the basic acoustical relationship existing between two members of a fifth or octave (and, of course, unison). The color changes inherent in all other intervals make it possible for occasional parallelisms to occur without injuring the sense of linear

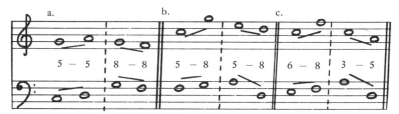

Example 17.1. Forbidden Parallel and Similar Motion.

independence of the participating lines. Extensive parallel writing of any kind will certainly weaken linear independence; but with perfect consonances, even a single instance of parallel motion has a dramatic, stultifying effect. Even when the motion is not strictly perfect-to-perfect (as shown in c. above) but *similar* motion to the interval of a perfect fifth, octave, or unison, it is considered undesirable. There is one exception to the last point — when the upper voice moves by step and the lower moves by skip.

The parallel and similar motion to which the preceding remarks were principally directed is the motion in two-part, or more than two-part, music in which the *outer* parts or *adjacent* parts have the relationships described. When three or more parts are used, the variables increase (the more parts, the more opportunities for taking freedoms) and some parallel motion is possible if it is unobtrusive (e.g., when the activity of a third part is strong enough to negate the effect of parallelism which may be present in two other voice parts).

Consecutive fifths, octaves, and unisons are not acceptable even when approached from the opposite direction. Hidden (or "covered") unisons, fifths, or octaves are forbidden except for the following infrequent instances:

a. When they are unavoidable in an imitative passage (this exception should
   not be interpreted too liberally);

b. When one voice (normally the upper) moves by step.

Unisons, fifths, or octaves should be avoided on successive, accented quarter notes (i.e., on adjacent beats). These same intervals should be avoided on successive, accented half notes. See Example 17.2.

Example 17.2. Successive Unisons, Fifths, and Octaves (Unacceptable Motion).

Unisons are permitted as the first and last intervals and, in whole-note motion, no others are permitted. In half-note motion, unisons are permitted on weak beats. Greater freedom is permitted in quarter-note motion where they may be used on weak beats and afterbeats.

When two different forms of the same note (e.g., C and C#) appear in two different parts on adjacent beats (or in otherwise strong positions in close proximity), they are forbidden. This practice is referred to as "cross relation" and is considered undesirable in many styles of contrapuntal and harmonic composition.

Voice parts may cross freely, but adjacent voices should remain within the interval of a tenth. An exception to the latter point is commonly found between the bass and tenor, where a larger spread is considered desirable (once again referring to basic acoustics).

It is not considered desirable to have more than four parallel sixths or thirds consecutively. Simultaneous skips in the same direction may not include fifths or minor sixths.

Imitation is widely used in this style. However, in the Gloria and the Credo of the Mass, owing to their longer texts and typically homophonic textures, it is not used as frequently. Imitation may take the form of strict canonic writing or it may appear as a free suggestion of a given line. Imitation is commonly used to begin sections but may be used freely at any point within a composition.

Dissonance Treatment

All augmented and diminished intervals (seconds, fourths, sevenths, and their octave transpositions) are considered dissonant intervals. The fourth is treated as a dissonance except when it is introduced on a weak beat over a stationary bass and tied to the next strong beat, where it assumes a stronger dissonant role by a change of the bass note and is resolved appropriately. The resolution must be in accordance with the demands of its second and strongest dissonant role as shown in Example 17.3.

Example 17.3. Fourth as a Relative Consonance.

Half notes may not be dissonant in a note-against-note style. Unaccented half notes may be dissonant when they follow a whole note or a suspended note. A dissonant note is never of longer value than a half note, nor is it approached by a value shorter than itself.

Dissonance must be approached and left by step. The single exception to this practice is the *nota cambiata*, a quarter-note dissonance approached by step from above, left by a descending skip of a third, and resolved up by step. The second of the four notes is the dissonant note and in effect receives an embellished resolve. The dissonant tone must fall on an unaccented portion of a measure and must be a quarter note. If the third note of a cambiata figure is a quarter note, it must be followed by another quarter note. This dissonant treatment is demonstrated in Example 17.4.

Example 17.4. Nota Cambiata.

Passing dissonances may appear only as half notes on a weak beat or as quarter notes on the weak portion of a beat. Accented passing notes are not permitted, except that either (but not both) of two quarter notes descending from an accented half note may be dissonant, thus allowing the first (when it appears as the dissonant quarter) to be an accented passing tone.

The third member of an accented group (i.e., beginning on a strong beat) of four stepwise, descending quarter notes may be dissonant if it causes a suspension in another voice and if the fourth quarter note is followed by its upper second (as in Example 17.5).

Suspensions are prepared by a tie to a preceding, unaccented, consonant note. They normally fall on half notes which must be on strong beats and re-

Example 17.5. Accented Passing Notes (Acceptable Forms).

Example 17.6. Typical Suspensions.

solved downward by step. The accompanying voice does not have to wait for the resolution of the suspension. Embellishments may be used in the resolution of suspensions. See Example 17.6.

Suspensions occasionally fall on quarter notes which must be on weak beats (never on afterbeats), are prepared by a tie to a preceding half note, and are resolved by step, either up or down, to a quarter note. All suspensions must resolve to imperfect consonances.

Anticipations are unaccented quarter-note dissonances approached by step from a quarter note or dotted half note above. The resolution is a repetition of the dissonant note as a consonant member of the following strong beat.

Lower neighboring-tone quarter notes are permitted on afterbeats. Upper neighboring-tone quarter notes are seldom used and then only when immediately preceding half notes or whole notes. Melodically the upper neighboring tone should be a semitone, if possible.

Double counterpoint (two-part invertible counterpoint), although of greater importance and more widely used in the Baroque era, may be found in Palestrina's works (also triple and quadruple counterpoint). Double counterpoint may be written at the octave, tenth, or twelfth. It is composed so that the upper part will work as well if its position is inverted with the lower. It is used to produce variety with the same material later in a composition. The intervals in double counterpoint at the octave may be determined by lining up two sets of intervals in reverse order (underlined intervals remain consonant when inverted):

$$1\ \underline{2}\ \underline{3}\ 4\ 5\ \underline{6}\ 7\ \underline{8}$$
$$\underline{8}\ 7\ \underline{6}\ 5\ 4\ \underline{3}\ 2\ \underline{1}$$

The same procedure may be followed for double counterpoint at the interval of the tenth or the twelfth (numbering 1-10 or 1-12 respectively). A passage in double counterpoint at the octave is given in Example 17.7.

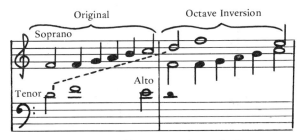

Example 17.7. Double Counterpoint at the Octave.

Three (and More) Voice Counterpoint

In the Palestrina style, the greater the number of voices one works with, the greater the amount of freedom one has, and, in some respects, the easier the process becomes. Although the guidelines suggested to this point remain in force beyond the limitations of two-part writing, in the context in which they have been presented, some of them can be interpreted more liberally when three and more parts are employed.

The guidelines that follow supplement and, in some instances, modify the preceding ones.

Regardless of how many voices are used, each is always completely independent. However, the amount of imitation between voices increases as the number of voices increases.

In three-part writing it is generally desirable to use as many complete triads as possible — in either root position or first inversion. The second inversion triad is not acceptable, owing to the dissonance of a fourth which results with the lowest sounding part. The more voices employed, the more essential is the use of full triads throughout the composition.

As indicated earlier, the more voices there are, the greater the amount of freedom possible; but whether or not momentary liberty may be taken is always determined by the amount of "coverage" provided by other voices. The musical results (interpreted strictly within the principles of this style) should always determine if the guidelines are to be interpreted freely. At no time should such liberties be numerous or lengthy.

Dissonances are always conceived in terms of the lowest sounding part. Tritones are acceptable between any combination of the upper voices but never in relationship to the bass. A skip into and out of a dissonant tone is accept-

Example 17.8. Skip into and out of a Dissonance.

able if that tone is doubled in another voice and is resolved properly in that voice. See Example 17.8.

A fourth above the lowest sounding part that enters on a weak beat, is suspended to a strong beat when it creates a sharper dissonance with another voice, and resolves properly in relationship to the two voices is acceptable and is called a *consonant fourth*. See Example 17.9.

A composition may begin and/or end with a complete root-position triad. In such instances the major third is preferred over the minor. Compositions may begin on a unison, open-fifth, or root-position triad. They may end on a unison, open-fifth, or root-position triad, or a triad without a fifth.

Unisons are acceptable between any two voices when they are approached and left correctly and when three or more voices are singing. All voices may meet on a unison only at the very beginning or the very end. Hidden fifths and octaves are acceptable between the outer voices when the upper moves by step. Adjacent voices may move by hidden fifths or octaves when three or more voices are employed.

Simultaneous skips in the same direction may not include fifths or minor sixths when in the outer voices and when all voices are moving in the same direction. But simultaneous skips in the same direction including fourths or larger intervals (except octaves) are acceptable when they occur between adjacent voices and when three or more voices are used.

Concluding Observations

Over one hundred recommendations or guidelines have been provided in the form of an introduction to Palestrina's style. Careful adherence to them will enable students to simulate quite closely the music of this composer.

Example 17.9. Consonant Fourth.

However, student effort will be lifeless and ineffective, even if totally "correct," if a musical stylistic sensitivity is not brought to the compositional effort. It is possible to compose correct lines that do not reflect a sense of good taste in the style. At the same time it is relatively easy to define the correctness of a line but infinitely more difficult to express what it may be that constitutes "good taste."

Palestrina's style is in many ways sharply defined. However, in practice the guidelines are seldom followed literally and the style is embued with endless subtleties, reinterpretations, and graceful, unpredictable twists. A strong imitative beginning may dissolve into remotely related linear contours or totally free counterpoint. A rhythm may be expanded or compressed by a single beat to reorient the relationship between two lines. Intervals of the imitation may change but clearly retain the intended logic and sense of the imitation. This can be seen even in canonic passages where a third becomes a second or a fourth as a single departure in an otherwise strict set of relationships, or a fourth answers a fifth at the outset of an imitation.

The strictness and clarity of this style should not be interpreted as rigidity. The fluidity referred to much earlier in our discussion is the trait we must most vigorously pursue. An intensive study of the works of Palestrina (not limited to the Masses) is essential to understand fully the breadth and subtlety of his style. Such a study would reveal the high degree to which his adherence to the guidelines pervades his music. But, more important, the principles and spirit of the style, which are so much more elusive, would be more fully recognized and assimilated for a complete understanding of and success with these compositional practices.

Summary

With the closing of our discussion of Palestrina's style, we complete our study of the principal compositional styles of the Middle Ages and Renaissance. Palestrina's style is the embodiment and refinement of compositional evolution in the entire period during which modality was the principal unifying force for all structural pitch relationships.

In the works of Palestrina there is a profound concern with each minute relationship but, at the same time, an omnipresent awareness of totality, of the significant contribution that each moment makes to the broad architectural design and the final artistic impact.

Palestrina's two-part writing appears as brief moments in extended works for three and more parts (more frequently for four and five parts). Yet it is the two-part writing that demands the greatest discipline, and it is from the two-part practices that the compositional decisions about the greater number of parts derive. The fewer the number of voice parts, the more strictly must the guidelines be followed. In the same manner the smaller the rhythmic values, the more strictly must the relationships be treated.

The singular purpose for the existence of this music was probably more carefully articulated for Palestrina's style than for any other known composer. It was to glorify God through the use of the sacred texts of the Bible and the songs of the Mass. The text was of primary importance and the music had to remain subservient to it. In aspiring to achieve this goal Palestrina developed and polished a compositional style more severely constricted than most others throughout history but one that, remarkably, gave the effect of musical fluidity and freedom.

summary, conclusions, and new directions

In this final chapter I am concerned with pulling together the diverse elements of the evolutionary forces of the approximately six hundred years encompassed by our study. However specific and detailed it may have seemed, it cannot be emphasized strongly enough that we have barely skimmed the surface of a vast and complicated subject. Although the study has provided insights into the evolution of our musical heritage and assistance to the aspiring musician who is acquiring rudimentary analytical and compositional technique, it can have provided only a point of departure for the achievement of a comprehensive understanding of the historical process. It is essential therefore that a foundation for the pursuit of such studies into the music of the seventeenth century be provided.

Two of the most important and exciting phenomena in the history of music which are interrelated and upon which our study of the compositional practices of the Middle Ages and Renaissance depended, occurred in the earliest centuries of the Middle Ages — the development of a viable notational system and the adoption of a controlled multi-voice-part technique of musical composition. All early contrapuntal musical decisions were dependent upon the possibilities inherent in the notation available. As notation became more flexible, the compositional process became more independent of it. The earliest problem was simply the graphic definition of abstract sound. This accomplished, the difficulty of defining the infinite possibilities of distributing sound through time became the principal notational problem — one that still involves more than the passing attention of composers. A clear evolution from the conventions of the rhythmic modes, through Franconian, Ars Nova, and white mensural notations can be traced. Each provided greater flexibility and more possibilities than those that preceded it. Refinements of the later centuries deal with such details as the accurate placement of text to music, the score layout, the shapes of notes, and eventually the introduction of bar lines and ties. Each of these was demanded by the music, and each, in turn, provided greater possibilities for the composer.

Tablature notation, which has had no more than passing reference in this volume, remains beyond the purview of our study. However, students should recognize that several different forms of tablature notation were used for instrumental music and that as instrumental music became increasingly independent of vocal music, and as it increased in its own contrapuntal complexity and began to be treated in ensemble settings in the later Renaissance, the use of tablature notation diminished and vocal notation was adopted for all Western music.

The main body of our study has been concerned with contrapuntal practices. However, counterpoint is the result of relating two or more lines to each other. To succeed in this process, one must begin by developing an ability to compose artistic lines. Historically this is represented by the vast, exquisite monophonic literature which precedes the first efforts at controlled multipart music. It is my opinion that it is impossible to write effective counterpoint in any style if one is not able to compose well-designed lines.

The first tentative efforts at multipart composition immediately revealed the need for making aesthetic decisions about the relationship of the parts. The tiny detail in organum that the perfect fifth or fourth became a tritone if it was not altered at the appropriate point in the composition and that the tritone was "offensive" was an acoustical taste decision that affected the entire evolution of Western music and immediately indicated the minutiae with which we were to be concerned. This kind of microcosmic concern vividly reflects Western mentality, which has brought us both the rewards represented by reaching the moon and the problems of the magnitude of environmental deterioration, resulting from the technology of a throw-away society which has had so disruptive an ecological impact in so many ways.

The gradual recognition of the inherent differences between intervals and the varying degrees of acceptability and the differing musical functions associated with them is a part of the process that has continued throughout music history. One result of this process has been that varying roles and judgments of taste have been associated with specific styles. The definition of individual contrapuntal styles often relies heavily on the treatment of vertical intervals and their function in relationship to each other.

Composers recognized quite early that as lines became independent the ear needed references to assist it in interpreting the intended artistic logic and meaning. A wide variety of devices serving a multitude of architectural and expressive functions were gradually devised, and they imposed their own evolutionary influences. Although I do not intend to imply a literal progression from one technique or device to another, this possibility cannot be ignored and must be assumed to have occurred at some point for some techniques. The following progressions are indicative of such possibilities:

1. Stimmtausch to canon (in its various forms) to imitative counterpoint to such imitative forms as the ricercare and the sixteenth-century motet;
2. Sustained tenor lines (cantus firmus) under melismatic or neumatic upper lines to isorhythm, to mensurated cantus firmus polyphony, eventually to the passacaglia of the Baroque.

Other techniques contributed to the compositional sense of order and variety, but their evolutionary relationships are not as apparent (if present at all): hocket, text painting, fauxbourdon, and invertible counterpoint.

Musical forms did not evolve independently. Since this music was almost exclusively vocal, it was very dependent on the text. Consequently throughout the period covered in this book, the poetic forms had the greatest influence on the broad musical design. Dimensions of the music broadened with the greater complexity of compositional technique. A variety of devices were used to distinguish large sections (e.g., the several imitative subsections of a sixteenth-century motet). Some new poetic forms developed, but more often old forms were refined or modified. Abstract architectural designs remained, for the most part, unknown until the latter part of the sixteenth century when instrumental music began to attract more attention and assume more independence from vocal music. One clear example of an evolved form of a much earlier poetic design was the one-stanza bergerette directly derived from the virelai.

One musical dimension far exceeds all others in its importance for the music of subsequent centuries. The evolution of definable harmonic relationships can be traced throughout this entire modal era. Although the significance of harmonic relationships was clearly sensed and pursued by composers during these centuries, it was not until the three succeeding centuries that the full significance and potential of these forces were explored.

The early concern with vertical relationships cannot accurately be considered an indication of harmonic awareness, for implicit in any discussion of harmony is the recognition of the horizontal motion demanded by vertical combinations. Decisions by early theorists and composers resulted more from concern with dissonance between distinct lines than from awareness of the forward motion which might have been inherent in that dissonance. However, one point in compositions that demanded the attention of composers – the cadence – presented harmonic questions even in polyphonic music.

The earliest widely adopted cadence in free two-part polyphony was the leading-tone cadence. The critical decision of adopting an altered tone to produce a more convincing resolution at points where this was required reflects the first distinct acknowledgment of harmonic demands in an otherwise exclusively polyphonic literature.

As three-voice writing gained favor, the leading-tone cadence continued to be the principal form of final resolve. In this context its third component reflected an even greater awareness of harmonic forces since the resulting triad was a first-inversion diminished chord. This chord embodies the tritone, one of the strongest components for harmonic motion in the entire subsequent tonal (harmonic) period. Although this interval had been rejected as *diabolus in musica* in earlier styles (e.g., organum), in the three- and four-voiced counterpoint of the thirteenth and succeeding centuries it became a vital element in a large percentage of the cadences.

The strongest basic chord in tonal music is the dominant chord with an added seventh. This chord, built on the fifth degree of any given scale, is almost fully realized in the three-voice, leading-tone, cadential triad. The only tone missing is the root of the chord which remains a vital element but only irregularly employed through the Middle Ages. However, throughout the Renaissance increasing use was made of that chord in root position, with a variety of other full root-position triads which began to assume harmonic relationships to each other. It is in the more extended preparation of cadences that these relationships become most apparent. I shall return to this shortly.

A second distinctive, three-voiced, cadential pattern gained considerable favor during this same period (the fourteenth century). It was derived from the leading-tone cadence and was called the Landini cadence. This cadential pattern has one important additional component (the sixth degree of the scale just before the final) that changes the character of the resolve from what we have subsequently identified as a dominant/tonic cadence to a subdominant/tonic cadence. The former is represented by root progression numbering V-I (fifth to first degree of the scale) and the latter by IV-I. These two cadential formulas subsequently became the primary harmonic pillars around which all tonal relationships of later periods radiate.

The evolution of basic cadential patterns through the 600 years with which we are concerned (1000-1600) can, in light of the preceding remarks, be summarized in the accompanying tabulation. As suggested earlier, lists such as this should not be interpreted rigidly. If the *spirit* of the interpretation of the evolutionary process is understood, this tabulation should be of considerable assistance to students who are attempting to understand the concepts involved in the evolution of ideas.

Toward the V^7-I	*Toward the IV-I*
Leading-tone (two voice)	Leading-tone (two voice)
Leading-tone (three voice)	Leading-tone (three voice)
Double leading-tone	Landini (under-third)
Octave-leap (Burgundian)	Double Landini
V-I	ii-I
V^7-I	IV-I

Example 18.1 demonstrates the cadences listed in the above tabulation for quick reference. These cadences reflect a vital aspect of the evolution of harmonic thinking, for the one position in a polyphonic context where the force of harmonic motion cannot be ignored is at points of resolve. However, by the late sixteenth century progressions of chords leading into the cadence and internal progressions of chords began to be intrinsically important, and the polyphonic concept of composition gradually lost its authoritative position in the composer's vocabulary. Chromatic alterations were used with increasing freedom and frequency, which brought the cadential harmonic relationships to internal chord patterns and provided for more remote or commanding progressions of chords.

Progressions such as those we looked at in earlier chapters (e.g., Example 15.3) began to assume greater importance in musical conception in the transition from modal to tonal thinking. This is especially apparent in the treatment of and motion toward cadences, and it becomes increasingly prevalent throughout compositions or large portions thereof. In a work such as the *Missa Sine Nomine*, which we considered in the discussion of Palestrina, almost every principal cadence consists of the progression iv-V-I. This is true in many works of the period and reveals the strong harmonic awareness that an-

Example 18.1. Principal Cadences of the Middle Ages and Renaissance.

ticipated the final affirmation of tonality in the Baroque.

In any study of harmony that must use as a point of departure the music of the Baroque, a more subtle set of relationships exists which, considered at length, is beyond the purview of the present study. However, it is appropriate that a few remarks be offered about substitute chords since even this more subtle harmonic phenomenon was clearly recognized by composers of the Renaissance.

For every chord in a tonally conceived composition there is another chord that can be used to produce a similar effect while providing some variation from the quality of the reference chord. The basic triads of I, IV, and V are used as reference chords, each of which has its own single or several possible substitute chords. The alternative triads can serve the same function and provide the basic effect of the principals, but they produce different strength and quality in that role. For example, the substitute for the IV chord is the ii chord. It can be used in place of the IV chord in approaching a V chord at a cadence (and frequently is). When used in that fashion, it will normally appear in first inversion, i.e., the third (middle tone) of the chord is in the lowest sounding part. In that position the bottom tone is the fourth degree of the scale, and it produces the same harmonic bass motion as does the IV chord in root position. The quality change results because in a major tonality, the IV chord is a major triad and the ii chord is minor. Similar relationships exist for the other principal triads.

Clear use of substitute chords in the music of the Renaissance, although not widespread, is prevalent and reflects composers' harmonic awareness well in advance of the arrival of the Baroque. It would also be possible to explore the moderate amount of harmonically conceived chromaticism used (especially by secular composers) throughout the sixteenth century. However, a greater understanding of the operations of harmonic relationships and the harmonic implications of alterations would be necessary than is required for this study. It would be better if interested students returned to these questions in greater depth after they studied the principles of harmony more intensively.

We have sampled a vast, rich music literature and have begun to uncover the characteristics that provide the sophistication, subtlety, and refinement of a highly developed, expressive art form. But the study has only begun. Students have been provided only with basics and with a rudimentary sense of the directions in which further study may be pursued. It is hoped that the appetites and interests of students have been sufficiently whetted so that they will return to this literature with the enthusiasm it commands and for the rich rewards it has to offer.

notes and bibliography

notes

Chapter 1

1. For a more extended discussion of plainsong square notation, see the introductory chapter, "Rules for Interpretation," in the *Liber Usualis*, p. xvii.

2. The only medieval theorist to use Greek names was Walter Odington (c. 1300), according to Willi Apel (*Harvard Dictionary of Music*, Harvard University Press, 1944).

3. The virga originally indicated a relatively higher pitch and the punctus a relatively lower one.

4. For an excellent discussion of the more subtle aspects of this notation, see Carl Parrish, *The Notation of Medieval Music*, Chapter 2; and Willi Apel, *Notation of Polyphonic Music*, Chapter 3.

Chapter 2

1. Some authors believe that the concept of forward motion conflicts with the spirit of plainsong, contending that it was never meant to go anywhere. I cannot accept this position. When different pitches are chosen and when they take place in time, a sense of direction results.

Chapter 3

1. The complete text for the Ordinary of the Mass and translations for each of its sections are provided in the Appendix.

2. Each letter represents a melodic section of the plainsong (upper case letters represent complete textual sections and lower-case letters are subsections within a complete section). A return to a given letter denotes a return to that musical idea.

3. Tropes were never used in the official liturgy.

4. Hereafter, letter representations of form will be used in the following manner: the return of a letter represents a return of the same music (whether a capital or a lower-case letter is used); a lower-case letter indicates that the same music recurs with *different*

text; a capital letter indicates the return of both music and text (e.g., material for a refrain).

5. The group was not a trained or professional ensemble. An informal audience provided the group singing.

Chapter 4

1. Such primitive types of multipart music can still be found in cultures like the Polynesian Islands and India.

2. See Guido's remarks concerning organum, which are given in Chapter IV of Hugo Rieman's, *History of Music Theory*.

3. So that notational considerations do not assume inordinate importance in our discussions, examples will be presented within the confines of the most compatible notations discussed to any given point in this text rather than retaining the original when it is beyond the scope of this study.

Chapter 5

1. Willi Apel, *Notation of Polyphonic Music, 900-1600*, p. 403.

Chapter 7

1. Gustave Reese, *Music in the Middle Ages*, p. 321.
2. *Ibid.*, p. 322.
3. Hugo Rieman, *History of Music Theory*, p. 177.

Chapter 8

1. "If they are called 'forms', it must be with reservation. For it is not so much distinctive formal structure as distinctive style that draws the line between them." See Gustave Reese, *Music in the Middle Ages*, p. 294.
2. *Ibid.*, p. 308.
3. *Ibid.*, p. 311ff.
4. Measure numbers are taken from the score of *Messe de Nostre Dame*, Hans Hübsch, ed.
5. Gustave Reese, *Music in the Middle Ages*, p. 357.

Chapter 9

1. W. Thomas Marrocco, *Fourteenth-Century Italian Cacce*, p. xii.
2. *Ibid.*, p. xii.

Chapter 10

1. Gustave Reese, *Music in the Renaissance*, p. xiii.
2. For a more extensive discussion of this subject, students are referred to Willi Apel's *Notation of Polyphonic Music, 900-1600*, pp. 368ff.
3. Willi Apel, *French Secular Music of the Late Fourteenth Century*, p. 12.
4. *Ibid.*, p. 13.
5. Dom A. Hughes and G. Abraham, *New Oxford History of Music*, Vol. III, p. 142.
6. For an excellent and more comprehensive study of the music of this period, see Willi Apel, *French Secular Music of the Late Fourteenth Century*.
7. *Ibid.*, p. 31.

Chapter 12

1. A table of principal dissonances considered in this study is provided in the Appendix.

Chapter 14

1. *Liber Usualis*, p. 957.

Chapter 15

1. Gustave Reese, *Music in the Renaissance*, p. 288.

2. *Ibid.*, p. 289.

3. Clement Janequin, *Chansons Polyphoniques*, vol. III.

4. Gustave Reese, *Music in the Renaissance*, p. 312.

5. *Ibid.*, p. 316.

6. *Ibid.*, p. 323.

7. Hermann Zenck and Walter Gerstenberg, eds. *Corpus Mensurablis Musicae, Adrian Willaert, Opera Omnia.*

8. Gustave Reese, *Music in the Renaissance*, p. 332.

9. *Ibid.*, p. 332.

BIBLIOGRAPHY

Books

Abraham, Gerald. *Oxford History of Music*, vol. IV, *Age of Humanism, 1540-1630*. London: Oxford University Press, 1968.

Apel, Willi. *French Secular Music of the Late Fourteenth Century*. Cambridge, Mass.: The Mediaeval Academy of America, 1950.

Apel, Willi. *Gregorian Chant*. Bloomington: Indiana University Press, 1958.

Apel, Willi. *Notation of Polyphonic Music, 900-1600*. Fifth ed. Cambridge, Mass.: The Mediaeval Academy of America, 1953.

Blume, Friedrich. *Renaissance and Baroque Music*. New York: W. W. Norton, 1967.

Brown, Howard M. *Instrumental Music Printed before 1600*. Cambridge, Mass.: Harvard University Press, 1965.

Bryden, John R., and Hughes, David G. *An Index of Gregorian Chant*. Cambridge, Mass.: Harvard University Press, 1969.

Bukofzer, Manfred. *Music of the Baroque Era*. New York: W. W. Norton, 1947.

Bukofzer, Manfred. *Studies in Medieval and Renaissance Music*. New York: W. W. Norton, 1950.

Crocker, Richard. *A History of Musical Style*. New York: McGraw-Hill, 1966.

Dart, Thurston. *The Interpretation of Music*. London: Hutchinson's University Library, Hutchinson House, 1967.

Donington, Robert. *The Interpretation of Early Music*. London: Faber and Faber, 1963.

Fux, Johann J. *Steps to Parnassus*. New York: W. W. Norton, 1943.

Gennrich, Friederich. *Formenlehre des Mittelalterlichen Liedes*. Halle: Max Niemeyer Verlag, 1932.

Goldron, Romain. *Music of the Renaissance*. New York: H. S. Stuttman, 1968.

Haar, James, ed. *Chanson and Madrigal, 1480-1530*. Cambridge, Mass.: Harvard University Press, 1964.

Hughes, Dom Anselm. *The New Oxford History of Music*, vol. II. London: Oxford University Press, 1967.

Hughes, Dom Anselm, and Abraham, Gerald. *The New Oxford History of Music*, vol. III. London: Oxford University Press, 1964.

Jeppesen, Knud. *Counterpoint*. Englewood Cliffs, N.J.: Prentice Hall, 1939.

Jeppesen, Knud. *The Style of Palestrina and the Dissonance*. London: Oxford University Press, 1927.

La Rue, Jan. *Aspects of Medieval and Renaissance Music*. New York: W. W. Norton, 1966.

Lang, Paul H. *Music in Western Civilization*. New York: W. W. Norton, 1941.

Parrish, Carl. *The Notation of Medieval Music*. New York: W. W. Norton, 1959.

Reese, Gustave. *Music in the Middle Ages*. New York: W. W. Norton, 1940.

Reese, Gustave. *Music in the Renaissance*. New York: W. W. Norton, 1954.

Rieman, Hugo. *History of Music Theory*. Lincoln: University of Nebraska Press, 1962.

Seay, Albert. *Music in the Medieval World*. Englewood Cliffs, N.J.: Prentice-Hall, 1965.

Strunk, Oliver. *Source Readings in Music History*. New York: W. W. Norton, 1965.

Sunol, Dom Gregory. *Text Book of Gregorian Chant*, 1930. G. M. Durford, translator. First ed., 1905.

Thomson, James C. *Music through the Renaissance*. Dubuque, Iowa: William C. Brown, 1968.

Waite, William G. *The Rhythm of Twelfth Century Polyphony*. New Haven: Yale University Press, 1954.

Music Collections and Facsimiles

Aubry, Pierre. *Cent Motets du XIIIe siècle* (vol. I, facsimile of Bamberg, Ed. IV 6), 3 vols. Paris: Rouart and Lerolle, 1908.

Aubry, Pierre. *Le Chansonnier de l'Arsenal* (facsimile of MS 5198, Bibliothèque de l'Arsenal). Paris: Geuthner, 1909.

Aubry, Pierre. *Le Roman de Fauvel* (facsimile of MS français 146. Bibliothèque Nationale de Paris). Paris: Geuthner, 1907.

Baxter, J. H. *An Old St. Andrews Music Book* (facsimile of Wolfenbüttel 677). London: Oxford University Press, 1931.

Beck, Jean. *Les Chansonniers des Troubadours et des Trouveres* (facsimile and modern edition). Philadelphia: University of Pennsylvania Press, 1927.

Casimiri, Raffaele, ed. *Le Opere Complete di Giovanni Pierluigi Palestrina*, vol. IV. Rome: Edizione Fratelli Scalera, 1939.

Dart, Thurston. *Invitation to Medieval Music*, vol. I. London: Stainer and Bell, 1967.

Davidson, A. T., and Apel, Willi. *Historical Anthology of Music*, vol. I. Cambridge, Mass.: Harvard University Press, 1954.

Dittmer, Luther A. *Madrid 20486* (facsimile). New York: Institute of Medieval Music, 1957.

Dittmer, Luther A. *Wolfenbüttel 1099* (facsimile). New York: Institute of Medieval Music, 1960.

Ellinwood, Leonard. *The Works of Francesco Landini*, Cambridge, Mass.: The Mediaeval Academy of America, 1939.

Frere, Walter H. *Graduale Sarisburiense*. West Mead, Eng.: Gregg Press, 1966.

Frere, Walter H. *The Winchester Troper*, vol. VIII. Henry Bradshaw Society, 1884.

Gleason, Harold. *Examples of Music before 1400*. New York: Appleton-Century-Crofts, 1942.

Hübsch, Hans, ed. *Messa de Nostre Dame*. Heidelberg: Willy Müller Süddeutscher Musicverlag (Novello, sole agents), 1953.

Husman, Heinrich. *Anthology of Music, Mediaeval Polyphony*. Cologne: Arno Volk Verlag, 1962.

Jeanroy, Alfred. *Le Chansonnier D'Arras* (facsimile). Paris: Societe des Anciens Textes Français, 1925.

Ludwig, Friedrich. *Guillaume de Machaut, Musikalische Werke*. Leipzig: Breitkopf and Härtel, 1954.

Marrocco, W. T. *Italian Cacce of the Fourteenth Century*. Cambridge, Mass.: The Mediaeval Academy of America, 1962.

Merritt, A. Tillman, and Lesure, François. *Clement Janequin. Chanson Polyphoniques*. Monaco: Editions de L'Oiseau-Lyre, Les Remparts, 1965.

Parrish, Carl. *A Treasury of Early Music*. New York: W. W. Norton, 1958.

Rokseth, Yvonne. *Polyphonies de XIIIe siècle* (facsimile of Montpellier Faculty des Medecins, H. 196). Paris: L'Oiseau-Lyre, 1935-1939.

Schrade, Leo, ed. *Polyphonic Music of the Fourteenth Century*, vols. I-IV. Monaco: Editions de L'Oiseau-Lyre, 1956.

Starr, W. J., and Devine, G. F. *Music Scores Omnibus*, vol. I. Englewood Cliffs, N.J.: Prentice-Hall, 1964.

Wolf, J. *Geschichte der Mensuralnotation von 1250-1460*, vols. I-III. Leipzig: Breitkopf and Härtel, 1904.

Zenck, Hermann, and Gerstenberg, Walter, eds. *Corpus Mensurablis Musicae, Adrian Willaert, Opera Omnia*. Dallas, Texas: American Institute of Musicology, 1966.

Manuscripts

All the following manuscripts were consulted at the British Museum, London, and have contributed to this volume in varying degrees. They are given below, with a brief comment about each, to provide students with some awareness of the nature of available sources. Each manuscript is identified by a name and number that indicate the collection of which it is a part.

Add. 5665, fifteenth-sixteenth centuries, the manuscript includes some red notes and the fermata, and consists of a collection of duets by anonymous English composers.

Add. 15102, c. 1487, a miracle play using Gothic notation on five-line staves; the F and occasionally the C lines are in red.

Add. 16975, thirteenth-fourteenth centuries, contains several hymns in two voice parts notated in square and diamond-shaped notes on staves of four or five red lines each.

Add. 29987, fourteenth-century Italian compositions in a fifteenth-sixteenth century manuscript which uses Italian notation, including open black, half black and half white, and red notes for cacce and istampida.

Add. 30091, thirteenth-century manuscript including motets and duets.

Add. 31922, a fifteenth-century manuscript with a set of rounds from the time of King Henry VIII.

Add. 34200, early fifteenth century, set in white mensural notation for three-voice chansons (anonymous) and includes an explanation of mensural symbols set in a circular diagram.

Add. 36881, twelfth-century, St. Martial School manuscript which uses four-line staves *scratched* on velum. This is a collection of mostly two-part Sequences and tropes.

Arundel 14, thirteenth-fourteenth centuries, contains Masses with a Kyrie set in three voice parts.

Arundel 248, early fourteenth century, uses square notation on eight- to ten-line staves for two-voice pieces and twelve- to fifteen-line staves for three-voice pieces. The manuscript contains Sequences and a Hymn.

Arundel 501, twelfth century, neumes set over words for miscellaneous pieces related to Germany.

Burney 357, twelfth-thirteenth centuries, a miscellaneous collection of short theological pieces including a two-voice Sequence.

Cotton, Titus A., xxi, early thirteenth century, contains only six pages of music in a miscellaneous volume of over 280 pages (including a discussion of shipbuilding). These pieces include three-voice Sequences.

Cotton, Titus A., xxvi, c. 1448, a collection of two- and three-voice chansons from northern Italy.

Egerton 274, a twelfth-thirteenth century manuscript which is beautifully illuminated and contains secular pieces, Sequences, and Hymns.

Egerton 2615, mid-thirteenth century, square notation on four red-line staves containing three-voice motets.

Egerton 3307, a fifteenth-century, illuminated manuscript which has been widely discussed in various professional publications.

Harley 746, late fourteenth century, a single song on the flyleaf of a volume not otherwise concerned with music — a very small fragment.

Harley 978, after 1226, square and diamond notes on five red-line staves, containing a variety of works, the most famous of which is *Sumer is icumen in*.

Harley 2942, fifteenth century, a variety of pieces in two and possibly more voices.

Harley 4664, early fourteenth century, set on two staves with four red lines each, includes a double-canon treatment of the Hymn *Nunc sancte* . . .

appendix

appendix

PERFORMANCE DIRECTIONS AND RHYTHMIC SYMBOLS
(ACCORDING TO THE SOLESMES INTERPRETATION)

I. *Directions*

Numerals: At the beginning of the chant, indicate the mode of the chant. Antiphons also have a letter (e.g., 8,G), which indicates the ending to be used for the psalm tone.

Asterisk: (*) Indicates change from cantor (soloist) to choir.

Repeat signs: (ij or iij) Direct the singer to perform the preceding phrase two or three times, respectively.

Custos (or guides): (✔) Small note guides at the end of a line alerting the singer to the first note of the next line.

Flat: Bb carries through a word or to the first bar line (irrespective of length) following its appearance. It may be presented at the beginning of a chant as a signature altering all B's in the piece unless they are otherwise adjusted.

II. *Rhythmic Signs*

Bar lines:

Quarter bar   Smallest melodic division — end of an incise.

Half bar   End of part of a phrase — performed with a slight ritard.

Full bar   End of a phrase (with diminuendo and ritard and a short pause before proceeding to the next phrase).

Double bar   End of a chant or section, or alternation of choirs.

247

Ictus: (′) A vertical episima that is a guide to note groupings but *not* an accent. It never occurs on consecutive single notes. It is the first note of every neume except the Salicus, where it is the second.

Horizontal episima: (–) Indicates a slight lengthening of a note and may be placed under or over the symbol. When placed under the Podatus, only the lower note is lengthened, as below.

Dot: (.) The dot approximately doubles the value of any note preceding it.

Repeated notes: (Without syllable change.) The note repeated is simply sustained for double its value (as with the Pressus).

BASIC LITURGICAL CALENDAR REFERENCES, THE MASS, AND PRINCIPAL CHANT BOOKS

The Liturgical Day (Divine Offices or Canonical Hours)
    Matins (at night, e.g., at midnight)
    Laude (at sunrise, e.g., 3 A.M.)
    Prime (6 A.M.)
    Terce (9 A.M.)
    Sext (12 noon)
    None (3 P.M.)
    Vespers (at sundown, e.g., at 6 P.M.)
    Complines (at nightfall, e.g., 9 P.M.)

The Liturgical Week

Dominica (originally Feria I)	Sunday
Feria II	Monday
Feria III	Tuesday
Feria IV	Wednesday
Feria V	Thursday
Feria VI	Friday
Sabbato	Saturday

The Mass (normal form — it changes for special occasions)
    Part of the Mass is sung and part is spoken. In both portions the texts for the Ordinary are fixed (invariable) but the texts for the Proper vary with the occasion.

    Two additional Ordinary chants are used as a prelude and a postlude to the Mass: the *Asperges me* and the *Ite, missa est*, respectively.

Sung		Spoken	
Proper	*Ordinary*	*Proper*	*Ordinary*
Introit (1)			
	Kyrie (2)		
	Gloria (3)		
		Collects (etc.) (4)	
		Epistle (5)	
Gradual (6)			
Alleluia or Tract (7)			
		Gospel (8)	
	Credo (9)		
Offertory (10)			
			Prayers (11)
		Secret (12)	
		Preface (13)	
	Sanctus (14)		
			Canon (15)
			Pater Noster (16)
	Agnus Dei (17)		
Communion (18)			
		Postcommunion (19)	

Note: Numbers in parentheses indicate the position of the section in the order of the Mass.

Principal Liturgical Chant Books

Antiphonale	Chants for the Office (includes the *Vesperale*, which contains music for Vespers).
Graduale	Chants for the Mass (includes the *Kyriale*, which contains music for the Ordinary).
Liber Usualis	Contains most chants for both the Office and the Mass. It is the "book for general use."

ORDINARY OF THE MASS

Kyrie eleison

Latin	English
Kyrie eleison.	Lord, have mercy upon us.
Christe eleison.	Christ, have mercy upon us.
Kyrie eleison.	Lord, have mercy upon us.

Gloria in excelsis Deo

Latin	English
Gloria in excelsis Deo.	Glory be to God on high.
Et in terra pax hominibus bonae voluntatis.	And on earth peace, good will toward men.
Laudamus te.	We praise Thee.
Benedicimus te.	We bless Thee.
Adoramus te.	We worship Thee.
Glorificamus te.	We glorify Thee.
Gratias agimus tibi propter magnam gloriam tuam.	We give thanks to Thee for Thy great glory.
Domine Deus, Rex coelestis, Deus Pater omnipotens.	Oh Lord God, heavenly King, God the Father Almighty.
Domine Fili unigenite Jesu Christe	Oh Lord, the only begotten Son, Jesus Christ.
Domine Deus, Agnus Dei, Filius Patris.	Oh Lord God, Lamb of God, Son of the Father.
Qui tollis peccata mundi, miserere nobis.	Who takes away the sins of the world, have mercy upon us.
Qui tollis peccata mundi, suscipe deprecationem nostram.	Who takes away the sins of the world, receive our prayer.
Qui sedes ad dexteram Patris, miserere nobis.	Who sits at the right hand of the Father, have mercy upon us.
Quoniam tu solus sanctus.	For only Thou art holy.
Tu solus Dominus.	Thou only art the Lord.
Tu solus Altissimus, Jesu Christe	Thou only art most high, Oh Christ.
Cum Sancto Spiritu, in gloria Dei Patris.	With the Holy Ghost in the Glory of God the Father.
Amen.	Amen.

Credo in unum Deum

Latin	English
Credo in unum Deum, Patrem potentem, factorem coeli et terrae, visibilium omnium, et invisibilium.	I believe in one God, the Father Almighty, Maker of Heaven and earth, and of all things visible and invisible.
Et in unum Dominum Jesum Christum, Filium Dei unigenitum.	And in one Lord Jesus Christ, the only begotten Son of God.
Et ex Patre natum ante omnia saecula.	Begotten of his Father before all worlds.
Deum de Deo, lumen de lumine, Deum verum de Deo vero.	God of Gods, Light of Lights, Very God of Gods.

Genitum, non factum, consub-
stantialem Patri: per quem
omnia facta sunt.
Qui propter nos homines, et
propter nostram salutem
descendit de coelis.
Et incarnatus est de Spiritu
Sancto ex Maria Virgine:
Et homo factus est.
Crucifixus etiam pro nobis:
sub Pontio Pilato passus,
et sepultus est.
Et resurrexit tertia die,
secundum Scripturas.

Et ascendit in coelum: sedet
ad dexteram Patris.
Et iterum venturas est cum
gloria, judicare, vivos et
mortuos: cujus regni non
erit finis.
Et in Spiritum Sanctum, Dominum,
et vivificantem: qui ex Patre
Filioque procedit.

Qui cum Patre et Filio simul
adoratur, et conglorificatur:
qui locutus est per Prophetas.

Et unum sanctam catholicam et
apostolicam ecclesiam.
Confiteor unum baptisma in
remissionem peccatorum
Et expecto resurrectionem
mortuorum.
Et vitam venturi saeculi.
Amen.

Begotten not made, being of one
substance with the Father, by
whom all things were made.
Who for us men and for our salva-
tion came down from Heaven . . .

And was incarnate by the Holy
Ghost of the Virgin Mary, and
was made man.
He was also crucified for us,
suffered under Pontius Pilate,
and was buried.
And on the third day He arose
again, according to the
Scriptures.
He ascended into Heaven and sits
at the right hand of the Father.
He will come again in glory to
Judge the living and the dead:
and of His Kingdom there will be
no end.
And I believe in the Holy Spirit,
the Lord and the Giver of life,
who proceeds from the Father
and the Son.
Who together with the Father and
the Son is adored and glorified,
and who spoke through the
phrophets.
And one holy, Catholic, and
Apostolic Church.
I confess one baptism for the
forgiveness of sins.
And I await the resurrection of
the dead.
And the life of the world to come.
Amen.

Sanctus, Sanctus, Sanctus

Sanctus, Sanctus, Sanctus Domi-
nus Deus Sabaoth.
Pleni sunt coeli et terra
gloria tua.
Hosanna in excelsis.
Benedictus qui venit in
nomine Domini.
Hosanna in excelsis.

Holy, Holy, Holy Lord God of
Hosts.
Heaven and earth are full of
Thy glory.
Hosanna in the highest.
Blessed is he that cometh in the
name of the Lord.
Hosanna in the highest.

Agnus Dei

Agnus Dei, qui tollis peccata
mundi; miserere nobis.

Agnus Dei, qui tollis peccata
mundi; miserere nobis.

Agnus Dei, qui tollis peccata
mundi; dona nobis pacem.

Oh Lamb of God, who takes away
the sins of the world; have
mercy upon us.

Oh Lamb of God, who takes away
the sins of the world; have
mercy upon us.

Oh Lamb of God, who takes away
the sins of the world; grant
us peace.

THE FOUR PROLATIONS

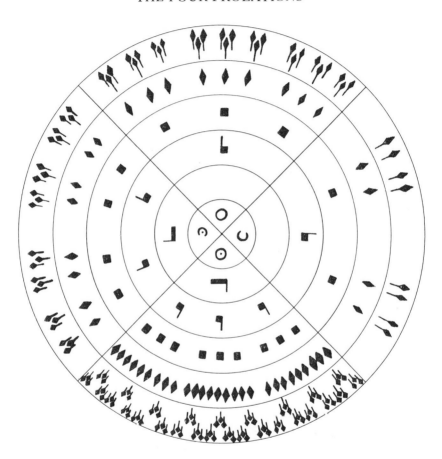

London, British Museum, Add. 34200, fol. 50 ro (excerpt). An attempt in a fifteenth-century manuscript to demonstrate the relationship of the Four Prolations.

NOTATIONAL EVOLUTION IN THE MIDDLE AGES

PLAINSONG (Square)

Period: c. 11th-12th centuries.

Pitch Symbols: Square and diamond neumes on a four-line staff with C and F clefs.

Neumes (examples)

Simple   Compound

● ¶ ⌐ ▪   ▪● ⋈

Strophici   Liquescent

Rhythmic Symbols: None with specific values. The dot and horizontal episema approximately doubled note values. Vertical bars dividing sections suggested conventional ritards. Other rhythmic decisions were left to the judgment of the performer.

Metrical Symbols: None

Rests: None defined, but text phrasings may have produced some between sections.

MODAL (Rhythmic)

Period: c. 12th-13th centuries.

Pitch Symbols: Ligatures derived from plainsong square notation; C and F clefs; staves of four, five, and six lines.

Ligatures (examples)

Binaria   Ternaria   Quarternaria

⌐   ▪   ⌐.   ⌐.

Rhythmic Symbols: Long and short (in respective forms of earlier virga and punctus) and rhythmic modal patterns derived from poetic meters. Position within patterns (ordines) provided values for member notes of ligatures. Entire system was predicated on continuous perfections (three-pulse groups) inherent in the meters (see below).

Metrical Symbols: None. Meter resulted from pulse inherent in each rhythmic mode:

Trochaic ♩ ♪   Iambic   ♪ ♩

Dactylic ♩. ♪ ♩   Anapaestic ♪ ♩ ♩.

Spondaic ♩. ♩. ♩.   Tribrachic ♪ ♪ ♩

Rests: None defined. However, a rest (incise mark) appeared at the end of each ordo according to the remaining value for the particular modal pattern.

FRANCONIAN

Period: c. 1260-1320.

Pitch Symbols: Ligatures derived from plainsong square notation; *C* and *F* clefs; staves of four, five, and six lines.

Ligatures (examples)

Ascending

Descending

Rhythmic Symbols: Longa and breve from Modal notation. Semibreve introduced. Values determined by ligature shape and stem location (e.g., stem left/up equals semibreve pair).

longa

breve

semibreve

Metrical Symbols: None. Meter was predicated on groups of perfections as in Modal notation but was freer (not restricted to modal groupings).

Rests: First system of clearly defined rests, with five rest values (PL, IL, B, MajSB, MinorSB) notated as vertical bars of different lengths.

ARS NOVA

Period: 14th-early 15th centuries.

Pitch Symbols: Several shapes of individual pitches; a few remaining ligatures; same clefs and staves as in earlier periods.

Notes and Ligatures

Maxima   Semibreve

Longa   Minima

Breve

Rhythmic Symbols: Each note shape had its own value related to the system of prolations (see below). The prolation symbols (not widely notated but understood) defined relationships among breves, semibreves and minima.

Metrical Symbols: Associated with the four prolations.

$\odot$ = ♩♩♩ ♩♩♩ ♩♩♩ C = ♩♩♩ ♩♩♩

O = ♩♩ ♩♩ ♩♩ C = ♩♩ ♩♩
        ♦ ♦ ♦   ♦ ♦
          ■   ■

Rests: Same as Franconian but adjusted for new values. Eight values recognized: PMx, IMx, PL, IB, B, SB, Mna, SMna.

255

PLAINSONG (Square)

Accidentals: Only Bb. Used primarily to avoid tritone but also for subtle linear differences (e.g., an upper auxiliary or descending passing tone).

Principal Forms:

Sacred	Secular
mass, hymn	virelai, lai,
sequence, psalms	rondeau
conductus	ballade

Principal Persons and Works:
  Musica Enchiriadis (pre square note)
  Guido d'Arezzo—*Micrologus*
  John Cotton—*Liber de Musica*

MODAL (Rhythmic)

Accidentals: Bb and Eb. Used for the same reasons as plainsong accidentals and to avoid the vertical tritone.

Principal Forms: Monophonic—same as earlier period. Polyphonic—several types of organum; conductus; and early motet.

Principal Persons and Works:
  Leonin and Perotin at Notre Dame
  Johannes de Grocheo—*Theoria*

FRANCONIAN

Accidentals: Bb, Eb, F#, C#. Flats used
as in earlier periods and sharps used
for raised leading tone (especially
at cadential points).

Principal Forms: Monophonic—same as
earlier periods; polyphonic—motet,
English discant, fauxbourdon, conductus, and earlier sacred forms.

Principal Persons and Works:
Franco (Cologne)—*Ars Cantus
Mensurablis*
Johannes de Garlandia—*De Musica
Mensurabili Positio*

ARS NOVA

Accidentals: Bb, Eb, Ab, Db, F#, C#,
G#. All used for the same purposes
as in Franconian notation.

Principal Forms: All former monophonic forms; and polyphonic
virelai, rondeau, ballade, caccia,
chace, madrigal, motet, and mass.

Principal Persons and Works:
Phillipe di Vitri—*Ars Nova*
Guillaume de Machaut—*Messe de
Nostre Dame*
Francesco Landini

TABLE OF DISSONANCES

Passing Tone: a note that is dissonant with others sounding simultaneously and that is approached and left by step in the same direction from and to consonant tones. A Passing Tone falling on a beat is referred to as an Accented Passing Tone.

Neighboring Tone: a note that is approached and left by step in opposite directions and that is dissonant to others sounding at the same time. The notes of approach and arrival must be consonances.

Anticipation: a dissonant note, normally on the second half of a beat, that is repeated on the following, normally strong beat as a consonance—widely used at cadences.

Suspensions: a note that is held over from a consonant position and becomes dissonant (normally on a strong beat) resolving by step down (although other resolutions are possible).

Appoggiatura: a dissonant note that is approached by skip (in either direction) and resolved by step. It may be accented or unaccented.

Échappée: (escape tone) the opposite of an appoggiatura, approached by step and resolved by skip.

Free Tone: a dissonant note that is approached and left by skip.

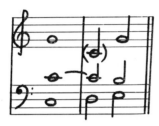

Nota Cambiata: a dissonant tone approached by step from above, left by skipping down a third which then is resolved up by step producing an embellished, descending scale line.

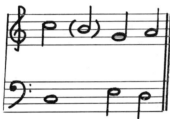

index

index

aBout the Book and author.

This textbook for the study of music theory uses an historical approach which enables the student to learn about compositional devices as they appeared and evolved in early Western music. This text and its accompanying workbook provide for the study of basic analytical and compositional techniques through the use of selected literature and original compositional assignments. With these materials techniques which have been employed periodically throughout history, even into the most advanced of contemporary composition, may be mastered and absorbed as an integral part of the student's understanding of the aesthetic principles of the art.

Lloyd Ultan is a professor and chairman of the departments of music and music education at the University of Minnesota. He is a composer who has had many commissions and whose works have been performed throughout the United States, Europe, and Asia.